The
Country
of
Football

Edited by PAULO FONTES AND
BERNARDO BUARQUE DE HOLLANDA

The
Country
of
Football

POLITICS, POPULAR CULTURE &
THE BEAUTIFUL GAME IN BRAZIL

HURST & COMPANY, LONDON

First published in the United Kingdom in 2014 by
C. Hurst & Co. (Publishers) Ltd.,
41 Great Russell Street, London, WC1B 3PL
© Paulo Fontes, Bernardo Buarque de Hollanda and the Contributors, 2014
All rights reserved.
Printed in the USA

Distributed in the United States, Canada and Latin America by
Oxford University Press, 198 Madison Avenue, New York, NY 10016,
United States of America.

A Cataloguing-in-Publication data record for this book is available
from the British Library.

978-1-84904-417-2 *paperback*

This book is printed using paper from registered sustainable
and managed sources.

www.hurstpublishers.com

In memoriam of Carlos Eduardo Sarmento

THE NEW BRAZIL

King's Brazil Institute Series
Editors: Michael Hall and Anthony Pereira

In recent decades, Brazil has become a more economically and politically stable country. As its wealth has increased, and it has become the sixth largest economy in the world, it has awakened the interest of outsiders. But Brazil is still not well understood. Its enviable image is one of a laid-back mixture of natural beauty—beaches, mighty rivers, rain forests, vast plains—and exuberant multiracial humanity, expressing itself in football, music, Carnival, and sex. This image attracts and seduces, but it also misleads. Brazil is more complicated than that.

This series is dedicated to exploring the Brazil behind the superficial images that dominate coverage of the country from the outside. It focuses on some of the country's major twenty-first century challenges. Fifty years ago, Brazil was an agrarian country, dominated by plantation agriculture, in which 70 per cent of the population lived in the countryside. Since then it has industrialised and urbanised. Large-scale internal migration and demographic growth, the latter pushing the population to over 200 million, have reshaped the country. The country has endured a military dictatorship, seen mass movements demanding a variety of civil, political, and economic rights, and undergone complicated and contested constitutional, legal, and political reforms. Many of its contemporary challenges stem from its explosive growth, and the struggle to adapt economic, social, and political institutions to the new realities of the country. Brazil in the twenty-first century is a country of contradictions, conflict, change, and growing global influence.

This series seeks to shed light on some of the most important contemporary issues in Brazil, and especially those that have played a big part in the recent transformation of the country. It will highlight Brazil's history, politics, and society, and examine conflicts that have made the country what it is today. One objective of the series is to bring some of the best recent Brazilian scholarship to an English-speaking public. Brazilian universities have grown and professionalised in recent years, without a corresponding increase in works in English by Brazilian scholars.

Contents

vii

CONTENTS

Acknowledgements

We would like to express our great appreciation to Professors Michael Hall and Anthony Pereira for their support and encouragement directed to the publication of this book.

The generosity and professionalism of the Museu do Futebol in São Paulo—especially of the Content Director Daniela Alfonsi—was fundamental to the identification of the illustrations.

Finally, we want to give our special thanks to Oliver Marshall, whose herculean, patient and elegant work of revision of the translations, accompanied by accurate and insightful comments, were decisive for the publication of this work in such a short space of time.

ABOUT THE AUTHORS

Fatima Martin Rodrigues Ferreira Antunes is a sociologist with a PhD from the Universidade de São Paulo (University of São Paulo/USP). Her thesis was a pioneering study on football factory clubs in the early twentieth century. She is currently a researcher at the Departamento do Patrimônio Histórico da Secretaria Municipal de Cultura de São Paulo (Department of Historic Heritage at the Municipal Office of Culture of São Paulo).

Clément Astruc is a French historian with a masters degree from the École Normale Supérieure in Lyon. In 2012 and 2013 he received a scholarship from the Embassy of France in Brazil for research into the development of professional Brazilian football.

Marta Cioccari is an anthropologist with a PhD from Museu Nacional (National Museum), Universidade Federal do Rio de Janeiro (UFRJ). She studied rural and urban workers from the south of Brazil. As an ethnographer, she is interested in the formation of working class values, such as honour and reputation. She has also extensively studied the military regime in Brazil, particularly social memory, biographies and trajectories.

José Paulo Florenzano is an anthropologist with a PhD from Pontifícia Universidade Católica de São Paulo (Pontifical Catholic University/PUC-SP). He is a professor and researcher in the Social Science Department at the same institution. He is interested primarily in professional football during the military regime in Brazil (1964–1984).

ABOUT THE AUTHORS

Paulo Fontes is an associate professor at the Fundação Getúlio Vargas (CPDOC/FGV) and a researcher for the Brazilian Scientific Research Council (CNPq). A historian of Brazilian labour and working-class culture in São Paulo after World War II, Fontes has studied internal migration from the north-east to São Paulo, the links between rural and urban workers, the role of place and communities in the formation of the working classes, and the cultural aspects of popular organisation and politics.

Christopher Gaffney is a geographer with a PhD from the University of Texas. He has experience in urban planning with an emphasis on sporting 'mega-events', and the role of football stadiums. He has received a Fulbright scholarship in order to pursue his research in Rio de Janeiro and has been a visiting professor at Universidade Federal Fluminense (Fluminense Federal University/UFF) since 2011.

Bernardo Buarque de Hollanda is an associate professor at the School of Social Sciences of the Fundação Getúlio Vargas and a researcher at the Center for Research and Documentation of Brazilian Contemporary History (CPDOC/FGV). His main topics of research include literary history and modernism, social thought and intellectuals in Brazil, the social history of football and organised soccer supporting groups.

Gregory E. Jackson received his PhD in Latin American History from Stony Brook University, with a special focus on the relationships between sport and social categories such as race, ethnicity, gender and national identity in modern Brazil. He is currently a lecturer at Western Connecticut State University.

José Sergio Leite Lopes is a professor of social anthropology at the Universidade Federal do Rio de Janeiro (Federal University of Rio de Janeiro/UFRJ). He has been investigating working class culture for more than thirty years, including sports in Brazil, and is the author of many articles and books on the topic.

Preface

Richard Giulianotti

In world football, Brazil is a nation that fascinates the global audience like no other. Here is a huge society that has seized upon football, making the game its own through a mixture of improvisation, dedication and celebration. In turn, much of the world seems to have been turned into 'football Brazilians' in appreciation of the perceived Brazilian style of play. Yet only rarely do international audiences gain a deeper insight or grasp of the Brazilian game that goes beyond the global stereotype of Brazil as a footballing nation *par excellence.*

This book—beautifully crafted by the editors, Paulo Fontes and Bernardo Buarque de Hollanda—is one of those rarities, offering an outstanding advancement to our wider knowledge and understanding of Brazilian football. The book 'raises the game', in large part by focusing on the historical, political and public dynamics of football in Brazil, both at the societal and the everyday levels. The contributors are leading scholars drawn from an impressive range of disciplines, notably anthropology, geography, history and sociology. The book itself is structured in broadly chronological fashion, so that we gain rich insights into the most significant phases in Brazilian football, and the close intersections between football, politics and society.

PREFACE

The book begins by considering the social genesis of Brazilian football, and the subsequent rapid and popular spread of the game. Charles Miller, a Scottish-Brazilian, is widely regarded as the founder of the Brazilian game, having returned from an education in England with a ball and football boots to organise the first football matches in São Paulo in 1895. As Fatima Martin Rodrigues Ferreira Antunes explains in the opening chapter, the game rapidly took off, particularly among Anglophone elites and then among the masses. Tours by the English amateur team, Corinthian FC, accelerated football's popularity, and of course came to inspire the name of one of São Paulo's great teams. More broadly, the popularisation of football was most significant among the working classes in Brazil's industrial towns, cities, factories and other workplaces.

Football was rapidly institutionalised in Brazilian towns and cities in the early twentieth century with the focus on civic and regional tournaments that were contested by leading clubs. The 1930s through to the 1950s was a crucial period for the game's development—the era of Getúlio Vargas's presidency defined by a political mix of authoritarianism, populism and nation building. As the chapter by Gregory E. Jackson details, professionalism came into Brazilian football in 1933 but did relatively little to change the 'master-slave' relationships that had otherwise characterised so much of Brazilian society, and which remained largely intact in the relations between players (particularly the vast majority drawn from the foot of the class and race hierarchies) and the *cartolas* who controlled the clubs and wider sports system, and held close ties with the press and political leaders. At the same time, Vargas utilised football as a tool for promoting national identity and integration, to pursue the production of 'eugenically fit and culturally orthodox citizens'. As Jackson points out, this broader context provides the basis for understanding the popular and political significance of the *Maracanazo*—the nation's epic, and in many ways defining, football failure, in which the Brazilian national team lost the final of the 1950 World Cup to Uruguay in Rio's Maracanã stadium before an estimated 200,000 shell-shocked spectators.

It is at the everyday or grassroots level that we come to grasp the importance of football, or indeed any cultural form, within different societies. In the case of Brazilian football, the amateur or lower-level game has a rich and diverse history in both major urban centres and smaller towns. The chapter by Marta Cioccari reveals how football is a colourful and dynamic cultural field in which workers (in this case, coal miners) are able to express and to explore themes of identity and belonging, solidarity and differentiation, and physical skill and creativity. Leading players in industrial towns may acquire local celebrity status, drawing comparisons, in both positive and negative ways, with the playing skills and turbulent lives of famous professional players. In cities such as São Paulo, amateur football has also introduced many millions of young players to the game. The chapter by Paulo Fontes further demonstrates how amateur football clubs were often established in informal ways by groups of working-class men, and these new organisations provided a social, cultural and political sphere that was at least partially separated from leisure activities otherwise controlled by employers.

At the elite level, Brazil is perhaps best renowned for a remarkable lineage of truly outstanding world-class players, including Leônidas, Zizinho, Didi, Garrincha, Nilton Santos, Pelé, Rivelino, Zico, Ronaldo, Ronaldhino, and many others. Yet perhaps the most popular and emblematic of these players is Garrincha, who is lesser known outside Brazil than many others, but whose death in 1983 prompted a remarkable national response. The paper by José Sergio Leite Lopes sets out in very vivid detail the events surrounding Garrincha's death and funeral, explaining the player's deeper social significance, particularly as a player drawn from an industrial-worker background and who slid tragically into alcoholism and poverty. Most notably, as a player, Garrincha had an exceptional style that, as Leite Lopes most perceptively reveals, was shaped by his unusual physiology (being born with bowed legs), remarkable technical virtuosity, playfulness (seeming to participate only for fun), and the fact that he fundamentally redefined the role of the outside-right within the team. Such qualities underpinned his adulation as a footballing genius and folk hero.

In broader terms, while most professional players in Brazil in the second half of the twentieth century were unable to match Garrincha's skills and popularity, they tended to have the same demographic characteristics, being drawn particularly from the working and lower-middle classes, and from 'mixed-race' or black backgrounds. As one would expect to find, football offered these players an obvious vehicle for social mobility, however fleeting, as the chapter by Clément Astruc explains. As a collective force in regard to labour relations, Brazilian football players were little different to those in other countries and continents: relatively fragmented, and unable to mobilise themselves in political terms, in part due to their competing interests.

PREFACE

In international terms, Brazil enjoyed years of success from the late 1950s to 1970, winning three World Cup finals and establishing a global aesthetic in terms of playing style before worldwide television audiences. Conversely, the 1970s and 1980s, when little international success was had, might appear as years of austerity. Yet in this period we find Brazil moving through some major social changes, particularly from the military regime (1964–1985) to democratic government, and football was not silent in these processes, as the article by José Paulo Florenzano makes clear. The military regime had sought to shape football and other sports according to its agenda, and to exploit for populist purposes whatever successes Brazil may have enjoyed. By contrast, the moves towards democratisation featured a marked contribution from the footballing world, as demonstrated by the explicit criticism of the military regime by the Atlético Mineiro player Reinaldo, and by the emergence of the famous 'Corinthians Democracy' movement, led by the players Sócrates, Wladimir, and Casagrande.

Brazilian football is also imbued with the stories and histories of its stadiums. The Maracanã in Rio is, of course, the most famous example, but other historic football venues include the Morumbi in São Paulo, and the Mineirão in Belo Horizonte. Many of these stadiums had vast capacities and relatively low and affordable admission prices for the lower classes, enabling huge crowds to gather for fixtures. In such environments, with the popular participation of tens of thousands, the Carnival-esque culture of Brazilian football was able to emerge and to play out at club and international level. These stadiums also provided relatively safe spaces for expressions of popular resistance or opposition to incumbent regimes.

The development of the Maracanã has gone through two major phases, first in its construction for the 1950 World Cup finals, and then its 'redevelopment' in advance of the 2014 tournament. As the chapter by Bernardo Buarque de Hollanda details, these processes have been deeply significant and contested within the public sphere.

The phase of redevelopment needs to be located within the wider endeavour of powerful political and economic forces to 'neo-liberalise' Brazilian football and society. Such processes have also, of course, been underway in other parts of South America and, for rather longer, in Europe. The result is a concerted commodification of football, in which there is a focus on the supporter as a 'consumer', and an attempt to reshape the football 'experience' in line with the lifestyle and spending preferences of middle- and upper-class, typically white spectators. Thus in Brazil, as the chapter by Christopher Gaffney indicates, we have witnessed the establishing of all-seated stadiums with comparatively low capacities but markedly higher admission prices, and an overall change in the types of spectator who can attend. For some commentators, this commercialisation and sanitisation of football stadiums—where the atmosphere at major fixtures is more akin to a television variety show than a mass public event—has clearly had a negative effect on the social and cultural foundations of the game.

The emerging issues here for Brazilian football have been thrown under the international spotlight in the build-up to the 2014 World Cup finals. Certainly, the levels of public expenditure on sport-related construction—the stadiums and infrastructure—are staggering, with the likelihood that many facilities will be seriously under-utilised after the tournament. At the same time, the 2013 Confederations Cup tournament in Brazil was an occasion for nationwide popular public protests and rioting on a variety of issues, partly on rising living costs (notably public transport fares), but also on the huge spending and details of corruption surrounding the hosting of the 2014 World Cup finals.

Indeed, no other sporting mega-event has experienced this scale of popular national criticism and opposition. And yet, aside from the normal anticipation prior to any tournament, the special global appeal of the 2014 World Cup—and, we should note, a crucial attraction for FIFA and its corporation partners—centres heavily on the extraordinary grassroots culture of football in Brazil. The long-term danger of course is that, as commodification and sanitisation take hold, Brazilian football's grassroots cultures will be destroyed, or given some kind of artificial 'life', such as through pre-match entertainment. Our grasp of these crucial contemporary issues in football is dependent on a full grasp of the historical context and detail. This collection of outstanding articles takes us a long way towards providing us with that understanding.

Richard Giulianotti
Professor of Sociology, Loughborough University/Professor II, Telemark University College, Norway
March 2014

The Beautiful Game in the 'Country of Football'

An Introduction

Paulo Fontes and *Bernardo Buarque de Hollanda*

In his occasional but recurring mentions of football, the historian Eric Hobsbawm made famous the expression that the sport had become the 'secular religion of the working class' in the world of the twentieth century. Its popularity is associated with a universal dialect or, to borrow an expression from the Brazilian professor José Miguel Wisnik, with the 'general idiom of a non-verbal language'.[1] With an ability to share symbols, practices and representations across the world, the phenomenon of football has also become one of the most powerful and profitable businesses of our time. To use the words of Hobsbawm once again, the sport bears 'the essential conflict of globalisation'.

In a growing picture of the 'globalisation of football', as well as the 'footballisation of the world', Brazil continues to occupy a prominent position on the international scene. Five times world champion, having participated in all nineteen FIFA World Cup tournaments held between 1930 and 2010, and host of the 2014 tournament, the country has long been seen as the source of many of the world's most talented players, including Leônidas and Domingos, Zizinho and Didi, Garrincha and Pelé, Zico and Sócrates, and Romário and Ronaldo, amongst many others.

Thus, Brazil has been internationally revered, sometimes rather stereotypically, as the home of a unique, beautiful and inimitable style of playing. As Eric Hobsbawm observed, 'who, having seen the Brazilian national football team in its heyday, can deny its claim to the status of art?'[2] The association between the sport and national identity is so strong in the minds of many Brazilians that the term 'the country of football' has become Brazil's own metaphor. It is likely that there is no higher form of recognition of 'Brazilianness' on the streets of any city in the world than the wearing of the shirt of the national team.

The striking link between the national imagined community and the sport has, however, no consensus or linear trajectory. It has been articulated historically with Brazil's twentieth-century model of economic and social development. It was a long process, riddled with social and political, racial and cultural tensions, which has been reconfigured and steadily updated through the narratives associated with the country. In this sense, it is not a complete surprise that large-scale street protests erupted in Brazil during the Confederations Cup in June and July 2013. In the environs of stadiums that had been constructed for the 2014 World Cup, some of the strongest ever popular demonstrations against a Brazilian government took place, with the protestors incensed by what they considered the abusive and irresponsible spending for the mega-sporting event that Brazil was preparing to host.

On the other hand, given the social range of football in Brazil, the contrast between the popularity of the sport and the belated recognition of its analytical worth by Brazilian social scientists and historians is striking. Such an initial framework, however, has been changing rapidly in recent years. Thus, it can be said that football in Brazil is now very much a legitimate object of analysis. If the pioneering studies in the 1980s by the anthropologists Roberto DaMatta, José Sergio Leite Lopes and Simoni Lahud Guedes aroused academic interest in football with their interpretive insights,[3] it was in the 1990s that the sport truly established itself as a field of systematic research.

Studies on sport, especially football, have resulted in dissertations and theses related to various disciplines ranging from physical education to psychology, media communication to anthropology and history. Beyond books and articles by individual authors, research groups have been established in universities and other research institutes in many Brazilian cities—in Porto Alegre, Curitiba, Belo Horizonte, Rio de Janeiro, São Paulo and Recife—and collaborative work has led to the creation of specialised journals.[4]

In order to familiarise readers with football studies in Brazil, we will briefly identify its main strengths and major contemporary trends. Dominating the agenda of most researchers is the relationship between sport and modernity, or that of sport and nation.[5] The objective is to explain how, historically and sociologically, a leisure market in Brazil was structured and what role modern sport played within it. In particular, researchers have sought to understand the way in which football has become one of the main vectors of condensing the idea of 'Brazilianness'. Among this subject's preferred sub-themes there has been research on the sport by state apparatus; the strategic and indispensable role of the media in the popularisation of sports; and debates among intellectuals and journalists about the significance of the practice of football.

The introduction in the late nineteenth and early twentieth century of various sports as elite pastimes, and the popularisation of some— most notably football—have been extensively explored by Brazilian scholars in parallel with crucial historical experiences since Brazil's transformation from a monarchy to a republic in 1889 (such as the nationalism and authoritarianism of the 1930s and the civil-military dictatorship between 1964 and 1985)[6]—football's historical significance forming another major strand of research activity.

Another theme of great prominence amongst researchers—one which is reflected in this book—is that of ethnic identity. Relating to the early decades of football in Brazil, immigrant groups (such as Italians and Portuguese in the early twentieth century) and their social networks (including their recreational and sport clubs) have been examined. Racial integration is also a theme of lively discussion, driven by the participation in football of people of African-descent which rapidly increased as the sport transformed in the 1920s and 1930s from an amateur to a professional pursuit.[7]

Discussions on Brazilian 'race' and 'culture' are guided by the writings of the journalist Mário Filho (1908–66) assembled in the form of the book *O negro no futebol brasileiro* (*Black People in Brazilian Football*), published in 1947.[8] This work is of huge importance, not least because it includes a foreword by the sociologist Gilberto Freyre (1900–87) who is well-known for his controversial studies on the historical origins of race in Brazilian society and his views of racial elasticity.[9] If Freyre is reputed to have overcome the concept of race in favour of a culturalist approach, learned during his years of study in the United States with the anthropologist Franz Boas, his essay was accused of being an apology of the 'racial democracy' in Brazil by the academics of the São Paulo universities, such as USP, in the 1950s and 1960s.

Aside from Brazilian-born authors, mention should be given to one of the first sports specialists to address the introduction of football to the country. In the early 1950s Anatol Rosenfeld (1912–73)—a German-Jewish refugee who spent most of his life in Brazil as a writer and journalist—produced a significant contribution directly linking issues of race and football in Brazil,[10] and forming a precursor to academic studies.[11] Rosenfeld's essay 'Football in Brazil' provides an accurate overview of the introduction of the sport to Brazil, with a clear and didactic periodisation, going on to present an excellent panorama of the players' practices and fans' representations of the sport during the first half of the twentieth century.

The specific stories of certain professional football clubs, such as Bangu, Corinthians and Palmeiras, as well as the anthropological and sociological analysis of the construction of 'belonging' to a club of organised supporters, are growing and converging themes of research.[12] The history of certain sporting institutions, the power structures that govern football and how sport overlaps with the political history of the country are topics of increasing exploration.[13] Also among the emerging areas of interest are the intersections between football, architecture and urban history, demonstrating the vitality and scale of new visions and new investigations.[14]

The intersection of the worlds of labour and football is a key field for intellectual production on sport in Brazil. Historians and social scientists have emphasised the close linkage of the genesis and development of sports with nationalism, urbanisation and industrialisation. Particular attention has been given to the processes of the formation of the working class since the nineteenth century, as well as their connections with the adoption of modern British sports in the country.[15]

The Country of Football: Politics, Popular Culture and the Beautiful Game in Brazil presents a significant part of this important and growing area of Brazilian academic production. This collection of nine chapters is made up of groundbreaking work by historians and social scientists, mainly from Brazil, but also from the United States and France, who examine, above all, the broad political significance of the sport in which Brazil has long been a world leader. In a panoramic view, the authors consider questions such as football's relation with the workplace and working-class culture, with the formation of Brazilian national identity, with race relations, with political and social movements and with social mobility. The articles range in time from the late nineteenth century, when the British introduced a modern form of football to Brazil, to the present day, when the 'country of football' has gained even more attention on the world stage as the host of the 2014 World Cup.

The first chapter of the book, written by Fatima Antunes, is a continuation of her work on football teams representing factories in the city of São Paulo in the early twentieth century. Of all the exponents of the sport in Brazil (church schools, leisure clubs and foreign-owned factories), Antunes focuses on factories as a way of understanding the success of football's spread in the country.

The wider context of these early days of sporting activity in the urban environment, especially in Rio de Janeiro and São Paulo, brings to the fore iconic figures drawn from the elite of these cities, most notably the young Anglo-Brazilians Charles Miller and Oscar Cox. Antunes also emphasises the roles in the proliferation of the sport of British engineers, who oversaw the development of railway lines deep into the interior of the country; of traveling technicians, who passed through harbour cities such as Santos; and of Brazilian students, who keenly imitated European fashions and readily adopted their latest novelties and tastes.

After this contextualisation, Antunes turns to an internal analysis of football in the industrial setting. The relationship between employers and employees becomes the focus of the chapter, mediated by the advent and success of this new game. Such practice soon showed itself to be effective in building collective identities and in the creation of negotiation spaces in the factory. Football imposed itself in industry and allowed for the blurring of boundaries, well-marked in the beginning, between work, leisure and free time in the urban order that was then flourishing in Brazil. Antunes explores individual cases and describes the trajectory of British and Canadian companies in São Paulo, a state marked in the First Republic (1889–1930) by progressive political leadership and extraordinary economic power. Antunes explores the ideological debates about the meanings of football within factories, seen either as a means of training workers or as a form of amusement for the masses.

Finally, before its move towards professionalism in the 1920s and 1930s, football had some bearing on the outbreak of general strikes in Brazil in the late 1910s, foregrounding Antunes's analysis of football and political ideology. The sport was the subject of heated discussions between communists and anarchists. The polarisation between these two ideological positions of the international Left would bring into opposition those who defended the potential benefits of athletic activity and those who identified it as a barrier to the class-consciousness of the workers.

The following chapter, by the historian Gregory E. Jackson, continues the book's broad chronological flow, focussing on the transition of Brazilian football to a phase of national popularity in the midst of the Getúlio Vargas government (1930–45). In part thanks to the advent of radio, a centralised national imagination emerged in the 1930s which progressively incorporated the football phenomenon. The state's need for moral framing grew as this centralisation occurred and vertical power structures were imposed in the so-called 'Vargas era'—of which there were three main periods: the revolutionary (1930–4), the constitutional (1934–7) and the dictatorial (1937–45).[16]

While Antunes accentuates the class elements present in the identity construction of football, Jackson emphasises the ethnic and racial dimensions. These elements had been the result of the emergence of black and *mestiço* players in the Brazilian national team and in the major clubs of Rio de Janeiro (then the capital of the Republic). To this end, Jackson makes use of a number of actors, institutions and events that emerged between 1932 and 1942. In this time frame, internal and external factors which contributed to the turn to professionalism of top-level football in the 1930s are analysed on a domestic and international scale.

Jackson goes back to 1923, when Vasco da Gama, a football club established by members of Rio de Janeiro's Portuguese community, won the state championship with a team of players from working class backgrounds. Based on the team's success, the clubs of Rio de Janeiro's working class (Vasco da Gama, Bangu and São Cristóvão) began to threaten and oppose both the amateur teams of the wealthy Zona Sul (Flamengo, Fluminense and Botafogo) and the long-established clubs of the Zona Norte (including América and Andaraí).

INTRODUCTION

Jackson follows the struggle for the recognition of football as a legitimate profession, a classification that would introduce contracts and wages. The clash was fought over and argued about by various sectors of the sports media, one of the main voices in favour of professionalism being the *Jornal dos Sports* (a periodical owned by Mário Filho) whose commercial interest led it to advocate the transformation of a sport that still maintained many elite features in a popular mass spectacle. In 1933, football's professionalism was for the first time officially recognised. Opposition, however, continued from amateur proponents until 1937, when 'pacification' was finally reached. Jackson explains how sports leaders, politicians, players, fans, club members and journalists participated in the confrontations between those favouring the original amateur spirit of the game and those advocating its new professional ethos.

On the international scene, Jackson illustrates how South American national teams entering Olympic football in 1924 and the newly inaugurated FIFA World Cup in 1930 enhanced nationalist rhetoric. Professionalism presented itself as the best way to obtain positive results in international tournaments. The rise of South America as a footballing powerhouse was confirmed by the major international tournaments that were won by Uruguay—the Olympic tournament in 1924 and 1928 and the World Cup in 1930. Uruguay's new dominance and the South American style of play showcased in international tournaments aroused the interest of European teams, in particular in Spain and Italy. Players from South America, some of them immigrants, were hired to play for European clubs or were even selected to represent European national teams at the 1934 and 1938 World Cup tournaments.

Based on his archival research and understanding of the wider literature of football, Jackson offers examples of tours by the Rio de Janeiro clubs to the so-called 'Old World', and describes the emergence of the first black Brazilian footballing idols, such as Fausto dos Santos. This description is extended to the changing representations and self-representations of Brazil, based on the shift in the meanings of race and culture, of which the work of the sociologist Gilberto Freyre is the most emphatic example. In the case of football, this change is represented by the formation of a multi-ethnic and inter-regional national team, able to overcome the racist discourse that had previously prevailed and to transcend regional disputes between Rio de Janeiro and São Paulo for the control of Brazil's nationally recognised sports entities and leagues.

Chapter Three, by Marta Cioccari, deviates from the panoramic periodisation of Brazil's footballing history and instead focuses on anthropological observations. She explores the history of football players of clubs linked to Minas do Leão, a mining community in Rio Grande do Sul's coalfield region of Baixo Jacuí.

Inspired by ethnographers such as Christian Bromberger and by sociologists like Norbert Elias, Cioccari considers the way in which the workers' footballing experience is articulated by the construction of masculinities and social identities. In her doctoral thesis, Cioccari made comparisons with the case of the coal mines of Creutzwald in France; in this chapter she reinforces the key role of football in the construction of 'small honour', a symbolic and social value among the miners, which was a complementary extension of the 'great honour' associated with their professional characters.

This highly localised study of the amateur footballing tradition in a community in southern Brazil is of great value for offering readers a specific case of an everyday reality that is usually overlooked in the conventional historiography of Brazilian football. Through interviews with players, ex-players and founders of the provincial clubs, Cioccari reveals the discourses relating to footballing skills and techniques, and the cases of valour and prestige that they considered memorable. Cioccari traces the proliferation of dozens of small street clubs in Minas do Leão, and some notable cases among the player-workers, whose stories are linked both to the mining companies that employed them and to political, urban and wider economic dynamics. Included are tales of extraordinary players who rose from street football to the amateur teams, managed to turn professional, and ended up at important clubs such as Internacional in Porto Alegre and Corinthians in São Paulo.

The competitions between these local clubs extended the web of local inter-relationships. These came to include not only the immediate neighbourhoods and families of the players, but also other communities near Minas do Leão (such Arroio dos Ratos, Charqueada and Butiá) that the town's two top teams confronted in competition. The internal rivalry of Minas do Leão's two workers' teams—Atlético Mineiro and Olaria (the former's reputation 'elite', the latter's 'popular')—is indicative of the way that unions and socio-spatial contrasts in Minas do Leão developed.

Chapter Four, by the historian Paulo Fontes, extends the preceding chapter's discussion on amateur street football. The text focuses on the period between the mid-1940s and the mid-1960s, the decades of so-called 'national developmentalism' and the age of industrialisation through import substitution. The greatest economic challenge that Brazil faced at this time was overcoming its delays relative to developed countries in restructuring according to the dependent and peripheral capitalist agenda. Industrialisation and urbanisation were accelerated by the state, the main actor responsible for the implementation of policies to increase the production of consumer goods and services, especially in the big cities. To this was added the institutionalisation of democracy, which lasted, albeit in an unstable and turbulent manner, from 1945 to 1964.

The geographic centre of the chapter is the city of São Paulo, a metropolis of vast and seemingly ever-shifting proportions. As Fontes points out, during this period the city's population grew rapidly, witnessing an extraordinary migratory flow, especially of people from the northeast of Brazil. Such dramatic urban change had direct effects on the character of leisure pursuits, free time and football among the working classes. Fontes places in a historical context the increasing restrictions on amateur football that were a consequence of land speculation and the confiscation of vacant spaces by the state and the booming private sector; the *várzeas*—considered the mythical public spaces in the development of 'authentic' Brazilian football, and the birthplace of many a great footballer—were an example of these spaces.

Fontes also articulates how amateur football was connected, through the appropriation and corporate recruitment of workers of northeastern origin who participated in amateur championships, to an expansion of working-class forms of associations and popular organisations, and the economic dynamics of industrial capitalism. Cases of this included important industrial organisations such as SESI (Industry Social Service) which from 1947 promoted the Workers' Sports Games (which were sponsored by specialised sports newspapers that extensively covered the event).

The relationship between employers and employees in the 1940s and 1950s encouraged competitions tied to the affiliation of certain professional groups, but Fontes also notes the involvement of labour unions, the Communist Party of Brazil (PCB) and various local forces in recognising football's strong appeal to the working classes. Legalised for a short period of time in the Cold War era, the PCB saw the promotion of neighbourhood games and amateur championships as something positive. The games used group identities and provided the PCB with a means to approach the urban workers of São Paulo without invoking historical prejudices against football still prevalent amongst many intellectuals.

Chapter Five constitutes a seminal essay by José Sergio Leite Lopes, professor of social anthropology at the National Museum of Rio de Janeiro. The text is devoted to Garrincha (1933–83), one of Brazil's great footballing idols. Originally published in French in 1989, the essay has become a key reference for the study of football in Brazil. 'The "people's joy" vanishes' begins with an emotional ethnographic observation of the melancholic death of Garrincha after a long and tortuous period of alcohol abuse and a series of subsequent hospitalisations. Through the press, the author follows what he suggestively defines as 'a media-age *chanson de geste*'.

Leite Lopes then focuses on the reconstitution of the history of Garrincha with a description of his meteoric career in football. Garrincha's success endured for just ten years (1953–63) before he plunged into a state of oblivion, from which he only emerged in 1983 when his death becomes a major public event. By illustrating the ambivalence of common people to individual stars in Brazil, Leite Lopes emphasises the intrinsic oscillation of the careers of football players. Transformed into national sporting heroes, they all too commonly fall suddenly into anonymity, with the loss of the mythical aura that once surrounded them. Thus, argues the author, the idolatry directed towards Garrincha—who twice starred for Brazil in World Cups—depended on newspaper stories which attributed to him stereotypical characteristics of purity and naivety, the heritage of a man of nature, a descendant of Indians or a carefree 'bird hunter' of the Brazilian rural hinterland.

Leite Lopes's argument demonstrates, however, that Garrincha was a paradigmatic athlete from the world of textile factories, a sector of fundamental importance in Brazil's initial industrialisation process of the late nineteenth to the mid-twentieth century. With this mythical discourse revised, Garrincha can instead be considered as a typical representative of the 'player-worker', alongside the likes of stars such as Domingos and Didi.

In chapter six, Clément Astruc explores football as a specific profession, drawing on the testimony of players who were selected to represent Brazil at World Cup tournaments from the 1950s to the 1980s.

INTRODUCTION

The sources that Astruc analyses form part of an oral history collection, with 120 hours of taped interviews with fifty-four former players, for the Centro de Pesquisa e Documentação de História Contemporânea (CPDOC/FGV, or the Centre of Research and Documentation of Contemporary History in Brazil) and the Museu do Futebol (Football Museum) in São Paulo. From this unique series of testimonies, Astruc investigates the meanings, ambiguities and specificities of the footballers' craft. His interest focuses on the professional conditions that made football unique in the historical period under examination.

In contrast with Gregory Jackson's article work, which discusses an era in which professionalism was still in the early process of development, Astruc highlights a period in which football had achieved the status of a profession. Even so, it was still poorly respected, riddled with hostile prejudices and received very different moral treatment when compared with most other working activities.

Having analysed the testimonies of forty-three footballers who had played for Brazil, Astruc identifies three research variables: 1. the social origins of the players; 2. the process of choosing the career; and 3. the promises of mobility, status and economic emancipation offered by the profession. Using these elements, Astruc identifies the random factors and constitutive risks in choosing football as a profession. For most respondents, football was far from a planned and rational option. Unlike the current, often glamourised image of players, many of those in Astruc's study highlight the negative perception of footballers that existed. In many cases, the choice of playing led to an ambiguous lifestyle more closely identifiable with vagrancy than with a traditional concept of regular and conspicuous employment.

In his examination of the footballing profession, Astruc proposes a far from homogeneous sociological profile. For this, he reveals a multiplicity of social, familial and geographical anchors. Within the limits of the group in question, Astruc observes that the players came from families from the lower classes and the middle strata of society. They were the sons of car mechanics, miners, teachers, bank clerks, metalworkers, police officers, attendants, housemaids and farmers. These narratives articulate a passage from childhood hopes and humble homes to swift and sudden enrichment provided by football—the commonly held dream of a poor boy who wishes to become a football player. With this would come benefits such as increased consumption, social status and, indeed, a change in living standards for themselves and their families.

Astruc then addresses one of the biggest issues surrounding the regulation of the profession of the player: the working relationship between player and club defined by the so-called 'Pass Law'. This system was until recently effective under Brazilian sporting law and became prominent in the country by binding an athlete to a club. More than in other professions, club officials controlled an athlete, dominated him on a legal and contractual basis through the exclusive ability to purchase or sell the player. Once signed, the contract restricted the athlete's freedom of choice, awarding power to the club at the expense of the individual. The domination imposed by officials prevented the player from deciding where he went to work or where he might be transferred. Astruc found that football players lacked any autonomous control over their own professional direction.

Afonsinho—a player with Botafogo—became famous in the 1970s through his court battles over the right to control his own fate. In turn, Astruc presents examples of lesser-known cases of similar situations. In particular, the author examines the case of the world champion defender Baldocchi, who, in the first half of the 1970s, entered into a prolonged and dramatic litigation against his club, Corinthians.

Finally, Astruc describes the precarious associations and the limits of corporatism amongst footballers. Often marked by exacerbated individualism, the construction of football's identity is frequently associated with the figure of the individual genius, a unique artist. Astruc provides, however, some examples of workers' unions and associations of athletes that were formed in the late 1970s in São Paulo and Rio de Janeiro when Brazil was firmly under military rule.

Chapter Seven, by the anthropologist José Paulo Florenzano, continues the chronological line of the book. The author sets his sights on the national political dynamic in the 1970s and 1980s. The final years of dictatorship, as Brazil began to turn towards democracy, between 1978 and 1984, is analysed in the light of their connections with Brazilian footballing life.

Florenzano begins by presenting examples of what he calls an 'authoritarian utopia'. The militarisation of football, in parallel to the military dictatorship in Brazil (1964–85), shows itself in a series of events in the 1970s. Among these events is the 1970 Mexico World Cup, as well as far less well-known events such as the Army Olympics, the Indian football leagues, tournaments sponsored by SESI and the Workers' Sports

Games. All these sporting dates and events connected to the military regime were aimed at framing football under the official slogan of a 'Great Brazil'. This superlative attempted to make the world believe in the miraculous strength of a country once hampered, but now promising; a young but mature nation; a territory originally wild, but able to overcome its feral past thanks to modern and heavy engineering, exhibited by the Itaipu hydroelectric dam, the Trans-Amazonian highway and the Rio-Niterói bridge.

The framework of moral and civic education and nationalistic slogans sought to produce a consensus, not only in political and economic terms, but also in culture and sport. Florenzano highlights the gaps, the reactions and the objections that radiated through football against the dictatorial status quo. To do so, he looks at players who, in a club environment, opposed the arbitrariness of coaches and managers with regard to behaviour, values, and even aesthetics. The insubordination of some players from clubs like Grêmio, Corinthians and Botafogo are at the root of what Florenzano calls a 'rebellion in football', one of the possible interpretations of the way the sport reflects, expresses and speaks to the wider issues of the state and surrounding society. Among the rebels of the 'Republic of Football', besides the previously mentioned Afonsinho, was Reinaldo—the Atlético Mineiro forward—who participated in a strike at the club in the late 1970s. His signature goal celebration was one raised arm with the fist clenched, a reference to the victorious militant African-American athletes at the 1968 Olympics in Mexico City.

Furthermore, Florenzano points out a series of events that marked the turn of the 1980s. Strikes by workers in the industrial ABCD Region brought to national prominence the name of the union leader Luís Inácio Lula da Silva. The political campaign for direct elections in 1984 accounted for an impressive level of popular mobilisation of civil society, following twenty years of dictatorship. Alongside these political developments, the failure of two Brazilian teams with completely different styles of playing in the World Cups of 1978 and 1982 inhabited the national sporting memory, while the most notable event at club level was the advent of the so-called 'Corinthians Democracy'. This expression came to characterise the participatory management approach of the club in the process of decision-making, valuing and incorporating the views of players—amongst whom the name of Sócrates stood out.

Chapter Eight, by the historian Bernardo Buarque de Hollanda, proposes a diachronic view of the two World Cup tournaments staged in

Brazil, the first held in 1950 and the second in 2014. The articulation of similarities and differences between these two events is traced by the history of the Maracanã stadium, built for the 1950 World Cup and the only venue of that tournament that would be used again in 2014.

Buarque highlights how the narratives of the two competitions in Brazil introduce a number of structural questions about national identity, regardless of the variances at each historical juncture. Along with the country's on-field performance, the level of development of the state is equally at stake—its capacity as a civilised and modern nation judged by its ability to organise and manage an event of international proportions, a global mega event. Buarque also observes that the behaviour of the fans, seen as a microcosm of the population at large, is an additional piece of evidence in this question, judged by their level of sporting education, their civility and their hospitality towards foreign visitors. The performance of the players, elected as representatives of the nation, renews the cyclical debate over the Brazilian style of play and the self-representation of the national squad as quintessentially offensive, individual and menacing.

According to the author's argument, the choice of the Maracanã allows a comparative analysis between the Brazil of the 1950s and the country of the present day. While the nature of the question is basically unchanged, the country itself, and football along with it, has gone through substantive and profound changes. Over this period of nearly sixty-five years, Brazil ceased to be a predominantly rural country, transforming into a highly urbanised one. The cities reached very high population levels without health, educational or housing facilities to meet their needs. As a result unwanted side effects have emerged; among them criminality, alienation, social segregation, loss of cultural roots, drug trafficking and paralysis on the roads. In sixty years, the demographic boom quadrupled Brazil's population, so that while in 1950 there were just over 50 million inhabitants, in 2014 the population is expected to exceed 200 million.

Regarding the Maracanã in particular, this chronological comparison allows the realisation of the difference between the original monumental stadium and its transformation into today's arena of private space, which no longer has a popular or democratic character. To demonstrate this point, Buarque discusses the activity of the football fans of the city following the 1950 World Cup. International matches, the 'Fla-Flu'

(Flamengo versus Fluminense) fixtures and the championships of Rio de Janeiro frequently lure large crowds to the ground. The stadium in the 1950s, 1960s and 1970s could easily boast an audience of over 100,000 ticket-holders, and regularly reached its full capacity of 150,000 spectators, making matches there the main source of income for locals clubs.

As Buarque notes, Brazil experienced in the 1980s and 1990s an acute economic and financial crisis. Football did not escape its effects. The Maracanã suffered a decrease in the average attendance at matches, violence between organised groups of supporters escalated, and the physical structure of the stadium itself noticeably deteriorated. Renovation of the ground was initiated in 2000 and intensified in 2007 when FIFA elected Brazil host of the twentieth World Cup tournament.

Buarque concludes with a question concerning the future. Following the 2014 World Cup, when the football clubs and their respective supporters reappropriate the new Maracanã, how will football adapt to being fundamentally configured as a spectator event centred on the demands of television and on the consumption of sports goods? A new clash between 'tradition' and 'modernity' lies in wait, a scenario still difficult to predict that will take into account conflicting political and economic forces and the social aspect of its actors.

The book's final contribution is by Christopher Gaffney, a geographer with a special understanding of the architecture of the South American stadiums and their football culture. Gaffney's contribution analyses the architectural infrastructure of the new Brazilian stadiums—in particular the twelve arenas that were built or refurbished for the 2014 World Cup—and the 'elitisation' of the social profile of their patrons.

His contribution begins with a retrospective panorama of the development of football in twentieth-century Brazil, based on an extensive survey of existing literature. From origins as the preserve of the social and economic elite in the first decade of the century, the game was gradually popularised, with the 1938 World Cup a defining moment for international exposure to the Brazilian team. In the immediate aftermath of the Second World War, football joined the discursive construction of the fiction of Brazil being a 'racial democracy'. The stadiums, especially Pacaembu in São Paulo and the Maracanã in Rio de Janeiro, sought to mirror this ideal of a multi-ethnic and inter-class nation.

After briefly discussing Brazil's victory in the 1970 World Cup final, the transition from dictatorship to democracy in the 1980s and the neoliberal wave that struck Latin America in the 1990s, as well as their communicative integration via satellite transmission and cable television, Gaffney arrives at the main focus of his chapter. This consists of an overview of the political economy of Brazilian football in the twenty-first century, culminating in the 2014 World Cup and the accompanying financial investment in promoting the event.

Legal tools and important federal laws regulating contemporary football are examined. As examples, Gaffney discusses the 1999 *Lei Pelé* (Pelé Law) which eased the player/club relationship; the Parliamentary Commission of Inquiry (CPI), which investigated alleged irregularities in the contracts between the national governing body of the sport, the Confederação Brasileira de Futebol (the Brazilian Football Confederation) and Nike (the multinational sportswear company) after Brazil's defeat to France in the 1998 World Cup final; and the 2003 *Estatuto do Torcedor* (Fan's Statute). The *Estatuto do Torcedor* originally came into effect to recognise football as a public good. This gave supporters rights in relation to their treatment and also provided them with more transparent and ethical relations with the management of their teams. In time, however, it ended up becoming a tool with which to repress and criminalise fans' associations which were considered to cause disturbances and violent acts both inside and outside stadiums.

Beside the legal apparatus, Gaffney uses statistical data on changes in the turnout of the public in the stadiums and analyses the effect of increased ticket prices from 2007, soon after the end of the Pan American Games in Rio de Janeiro in the wake of Brazil being chosen to host the 2014 World Cup. The author's aim is to assess the revenues of sports entities and professional clubs since 2007. Transnational governance of football by FIFA is taken under the baton of new revenue sources, primarily anchored by income from broadcasting rights, multi-million dollar transfer deals of players and sponsorship by multinational companies.

Without internalising the official jargon and the institutional vocabulary, Gaffney rejects the idea of an inherent 'legacy' on sport, society and the economies of the twelve 2014 World Cup host cities or of a self-accomplished prophecy. He deconstructs terms such as urban mobility, the tourism industry and the modernisation of the broadcasting network, providing an invaluable critical perspective for deciphering contemporary Brazil.

1

The Early Days of Football in Brazil
British Influence and Factory Clubs in São Paulo

Fatima Martin Rodrigues Ferreira Antunes

Football arrives in Brazil

Charles William Miller is generally acknowledged as a central figure in the introduction and popularisation of football in Brazil. Although prior to Miller's involvement football did have a limited presence as a leisure and educational activity in some schools, he can claim the credit for efforts to promote the sport in the city of São Paulo and, from 1895, introducing a set of rules that were accepted and strictly observed.

Since 1886, football had been an accepted physical activity at Jesuit schools in Rio Grande do Sul, in the far-south of Brazil, as well as at Marist schools in Rio de Janeiro.[1] In the same decade, teachers and students of Colégio São Luís, in the city of Itu, São Paulo, regularly congregated in the schoolyard to play 'hit-the-ball' (*bate-bolão*), a game that involved kicking a ball against a wall.[2] In 1894, football was further organised at Colégio São Luís, with teams being made up of eleven players and opposing sides wearing different uniforms.[3] During the 1890s, Colégio Pedro II in Rio de Janeiro introduced a game following a similar structure.[4] Mário Filho—a Brazilian journalist and author noted for his interest in football—found that in the 1890s a number of Brazilian schools took up the game. For example, in 1896, priests introduced football at Petrópolis's Colégio São Vicente de Paula as a useful means to resolve disciplinary problems:

The *Peluda* (as they called a ball of poorly-tanned leather that was made by the priest Manuel González) solved all relationship problems aroused during class breaks. Even the most serious of them: the cliques in the courtyard, the conversations among the students, the priests were kept out of the conversation, hearing nothing. As a priest approached, the talking stopped.

Nobody could talk while playing football. Therefore, during the afternoon break students were invited to play football, forming teams of around thirty to forty players, the priests in their midst, their cassocks tucked up, giving kicks, getting hit on their ankles.[5]

The game became so popular among Brazilian school students that many of them joined the teams that were being formed by their local clubs, which were always keen to identify talented young players. Filho observed that the scarcity of players during the early years of the sport in Rio de Janeiro forced the football league to allow them to play twice in a single day, representing different teams. This expedient, however, was gradually abandoned:

Every year, more and more players emerging from high school made their way to the clubs. Clubs were increasingly less in need of attracting more footballers to constitute their teams. Some even dared to have more than two teams.[6]

Despite these early pioneering efforts, enthusiasm for the formation of teams was limited until Charles Miller became involved with football in Brazil in the mid-1890s. In contrast, football in Britain was already a well-established and professional activity, while the sport was steadily attracting attention across Europe, as well as in other countries with which Britain maintained close commercial ties. Football was gaining the structures of an urban sport, suited to both industrialised countries as well as those in process of industrialisation.[7] Miller, who had played as a forward in England, was able to capitalise on the germs of interest in the sport in Brazil while adopting the formal approaches that he had experienced in England.

Charles Miller was born in São Paulo in 1874. His Anglo-Brazilian mother came from a well-connected family whose wealth was based on their engineering business which held construction contracts with the São Paulo Railway Company. Miller's father came from a humble Scottish background, but in São Paulo he reinvented himself as a successful merchant dealing with goods imported from Britain.[8] In 1884, at the age of just nine, Miller was sent 'home' for schooling in Britain. This was typical for sons from wealthier sectors of Anglo society in Brazil, their families being keen that the younger generation would maintain a strong sense of 'Britishness'. Miller was enrolled at Banister Court, a small, rather obscure private boarding school in Southampton. It was there that he first played—and developed a life-long passion for—football. Football was increasingly popular in English schools and Miller soon made his mark with Banister Court's squad in inter-school matches. Miller's footballing skills were soon noticed by non-school sides and he joined both St Mary's Football Club (which eventually became Southampton Football Club and has always been known as 'the Saints') and Hampshire County. From 1892, he occasionally played with the London team Corinthian FC, a side that was proudly amateur but attracted many of the best footballers in England.

Upon completing his schooling in 1894, Miller chose to return to Brazil and was surprised to find that football was almost unknown in the country of his birth, despite its pedagogical use in some schools and the very noticeable and influential presence of the British.[9] Although the British community in São Paulo was familiar with football, they mainly played cricket and occasionally rugby or, in the case of elite members of society, tennis. Thus Charles Miller, who had developed considerable footballing skills and techniques with leading English clubs, found no suitable opportunities to play his beloved sport once he had returned to Brazil. As a consequence, Miller dedicated himself to encouraging British residents of São Paulo, with whom he mainly mixed with socially, to take up football. Although pursuing a career with a succession of British-owned companies, Miller's real interest lay in setting about teaching young men in the British community the rules, techniques and tactics of football, with the aim of forming teams and tournaments.

The first Brazilian match in which official rules of football were strictly observed, took place in São Paulo, in 1895, just one year after

Miller had returned to South America. The venue was the Várzea do Carmo (the Carmo Floodplain), a large expanse of land on the edge of São Paulo's historic centre, which would later become the Parque Dom Pedro II.[10] It is likely that the teams representing the British-owned gas company and the São Paulo Railway each comprised six or eight players without proper uniforms or boots—items still unavailable in Brazil.[11] Two more training sessions were held at the Várzea do Carmo before São Paulo's first football pitch was created on the Chácara Dulley in the Bom Retiro neighbourhood. Here the São Paulo Athletic Club (SPAC) maintained a cricket field which was adapted for playing the new game of football. It was during these early matches that Miller formed the official SPAC football team.

Copying the British, Mackenzie College students established in 1898 the Mackenzie College Athletic Association, primarily composed of young Brazilian members of the city's elite. Slowly, football was developing a wider following. Interest in the game was extending beyond employees of British companies, and now also included Brazilians of the higher social classes. In 1899 another club was formed, the International Sport Club—its name reflecting the mix of nationalities of its members who included Brazilians, Germans, British, Portuguese and Spanish. In the same year, the Sport Club Germânia was founded under the auspices of Hans Nobiling from Hamburg, who would also go on to contribute a great deal to the spread in popularity of football in Brazil. In 1900, it was the turn of the Paulistano Athletic Club to be established, its board of directors drawn from the so-called 'coffee aristocracy' of wealthy landowners. In the following years, many more football clubs emerged. These clubs felt the need to establish a league to regulate their relationship and to organise championships. With this goal, the Liga Paulista de Futebol (São Paulo Football League) was founded on 14 December 1901. It was the first of a series of bodies aimed at the regulation of the sport.

In Rio de Janeiro (then the Brazilian capital), Oscar Cox, the son of a British father born in Guayaquil, Ecuador and a Brazilian mother, made a contribution to Brazilian football analogous to that of Miller in São Paulo. After completing his studies in Switzerland, the seventeen-year-old Cox returned to Brazil in 1897 where he soon took up an active interest in football. In Rio he joined the Payssandu Cricket Club which had been founded by the British in 1892. Excited by the growth of football in São Paulo, he proposed the first contests between São Paulo and Rio. In October 1901, two games were held between the cities at the Velódromo in São Paulo. British cultural traditions heavily influenced the tone of the gatherings after the matches:

The tie in the first game (1–1) was celebrated by both sides, whose components gathered at night, to dinner at the suggestive Rotisserie Sport. The banquet ended with a toast to the King Edward VII—from England, of course—and the Brazilian President, Campos Salles, who was born in São Paulo.[12]

Soon after, in 1902, Cox helped to establish Fluminense Football Club, becoming its first president. In an era marked by the growth of British technology and investment in Brazil, skilled British workers in cities such as São Paulo and Rio de Janeiro brought their habits and culture into Brazilian sport. Leonardo Pereira highlighted the importance of the British presence in Brazil at the time that Brazilian football was emerging:

For them, football appeared to be a kind of celebration of British identity. Significantly, the Rio de Janeiro Cricket Association hosted a party in 1902 in honour of the coronation of Edward VII, the main attraction being a football match. The British decidedly contributed to the diffusion of the new game. And they did that by participating in clubs formed in the British colonies in Brazilian cities, and introducing the sport in their workplaces. They were not alone in this endeavour, but they were among the key players.

English supremacy during the beginnings of football practice in Brazil contributed to a larger development of the sport in São Paulo, where foreign migration was much more intense in the period.[13]

In São Paulo, apart from the British, only members of the upper class were able to take part in the new sport. Playing football was an expensive activity, because the sport demanded imported equipment, including uniforms, cleats, shin guards and balls. As a consequence of this, for some time football maintained an elitist character and remained an amateur practice. The audience of the initial matches was also exclusive. Newspapers at the time reported that well-dressed men, elegant ladies, girls and boys went to the football fields to cheer on their sons, brothers, cousins and friends.

But despite the financial demands of participation, it was not merely from the elite of São Paulo that football drew support. Amongst the poorer socioeconomic classes, especially workers, football slowly attracted interest. The early football practices of the British at the Chácara Dulley aroused popular interest:

These private tests of the Britons had much worth, although it may not seem so. They made the city notice that 'nearby the neighbourhood of Luz, the Bom Retiro, a group of passionate Englishmen occasionally kicked something akin to an ox bladder, which gave them great satisfaction and regret, when this kind of yellowish bladder entered in a rectangle marked out by poles'.[14]

People increasingly wanted to know what it was that the 'Englishmen' were doing in Bom Retiro—how to play this strange game. Curiosity led to early attempts by locals to try it:

Shortly, the 'nearby Luz, the Ponte Grande', rubber balls were not exclusively played with and thrown by the hands. The feet also came into contact and started having a decisive usefulness. Stones were used as 'beams', and kids in the streets became familiar with the ball and how to use it, differently from how it was previously done. Although not knowing exactly how to play football, these boys, years later, as adults, would be the central figures of football matches at the city's floodplains.

People in the streets mimicked the Englishmen at the Chácara Dulley in the same way that they would subsequently mimic the inaccessibility of the stadiums.[15]

The success of football among the poorer socioeconomic classes was predictable due to the very nature of the game. Easily assimilated, football could be played without previous arrangements. It could encompass any number of players, regardless of any age gap; it could be played outdoors and in any weather, with a ball made of fabric, paper or rubber. In the city of São Paulo, alive with progress and industrial development, and amongst a population still sparsely distributed with plenty of space available for occupation, football would become an accessible leisure activity, the favourite of barefoot boys in working class neighbourhoods. The sport previously played by the British elite was becoming popular.

At the time of the Chácara Dulley, boys and young men started playing football in an improvised manner wherever they could—on the streets and pavements, backyards and schoolyards. As their interest in football grew, they sought more appropriate sites, playing alongside the British and members of the Paulistano Athletic Club. People flocked to the Várzea do Carmo, which had hosted the British players' first training sessions. It was here that the sport became further organised and became known as 'floodplain football'.

The first football fields for this wider body of participants appeared around 1902 and soon surpassed those of São Paulo's fashionable neighbourhoods. Their number grew dramatically, as Neiva described: 'We saw three new fields before going to sleep, and when we woke up, there were half a dozen more of them, already free of grass'.[16] From the Várzea do Carmo, football fields spread across the city, especially in working-class neighbourhoods. In these places, many new clubs emerged, with Brás, Belém, Penha, Bom Retiro, Canindé, Ponte Grande, Santana and Ipiranga having the highest concentrations of floodplain clubs.[17] In addition to maintaining football teams, these clubs organised social activities such as dances, picnics, excursions and fishing trips, in which women and children were also allowed to participate. The championships organised between these teams drew the attention of the public and official competitions were promoted by the Liga Paulista de Futebol. Gradually, star footballers emerged from the floodplains, and these men were sometimes signed to the main football clubs of Rio de Janeiro and even chosen to play for the Brazilian national team.

The popularisation of football in São Paulo occurred mainly through the floodplain teams and clubs that were formed inside factories. The latter, as we shall see, were confined to participating in tournaments between the factories, with their players and teams rarely turning professional. In this, São Paulo did not follow the British example, in which clubs in factories or companies (such as Arsenal, West Ham and Manchester United) and even in churches (Southampton) went on to achieve professional success.[18]

Factory teams are formed

Bangu, in Rio de Janeiro, is probably Brazil's best-known works team. The Bangu Athletic Club was founded in 1904 by British skilled professionals at the Companhia Progresso Industrial do Brasil (Company of Industrial Progress of Brazil), a Brazilian and Portuguese-financed textile company. The team was initially composed of seven Britons, an Italian and a Brazilian, who had the approval of the company's directors to play football during their spare time.[19] The factory bought the team's shirts and allowed a football field to be installed on their property. Without such help, the sport would have been unfeasible. There were not, however, sufficient British players at Bangu to form two complete teams to play against each other. Furthermore, the factory was located in one of Rio's peripheral neighbourhoods, and transport difficulties discouraged other British players, working with other companies, to travel there to compete. The solution was to enlist other workers of the factory, and most of them were certainly very willing to try to kick a ball around. As a consequence, workers there had access to a game that had previously been the almost exclusive preserve of the British colony and elements of the upper classes. The Bangu Athletic Club initiated the popularisation of football in Rio.

The Bangu Athletic Club was unique for having been created as a factory team and, from the start, for allowing workers to participate in the game without restriction, unlike the elite clubs of Rio de Janeiro and those of the British. The case of Bangu became well-known because the club quickly reached football's top division, and soon was playing against Fluminense, Botafogo and other clubs. Bangu, however, was not the first Brazilian factory club. Some previous and isolated initiatives arose spontaneously, such as the Votorantim Athletic Club, which was founded in 1902 by Italian engineers and technicians working at the British-owned Fábrica de Tecidos Votorantim (Votorantim Textiles Factory) in Sorocaba in the interior of the state of São Paulo.[20] In addition, Regoli & Cia Ltda in the Mooca neighbourhood of the city of São Paulo had a football club. When the textile factory was purchased by Rodolfo Crespi in 1909, the workers' team was renamed Crespi Football Club. Years later, in the 1930s, the team was renamed again. Under its new moniker, Athletic Club Juventus, the football team would soon become better known than the textile company itself, just as had occurred with Bangu and, to a certain extent, the Italian club that inspired its name, Juventus (which had been created in Italy as a workers' team for Fiat, the automobile manufacturer).

Factory teams quickly spread across São Paulo, steadily increasing in number from the early decades of the twentieth century. Soon it was difficult to find an industry that did not have at least a small team. Amateur football, the sport played in clubs created in factories by the workers themselves, became a new tradition in the city. In most companies, the board of directors contributed to the initiatives by funding the teams and providing material support. This contribution was of foremost importance to promote the sport.[21]

Many clubs emerged from informal football matches played on the streets or factory yards during lunch breaks. The game gradually became organised. As many people wanted to participate, separate teams soon began to be formed within individual sections of a company. With the growing number of teams, more matches were being held, and more playing time demanded. Therefore, playing only during lunch breaks provided insufficient opportunities and the activity was extended to weekends. As the taste for football grew, people wanted to improve the conditions of their game: they wanted to play as the British did, with full complements of players on teams, uniforms, a leather ball, a proper field, a place to meet and store their sporting equipment. In short, they wanted football clubs. But how was it possible to fund such initiatives? Collecting contributions from stakeholders was an early idea, but it was not enough to sustain the high standards desired of football, while the workers themselves paid paltry, almost symbolic fees. Turning to a company's board of directors was a feasible solution, possibly the only one. This idea was justified by the affinity between factories and football teams that had been formed due to friendly relations established in the workspace. When the board of directors agreed to collaborate, the organisation of the football club adopted different contours.

All the activities of these football teams were subsidised, with the football field and clubhouse installed on company-owned land. In some other cases, the company contributed to the payment of rent. Each month, an agreed sum of money was supplied to the club, thus supplementing its budget, and allowing the payment of expenses related to maintenance, taxes, transport, energy supply and the cleaning of uniforms. As for sports equipment, the companies provided the shirts, balls and cleats. Clubs formed in factories were not limited to football, they also maintained their social activities and enjoyed a high attendance of workers and their families; to support them, clubs requested supplementary resources.

The board of directors contributed to the factory's club, but demanded a return on their investment. They wanted to know how the money was used: what were the activities and how much had been spent. Clubs had to communicate their activities by reports and supplying monthly or annual balance sheets—accountability was an initial form of control over them. The increasing breadth of activities maintained by factory clubs required organisational improvements. To meet this end, clubs established their own boards of directors, whose members had managerial tasks. Officers tended to be recruited from the company's own bureaucratic staff, as chiefs, directors and managers. It was also common that the owner of the company would occupy a senior position in the club, such as honorary president, as a sign of recognition for having contributed to the club. In the meantime, the workers, who organised the football team, were either left to play and watch the games or to occupy subordinate positions in the administrative staff of the club.

Club directors, along with the members of the supervisory and deliberative councils, decided on internal regulations and statutes, and defined the rights and duties of their members. These documents, however, were submitted to the factory's board of directors for approval. The company wanted to know what was going on inside the club, making sure that order and discipline was being maintained. The Brazilian state also had a hand in deciding how football clubs within the factories would be administered. During the Estado Novo (1937–45) and the dictatorship of President Getúlio Vargas, the Brazilian government promoted an organisational and bureaucratic intervention in all sports associations. The National Sports Council defined the model of the statutes to be adhered to by clubs throughout Brazil.[22] Class-based football leagues, representing entrepreneurial sectors—the Liga Esportiva Comércio e Indústria (Commerce and Industry Sporting League) and the Associação Comercial de Esportes Atléticos (Commercial Association of Sports Athletes)—also emerged during that time, and they organised tournaments between companies which were used for government propaganda.

The vision of entrepreneurs

Observing the process of how factory clubs were organised and how their relationships with the companies to which they were attached developed, one might ask what motivated companies to adopt these sports associations created by their workers, contribute to their maintenance and exercise some control over them. Anatol Rosenfeld raised the hypothesis that the encouragement of football by a company amongst its workers would be a means to tame the workforce and instil in them a sense of group identity in support of the firm.[23] Equally, Waldenyr Caldas rejected the argument that industrialists used football to improve workers' physical disposition to work and thereby increase production— if this was plausible all workers would have access to football, which was not the case.[24] Aiming at the success of the team—and, by extension, of the company—factories started rigorously selecting footballers. Only the best would be employed, and few, indeed, would be able to compete for a position in the team's factory. As for the others, those who simply played for fun would have to accept the role of spectator.

In studying the spread of football in France, Alfred Wahl reported that entrepreneurs had a clear interest in promoting the identification of the club and the company as a single whole, encouraging the belief that players, workers and bosses together formed a large family.[25] Footballing victories would increase pride amongst the workers for the club and, by extension, the company. This feeling of integration could thus reduce workplace conflict and optimise production. Entrepreneurs especially believed that their employees' clubs served as useful promotional tools.

A new way to promote and sell the products of companies was being opened up as the club boasted the name of the factory. Business leaders were concerned with maintaining order and discipline in factory clubs as a sign of the organisation and efficiency that would eventually lead to success. The prestige of factories did not rely on the performance of the football team, but success would certainly help promote the company. Workers' teams somehow played the role of a calling card for the companies: they used the same name, in effect publicising their products. Early on Brazilian manufacturers realised the important value that football played as an advertising vehicle.

Anatol Rosenfeld also mentioned the promotional function of Bangu A.C., as well as the consequences it brought, not only to the practice of football, but to the working conditions of many of the textile workers. Through the workers' team, men from humble backgrounds had access to a previously unknown cultural good which, once appropriated and reworked, opened other opportunities beyond mere amusement. Rosenfeld pointed out that when football became an offshoot of employment at the factory, workers who made the team earned benefits. The footballers, he noted, were awarded time off for training, given lighter work and were promoted faster: 'generations of young people [were given jobs] because not only did they work well, but also because they played well'.[26] After all, with good players the team could achieve better results, which would increase its prestige and fame. Meanwhile, for the less affluent, to play football in the factory club brought the possibility of a career as a worker-footballer.

THE COUNTRY OF FOOTBALL

Football and the workers' movement

During the early decades of the twentieth century, the diffusion of football amongst the working class was acknowledged by anarchists and communists as a reality. Some unions viewed football as a bourgeois sport, a powerful opiate that would undermine the unity and organisation of the working class. While these groups debated heatedly over whether football should or should not be accepted, workers continued to be attracted to the sport. Devotion to their political beliefs prevented anarchists and communists to understand that football was already part of working-class culture.

From the late 1910s, the propaganda events traditionally promoted by anarchist unionists were replaced by festivals, picnics and excursions. Most of these activities occurred in public spaces, and were mainly aimed at leisure and fun. Among them, football matches held a prominent position. Anarchists criticised popular parties, such as Carnival, and other traditional festivities and football matches for being bourgeoisie cultural elements; however, they grew to tolerate football in their festivals, as long as they would contribute to the effectiveness of libertarian preaching.[27]

In the late 1920s and early 1930s, anarchists' attitudes towards football changed. During this period, the labour press denounced the presence of the dominant class in popular neighbourhoods and their attempts to control the working class through football, as well as by other means. The anarchists, who had tolerated football matches among workers, placed themselves alongside communists and positioned themselves against the practice of the sport, arguing that it would weaken the fight for better working conditions. Football, especially in factory clubs, would divide the working class, putting workers into confrontation with each other in defence of certain company names.

While anarchists continued to be opposed to football, some unions and groups with communist allegiances changed their way of acting and tried to organise leisure activities appealing to the working class, in contrast to what they called the bourgeois culture. They began to promote trade unions as centres of educational and recreational activities, the aim being to increase and foster class awareness among the proletariat. They proposed that workers themselves should manage football clubs and initiated a campaign of 'proletarianisation of the sport' in an attempt to attract young people to trade union activities.[28] Communists wanted to treat football differently to the way they believed the bourgeoisie did. Instead of using it to control and divide youths, the communists wanted sports activities to be a unifying element of the working class, a field of struggle for the liberation of all forms of misery and oppression. The communists, who had long been stridently opposed to the adoption of football by workers, now developed exaggerated expectations of the sport, even proposing the creation of a federation of football clubs organised by unions.

To the anarchists' criticisms that football would divide the working class, communists argued that if workers did not have access to the sport within the union structures, they would seek it elsewhere. The communists recognised that football had won over support from all social strata. Instead, it was felt that it would be better to accept the sport, have the workers control their clubs and end some of the exploitative practices, such as the small payroll deductions to maintain the factory club or the convening of workers to perform additional services when they were gathered at the club during their leisure time.

Although anarchists and communists were reluctant to accept football amongst workers, their objections were defeated and they eventually acknowledged that the popularisation of the sport and its adoption by the working class was irreversible. Even so, they felt it was necessary to subvert the main characteristics that the bourgeoisie had imposed on football. Having achieved this intent or not, the fact is that both anarchists and communists played important roles in the spread of football to the working class, especially among workers who were members of unions or class associations.[29]

The professionalisation of workers' teams

As football grew more popular and gained status, professional sporting opportunities for workers arose. With its popularisation, football spread the professional horizons of many labourers who started to dedicate themselves to sports inside the factory as a normal kind of work. In working places, the support of employers of football clubs encouraged the professionalism of the sport, a process that peaked in the 1940s and 1950s.

At the start, the support provided by companies to clubs was limited to financial assistance for purchasing sports equipment, paying the rent of football fields and other expenses associated with the game. Subsequently, competition between clubs made many companies assemble more competitive and competent administrative teams and footballers of better technical ability. The sports capital of workers began to be valued in the labour market with some companies preferring to hire a good footballer ahead of a good worker. Extra payments began to be offered to workers who played football, taking the form of small gifts and services, gratuities and even a second salary. Many workers were motivated by the possibility of additional earnings represented by the bonuses (*bichos*)[30] that players received. Attracted by the possibility of additional earnings, workers who believed that they had footballing skills often engaged in bitter infighting for a position on the team, which was the reason for many workplace conflicts.

The specialisation of sports within factories, however, excluded most workers who simply wanted to play football for fun. This element was being replaced by those who regarded football as a professional undertaking. Although the main occupation of these men continued to be in the factory, they devoted time after work to training as well as weekends for matches. Many of them were dissatisfied with this situation and wanted to go further. They were what Simoni Guedes called careerists:[31] workers who judged the position of footballers in factory teams as the first step of a professional footballing career. They were focused on the sport and had well-defined ambitions.

Those playing in factory clubs usually concentrated on attempts at trying out for professional clubs. Some men were successful; most, however, had to abandon their dreams of being a first division player. Even so, they did not give up playing football; the sport still had practical value as success in a workers' team could lead to better employment conditions. They were fully aware that the workers' team could help them to get a choice job in a factory. Football became a supplementary professional activity for them, with earnings, in the form of bonuses or a second salary, supplementing their monthly income. They would spend the week at the factory and the weekend on the football field. Such were the characteristics of professionalism within the sport that for most workers were the only feasible hope.

Few worker-players made it into any of the professional football clubs of the first division. When professional football started in Brazil (officially, not until 1933), some outstanding factory club players joined major teams in São Paulo and Rio de Janeiro. But, as a rule, the income

of a footballer at a professional club was not enough for their maintenance. Thus, even after football became an individual's main professional activity, he would need a supplementary job. Other footballers
went in the opposite direction to worker-players: having been recruited
by a major professional club, they sought a second job in a factory. In
other cases, industries enrolled professional footballers as employees
exclusively to play on the workers' team, in an attempt to improve the
performance of the club in the championships between companies.
Alfred Wahl called such fraud 'coverage employment', a practice also
common in French factory clubs at this time.[32]

Eventually, however, footballers could become full-time, professional
athletes, exclusively relying on income derived from the sport. The
example of those who achieved fame as professional players in major
clubs strengthened the dream of upward mobility through football. The
most emblematic case involved Manuel Francisco dos Santos, popularly
known as Garrincha. Born in 1933 in Pau Grande, a district of the town
of Magé in the interior of the state of Rio de Janeiro, as a child
Garrincha worked in Pau Grande for the Companhia América Fabril,
which produced textiles. In 1949 Garrincha began his footballing career
by playing for the Sport Club Pau Grande, a team organised by employees of the factory. Due to his excellent footballing skills, Garrincha was
able to continue working at the factory despite constant conflicts
between workers and employers—conflicts which often ended with the
dismissal of the former. According to José Sergio Leite Lopes,[33]
Garrincha's indiscipline and absenteeism were tolerated by the factory
due to his outstanding performances on the football field. Everyone
believed that Garrincha had a promising career ahead of him, a predic-
tion eventually confirmed. Despite several unsuccessful trials with Clube
de Regatas Vasco da Gama, Fluminense Football Club and São
Cristóvão de Futebol e Regatas, Garrincha spent much of his professional career with Botafogo de Futebol e Regatas and became famous for
his role in the Brazilian national team, including being part of the winning squads in the World Cups of 1958 and 1962.[34]

Many footballers emerging from factory teams were destined for the
major clubs. Except for a small number of superstars—players of the
highest technical level, such as Garrincha—few of these achieved financial success. Most footballers, though improving their personal standard
of living, would face an uncertain future at the end of their careers.

Despite playing professionally, they played supporting roles, never quite reaching the spotlight. They came and went on the fields, not being particularly inspirational players, and not benefiting greatly from earnings from the sport. There is no doubt that playing football enabled some employees to acquire a trade or start a small business, but that was certainly not the general outcome. For most ex-professional footballers, factory clubs represented an important means to secure a new job. In these cases, they needed to know how to use former relationships to secure a position back at the factory and thus get involved in workers' teams as players or coaches.

In summary, in addition to developing a special type of professionalism, factory clubs had a close relationship with professional football: they served as development centres for players who were hoping to be signed by the major clubs and welcomed them back at the end of their professional footballing careers. The popularisation of football brought new symbolic, ideological and socioeconomic meanings. The sport became a social phenomenon of great significance, involving a complex network of social relationships and interests which sometimes diverged. Football's diffusion amongst workers led entrepreneurs to encourage the organisation of clubs within factories not only as a form of entertainment: these associations spread the name of the company and its products by participating in official championships. The resulting appreciation of the sporting ability of workers gave rise to a process of social mobility in the workplace, of which only a small portion of workers had effectively benefited.

The Sociedade Esportiva Linhas e Cabos: a special case

Founded in Toronto, Canada in 1899, the São Paulo Tramway, Light & Power Company Limited, was one of the companies based on foreign (predominantly British) capital that dominated key sectors of the Brazilian economy from the late nineteenth century and included railways and urban transport, telephone and the production and distribution of gas and electricity.[35]

Since it started operating in São Paulo in 1900, the 'Light', as it became known, became deeply involved in the promotion of football, frequently awarding trophies and medals to outstanding teams participating in the city championships. For example, in 1903, the Light's board of directors gave medals acquired in London to the footballers of the São Paulo Athletic Club, twice champions of São Paulo's football league tournament.[36] The Light also supported the formation of football teams drawn from its own employees. The company was especially proud of having organised the first night-time match ever held in Brazil (indeed the first such event held anywhere in the world), an event that was internationally recognised. The match—between Sociedade Esportiva Linhas e Cabos (which was made up of employees of the Light) and Associação Atlética República (a club of the city)—took place on 23 June 1923 at a company-owned football field that was located at Rua Glicério, in the Cambuci neighbourhood of central São Paulo.[37]

By 1934, the company had 7,008 employees, distributed between seventeen departments of the São Paulo Tramway, Light & Power Co. Ltd and eleven other companies that over time had become part of the corporation.[38] The management of this conglomerate was based on a rational-bureaucratic model that fundamentally differed from the standard of family business prevailing in São Paulo at this time, where decisions were often dependent on the whim of a single person. The Light was a service company, not a manufacturing industry. Features such as the large size of the business and the high number of employees, the centrality of foreign capital and complex management structures, gave football there certain peculiar features. In terms of organisation and function, the Light's clubs did not noticeably differ from those of the factories. Football was decentralised since the Light's general management did not demand a specific model of sports association. When the company's directors changed, the interest in clubs and sports also changed. Thus, the idea of a central workers' team, able to attract all the company's staff to one place, could not develop. Instead, small groups within recreational sections were formed, gathering co-workers who maintained daily contact. At best, these nuclei encompassed employees of the same department. In the case of companies associated with the Light elsewhere in the state of São Paulo, each had a small football club.

The Sociedade Esportiva Linhas e Cabos (SELC) stood out amongst the smaller football clubs. Founded on 17 September 1920, the SELC drew its membership from employees of the Light's Section for Lines and Cables (subsequently named the Division of Distribution), which was responsible for the installation and maintenance of the power grid. The organisation of the club did not differ from other factory clubs. There was a board of directors and an advisory council, who reported the SELC's activities annually to the company's general superintendent. In return, the company agreed to assist the board of directors in maintaining the SELC's social and sports headquarters. In recognition of this support, some senior company officials were appointed honorary directors of the SELC, endorsed by its general assembly. Over the years, the board of directors remained virtually unchanged. In 1934, the SELC had 141 contributing members, accounting for 20 per cent of the employees of the Division of Distribution. Football was the main activity of the club with thirty of the members, including many club officers, playing football in the SELC's first or second teams. The Light ceded the football field at Rua Glicério to the SELC.

In 1929, the SELC moved to a site at Avenida Estado in Cambuci, also owned by the company. There, alongside the football field, they built a new headquarters with space for parties and meetings, as well as a playground and a boules pitch, the game being popular in São Paulo at the time, especially with Italians. The company provided funding and building materials, while in their spare time club members helped with the building work. Although they were grateful to the company's managers for the contribution to the club, the SELC's directors were keen to stress that all the assets of the club were gained through the struggles of its members themselves. Dated 23 September 1931, a letter from Severino Gragnani, the SELC's president, reveals a strong sense of identity and pride for the club:

Being honest, hardworking and honourable, these individuals [members] earned an honourable past for the Company and even succeeded in forming an appreciable patrimony, thanks to their efforts, perseverance and good will.

So it is, that the Company already has its sports arena, thanks to Dr Souza's [the Light's general superintendent] benevolent land concession, emphasizing that the football field constitutes the main index of its progress. This field was built by the members themselves during the few off hours in weekdays and during the holidays and Sundays.

[…] All of them, indistinctly, work for the greatness and prosperity of the Society.[39]

Feelings of identity and pride were typical for members of sports clubs. But for the SELC this identity was sometimes clothed by a class bias that differed from the remaining small clubs of the Light. Some of the SELC's founding members and footballers were in the União dos Trabalhadores da Light (Light's Workers' Union),[40] a communist-oriented union, which had as its mouthpiece the newspaper *O Trabalhador da Light*.

During the 1930s, the SELC organised annual festivals, similar to those organised and sponsored by communist and anarchist newspapers, to mark its own anniversary and to celebrate International Workers' Day.[41] The programmes included recreational activities for children, young people and women such as sack races and tugs of war, and the game of boules for adult men. But the main event at these festivals was always a football match between the SELC and a guest team, typically a factory club that was also affiliated with the Liga Esportiva Comércio e Indústria (Trade and Industry Sports League), which in turn was an affiliate of the Associação Paulista de Esportes Atléticos (São Paulo Athletic Sports Association), the predecessor of the Federação Paulista de Futebol (São Paulo Football Federation). Festivities ended with a family party, sometimes preceded by a rally of the União dos Trabalhadores da Light.

In the 1920s and 1930s, festivals celebrating 1 May were common among anarchist and communist groups, including unions. The day was celebrated with a party organised by the workers themselves. No other sports club at the Light celebrated this date as the SELC did— even the AAL&P, a contemporary of the SELC, never organised a celebration for this purpose. The SELC dance and sport festivals had the style of those of the unions and the labour press and were substantially different from the grand official parades and rallies, inspired by the quasi-fascist ideological propaganda of Getúlio Vargas's government in the late 1930s and early 1940s, that marked 1 May. From the late 1940s these festivals were replaced by the Jogos Esportivos Operários (Workers' Sports Games), sponsored by Serviço Social da Indústria (Industry Social Service), an organisation created in 1946 by industrialists to provide social, educational and leisure services to workers. However, in the Jogos Esportivos Operários, workers were no longer necessarily participants, but rather spectators. More concerned with victory than with employee participation, many companies were represented by professional and semi-professional athletes. The meaning of the 1 May celebrations, as conceived of by the directors of the SELC, had been completely forgotten.

The Associação Atlética Light & Power (AAL&P) was founded on 16 March 1930 with the aim of uniting the sports associations spread across the departments of the company. Its founders, administrative workers in the head office, had favoured tennis and gave most support to this sporting activity. Football, on the other hand, was played by the more humble employees, in particular those in junior or manual jobs. The AAL&P was affiliated with the Federação Paulista de Tênis, where some of its members occupied management posts. The AAL&P also developed basketball, athletics, rowing and swimming. It maintained a football team that took part in the championships of the Liga Esportiva Comércio e Indústria (LECI) and, for a short period, in the tournament of the Associação Paulista de Esportes Atléticos (APEA). When the APEA turned to professional football, the AAL&P left the association as it was committed to the spirit of amateurism. The AAL&P football team mainly consisted of employees drawn from different departments across the enterprise.

In 1931, the AAL&P invited the SELC to merge, as the Bonde Team (Tram Team), the Medidores Team (Meters Team) and other small factory clubs had done. The president of SELC explained his refusal to agree to the merger by arguing that the two associations represented different social classes and were thus incompatible with each other. Although the AAL&P were willing to encompass all employees of the company, it was still a club of head office staff, with better levels of education and higher wages. The SELC, in turn, represented labourers in the Division of Distribution.[42] Moreover, a merger would imply the loss of a hard-won heritage and the privilege of controlling an exclusive and desirable football field:

We are very honoured by your kind invitation to enter and form a large guild, a united front of all sports societies at the Company.

Now we have the duty to explain to you the reasons that prevent us from accepting your suggestion.

[...] Our members are not only interested in having the Society as a simple sports centre for recreation, but also for congregating with their families and socialising during leisure time with the same strong ties that unite them in everyday drudgery. And also, the Company will be able to find them at all times and for any emergency, whenever needed.

That is, we do not believe that we could gather our members conveniently under the mantle of your great sports college, mainly due to the ways and customs of the classes in question.[43]

Severino Gragnani, the president of the SELC, had never shown sympathy for the AAL&P. Similarly, the AAL&P seemed dissatisfied with the independence and autonomy that Gragnani had achieved for his SELC. Apparently contradicting the independence of the SELC, at times its directors directly addressed the general superintendent of the Light, especially over issues concerning the preservation of its headquarters. It was, in fact, a survival strategy. The SELC's managers knew that the continuity of the club depended on the goodwill of the company's administration.

In 1937, the company performed work to a pipeline under the SELC's football field. The club's directors had unofficial information that the Light was planning to demolish the headquarters next to the field in order to complete the works. Under the threat of losing almost the entire sports arena, on 12 July Severino Gragnani wrote to Odilon de Souza (the Light's general superintendent) to try to convince him of the advantages for the company of keeping the headquarters and, by extension, the sports club. If employees could gather in the sports arena, they would always be available to provide emergency services:

There [the football field] was the meeting point for employees of the Section of Lines and Cables. On Sundays they would go there to have fun by watching a football match and other sports competitions that were staged at the headquarters.

Aiming to provide good services to the company, this society always tried to gather employees of the Section of Lines and Cables in a single environment, because it has often happened that when they were gathered in joyful recreation in the club, they were called to undertake emergency services for the company, and went in good humours to repair electrical lines or to provide any other services that might have been required.

[...] This society will probably be deprived of the privilege to continue using their facilities and the above mentioned sports field. Therefore, the Sociedade Esportiva Linhas e Cabos, very respectfully, asks your permission to inquire whether you or the Superintendent has the intention of granting another meeting point for installing the club in any of the properties of the company that suits this purpose?[44]

The arrangement for enlisting workers for the possibility of being called to provide extraordinary services was criticised by the workers' press. On 8 August 1934 the newspaper *Nossa Voz* denounced the supposed fact that during the 1919 strike at the Light, the 'population of clubs' was called to replace the striking workers.[45]

In January 1942, the SELC faced serious financial difficulties. Administrative changes in the company reduced the number of employees of the Division of Distribution from 678 in 1934 to just forty-five in 1944.[46] As a consequence, the number of SELC members also fell, which immediately caused a decrease of funding raised through membership fees. With dwindling resources it became virtually impossible to keep the club running. Given this situation, the board of the SELC appealed to the management of the Light, asking to award a monthly donation. The request was granted and the company went on to contribute a monthly sum of 150,000 réis, an insufficient amount in the face of the SELC's needs. The club struggled with financial difficulties for another year, until in April 1943 Gragnani eventually decided for a temporary interruption of sporting activities. They never resumed.

The Light: restricted support to the workers' clubs

Many companies used their football clubs as tools to advertise their products. The encouragement that they devoted to the formation of teams that might be able to participate in official tournaments was due to their interest in better promoting the company's name. They were not primarily concerned with providing their workers with leisure activities or entertainment. Although the Light's administrators supported the creation of spaces for the practice of sports by employees of the company and allowed them to form their own clubs, the company never took the initiative. As employees did not have sufficient resources to maintain their clubs, they resorted to asking the company for help. The company, in general, met the basic demands that were made, but was cautious in how it released funds. In so doing, the company extended its control over the practice of sports, simply because the implementation of any initiative that was not supported by the company was not feasible.

In this context, the workers' football clubs at the Light had always encountered difficulties in their development. All attempts to create new clubs were driven by a mix of identity and pride for the company and by the struggle for what was considered a basic right. Numerous businesses in the city maintained football teams. Employees of the powerful São Paulo Tramway, Light & Power Company Limited, however, did not benefit in this way. They resented the lack of spaces for leisure and sport and felt that given the Light's size and importance within the city and the state of São Paulo, the company should provide them with strong clubs.[47] For them, it was natural that such an important company as the Light would have well-equipped clubs and successful teams in the championships. But in terms of sporting achievements, except for the period of activity of the AAL&P, the Light had little to boast about. In fact, the elitist character that marked the early years of the AAL&P was intended to promote the club and raise the social status of its members, though by a different route than that of competition between workers' clubs.

Workers' clubs in the Light were marked by discontinuity, both from the standpoint of time and space. They arose separately in each section, in several power plants in the state of São Paulo, as spontaneous and collective sporting organisations. Attempts to centralise the activities of these small clubs into a single, larger one were unsuccessful. Although the Canadian company would support sports activities, it maintained a restrictive stance in allocating resources to these clubs. Unlike other companies in the same period, the Light showed no interest in promoting itself through the football clubs of their employees and, thus, the company did not prevent its clubs from perishing.

The cases discussed here illustrate how football unfolded within São Paulo's factories and workplaces, and record a specific experience of the working class in the city. In different political and social contexts, football was thought of as an activity of leisure and recreation, a means to promote a factory and its products, a way to achieve individual benefits in the place of work or in a future career as a professional player. Football also fed the struggle between different professional categories that dedicated unequal attention to the social advantages that they could achieve with the sport. This chapter has shown how bourgeois cultural imposition over the workers could be a matter of both rejection and resistance. Finally, football in the factories represented a space of mobilisation and organisation for workers around the sport, involving political and symbolic fights.

2

Malandros, 'Honourable Workers' and the Professionalisation of Brazilian Football, 1930–1950

Gregory E. Jackson

Introduction

The rise of the poor of predominantly mixed and African ancestry in Brazilian football after 1933 offers examples of the broader changes occurring during the period in society at large. Multi-ethnic football became the norm with professional clubs and the national team. The shift in player selection from mostly white upper-class players reflected the optimism of the era in national history, which promoted the idea of *mestiçagem* (miscegenation) as the strength of Brazilian society. Paradoxically the idea of a *raça brasileira* was built upon the central premise that Brazilians, since the early twentieth century, had transcended the idea of race itself.[1]

That era was dominated by Getúlio Vargas, one of the most influential figures in Brazil's national history. It was during his long and complex political career on the national scene that spanned more than two decades, from 1930–1954, that the professionalisation of the national game became intimately connected to the new vision of Brazilian society taking shape. This chapter focuses on the years 1930–1950 and analyses how the professionalisation of football, as well as 'the pacification' of the game's sporting directors and governing institutions, played a critical role in articulating Brazilian modernity. Both of these processes unfolded amidst rapid, ambitious and far-reaching reforms strategised to transform Brazil during the inter-war years and the Second World War.

After World War II the United Nations sponsored an extensive study of Brazilian civilisation to better understand what appeared to the outside world to be a successful transition from slave to free society without catastrophic ethnic- or class-based confrontations among the evolving citizenry.[2] When compared to the Jim Crow segregation of the US South or South African apartheid, social relations in Brazil seemed to be a model worthy of emulation. In Brazil, social stratification and economic stability correlate to multiple social categories such as race, ethnicity and social class in a historically specific manner. Those categories are also at work throughout Brazil with meanings attached to the colour of skin, the texture of hair or regional ties. The 'flexibility' that exists in how such terms are used make the use of stark, artificial binaries regarding racial thinking impractical when talking about social life in Brazil.[3] Nevertheless, football culture there, like elsewhere, is littered with essentialist claims regarding the 'origins' of playing style and fandom.

When Brazil hosted the first FIFA World Cup after World War II, much more than football was at stake for the South American nation. In addition to the usual pressures which now face the organisers of modern tournaments regarding the logistics of security, infrastructure and tourism, Brazilians faced the additional pressure of refuting the many negative stereotypes associated with miscegenation and prospects for western-styled development in the tropics. The hosting of the international event and the outcome of the championship itself each carried symbolic importance for upper-class sportsmen who were plugged into the global economy and international diplomatic affairs, and had eagerly lobbied to host the tournament. Football, which underwent far-reaching reforms throughout the Vargas years, offers an insight to the ways in which the game played a central role in the daily life of the average individual, as well as the vision the sport held among elite sportsmen and government reformers for the future of race and nation—a vision that was to be showcased at the 1950 World Cup. This fact is critical to understanding the stakes and impact of the stunning come-from-behind win by Uruguay in the final known as the *Maracanazo*.

The national game under Vargas connected influential members of society throughout Brazil as it had during previous decades. However, an authoritarian phase was underway in football as early as 1934 and continued through to the end of the Estado Novo in 1945. During that period, the Vargas state focused the energies of sportsmen towards the goals of the nation. Football under Vargas represented a pedagogical tool to eugenically build fit and culturally orthodox citizens. Though in reality football never approached such efficiency in transforming those who came into contact with the game, the manner in which it was conceived by scholars, government ministers and members of the military is instructive as to the general complexity of organised sport in Brazil. High levels of participation and the particular nature of sporting culture made football in Brazil an attractive heuristic for explaining modernisation to the masses.

For both specialist and lay readers alike, football reveals a cross-section of the Brazilian social universe.[4] Unlike previous governments who showed a passing interest in the game, under Vargas football and its institutions became organs of the state geared towards the building of the new Brazilian man and a modern Brazil. The evolution of the Brazilian game and its institutions since 1894 tells a story of how members of the national elite viewed the strengths and weaknesses of its people according to how they organised the spectacle of modern sport. By analysing how the game was organised, we gain great insight into other aspects of social history. Throughout the 1920s and 1930s, many sports enthusiasts from all walks of life debated sports themes in the press, in the clubs that sponsored teams, and in the streets among supporters who could not afford membership to the clubs to which they had thrown their allegiances. But *cartolas*, the upper class sportsmen who held directorships on numerous boards associated with the clubs, leagues and regional sporting institutions, held disproportionate sway in the process of player selection. Their vision regarding who was equipped to honour the colours of club and country was, of course, shaped by the larger intellectual currents of the period.

It is for that reason that football culture in Brazil offers a rich field for analysis on the changing dynamics of racial and class meaning during a pivotal moment in Brazilian history. More generally, the history of sport in Brazil offers a unique look at a transitional period for a post-slave society. Since footballing culture and sporting institutions did not evolve in a vacuum, the transformations which occurred in Brazilian football offer a significant insight into the changing meaning of race in the Atlantic world, at a time when social Darwinism and determinist attitudes were only softened by multiple world wars. Football in Brazil during the 1930s offered honourable work to worker-players who had previously existed on the margins of urban society. Many of the worker-players who benefited from professionalism were *mestiço*, or of 'obvious' African ancestry. Consequently the game and the image it evoked were transformed by the new interpretations of the British game which had been dominated by white upper-class Brazilians since its arrival in 1894.

The game would become the focus of social and cultural engineering of a new kind of Brazilian man and, through that patriarchal vision, a new society. This chapter explains how the professionalisation of football in Brazil was attached to larger ideological currents in the Atlantic world and played a role in formulating new social relations and attitudes about race, while retaining subtle aspects of white supremacy. Those changing attitudes were reflected in the institutional reforms and strategies pursued by Vargas and his ministers through 'the pacification of sport'.

Football and the Vargas regime, 1930–1945

The entrance of Getúlio Vargas onto the national political scene in November 1930 altered the trajectory of Brazilian history. Described years later by supporters as a 'revolution', Vargas was a break from Brazil's oligarchic past. Vargas's reforms from 1930 to 1945 were focused on urban centres and, among many political promises, aspired to redefine the value attached to labour in Brazil. During the Vargas years, to be a worker was a badge of honour rather than a mark of shame. Vargas was himself a native of São Borja in Rio Grande do Sul, and energised a movement known as the Liberal Alliance which sought to bring into the fold regions throughout Brazil that had been neglected by previous governments, with a primary focus on the affairs of the states of São Paulo, Minas Gerais and Rio de Janeiro. The reign of Getúlio Vargas spanned three distinct phases between 1930 and 1945: as a member of the Liberal Alliance, the 1930 'revolution' and the provisional government established thereafter; as president of the Second Republic as outlined by the 1934 constitution; and as president of the Estado Novo, an authoritarian regime which overthrew itself on 10 November 1937 to defend against a fabricated communist plot.

Vargas, with the support of the military and through rational deployment of state ministries, such as the Ministry of Health and Education, attempted to build a new modern Brazil on the basis of rational positivist approaches and untethered by the impracticalities of democratic politics. Reforms of sport under Vargas would create both institutions and a professional culture that survives somewhat intact in contemporary Brazil. Nevertheless state paternalism and individual demagoguery had run its course in Brazil by 1945 and at the end of World War II, Vargas was deposed by many of the same military high command that placed him in power in 1937 and had supported the 'revolution' seven years prior.[5] After Vargas's removal from office in 1945, he returned to the national political scene as a democratically elected official in 1950 and remained in office until his suicide in 1954.

Sport offered reformers an effective path to members of the working classes who often evaded or resented government vaccination and sanitation programmes viewed as intrusive.[6] Worker-players often had origins in such communities. Consequently, programmes centred on the development of sporting institutions in the poorest parts of Brazil were welcomed by residents of such communities and viewed by many as a way out of poverty. By registering with neighbourhood clubs that were themselves linked with municipal, regional and national governing bodies formed under Vargas, aspiring players of all levels had access to basic hygiene and medical services connected to the physicals required for club registration.

The most intense period of institutional reforms took place between 1934 and 1945. Those reforms aspired to remake Brazil from the ground up, through top-down programmes devised by teams of experts on physical fitness, propaganda and social engineering. The game's popularity, together with the historically elaborate networks among the upper classes throughout Brazil, combined to generate strong grass-roots networks dedicated to using the game for social ends. The professional character of the sport by the 1920s linked working-class virtuosos who penetrated an elite-only game with a state-directed sporting infrastructure that could properly promote the game and its newest untapped natural resource, working-class players, on an international scale. As such football held the potential to raise Brazil's profile in the global community through success in the Olympics and World Cup. At the same time positivists and social reformers saw another way in which the promotion of sport could advance Brazil. The eugenic aspects of the game and culture which promoted it had the potential to rehabilitate and regenerate the *raça brasileira* emerging from a slave system, miscegenation, and tropical decay—all theories which pessimistically predicted perpetual underdevelopment in Brazil.[7]

Prior to 1930, and for much of the first two years after Vargas assumed office, Brazil was fragmented by regional cultures, partisan politics and the lack of any universal sense of national identity. To Vargas's ministers such as Gustavo Capanema, the head of the new Ministry of Health and Education, football brought people of vastly different backgrounds together and by the 1930s governmental studies on the game claimed football specifically facilitated assimilation among new arrivals flocking to urban centres from the interior and abroad.[8] Together with strong doses of state-suggested patriotism and discipline, the habitus of football could quickly and efficiently alter the nation's deterministic path through rational scientific approaches grounded in eugenic principles.[9]

Though no documents link the state directly to professionalism, some of the earliest reforms initiated by Vargas's cronies indicate the influence of the political climate building within and around the game before the formation of the Estado Novo. The transition to a multi-ethnic, professional game which valued the contribution of workers in the making of modern Brazil clearly conformed to the orthodoxy of the regime. Dr Luis Aranha, the younger brother of Oswaldo Aranha, a long-time ally from Vargas's home state, was appointed to accompany the national team to Italy in 1934 for the FIFA World Cup. Aranha assumed control of the Confederação Brasileiro Desportos (CBD) during the transition to authoritarianism and oversaw the many changes that would occur within the game from 1937–45.[10]

The *reforma Capanema* was the means by which those ambitious reforms were undertaken by the minister of health and education, Gustavo Capanema. Following several months of analysis and deliberation, the reforms began to be implemented in earnest after 1937 and the creation of the Estado Novo—though several aspects of the larger programme were underway since at least 1934. Billed as a modernisation campaign, interventions into the affairs of private sporting associations by the Vargas government were connected to issues of national security on the eve of World War II. Those interventions were an extension of governmental 'pacification' of rogue sporting associations attempting to individually represent Brazil in international sport. Regional sporting bosses were reigned in and co-opted through government appointments to special sporting committees aimed at glorifying the nation through sport. The interventions by Vargas after 10 November 1937 followed several months of study by national security advisors on the activities and usefulness of clubs in war-time preparations and civilian efforts to modernise the nation. The new institutions created by Capanema and fellow reformers built upon the pre-existing sporting networks which reached deep into the heart of Brazil. Reforms specified the desire to improve the eugenic fitness and civic literacy of the masses. Football for progress was central to both the populist and corporatist strategies employed by Getúlio Vargas and his political advisors.[11]

By the 1938 World Cup, professionalism was accepted throughout Brazil as part of a deal brokered by Luis Aranha on behalf of Vargas, the military and Capanema. The schism over the amateur or professional trajectory of Brazilian sport dating back to the 1910s was rendered moot by the imposition of new supra-national sporting institutions like the Confederação Nacional Desportos (CND) in 1940. This new institution superseded all previous claims to sporting hegemony and facilitated Brazilian participation with international organisations such as the IOC and FIFA. Under this umbrella institution, international and domestic sporting responsibilities and fiscal budgets were assigned and reassigned to split the oversight of all domestic football leagues throughout Brazil from the organisation and funding of the *seleção*—the national football team. Appointments to prestigious posts were used as insurance and incentives for the implementation of top-down directives coming from the CND. Ultimately sport and the nations' sportsmen answered to Vargas himself or, in his absence, the minister of health and education. The CND brought together experts on physical education, medicine, culture, civic education and military in an effort to deploy sport for the purpose of making a modern Brazil.

In 'sporting nationalism', Vargas and his ministers believed they had found a proven strategy for redefining national identity. Both Mussolini in fascist Italy and Adolf Hitler in Nazi Germany had resurrected the image of its people and institutions among many in the global community by successfully hosting and competing in the 1934 FIFA World Cup and the 1936 Olympic Games, respectively. The international community had demonstrated significant sympathy for authoritative approaches for social organisation grounded in the discipline and culture of modern sport. Whereas Nazi Germany and fascist Italy expressed little tolerance for ethnic mixing, Brazilian sport under Vargas promoted a multi-ethnic expression of the game as authentically Brazilian. The democratic openings which appeared in the Brazilian game with the coming of professionalism in 1933 provided the cultural and material transformations in the production of popular culture which made the game appear to support governmental claims that Brazil was indeed a racial democracy.

From crisis to harmony: professionalism from a transnational perspective, 1923–33

The mixed messages conveyed through sport were doubly vexing for working-class Brazilian players of all ethnic origins involved in false amateurism, known locally as *amadorismo marrum*. In other walks of life non-whites and the poor were cast as obstacles to progress. The presence of players who fit that description during the early days of football in Brazil was viewed as an embarrassment by elites. From the perspective of players who laboured under those arrangements, many viewed their efforts on the field of play as honourable work and a form of agency. The trivialisation of their efforts by critics of professionalism within the amateur game as 'play' invalidated to some extent the potency of their acts. Numerous individuals that laboured for *bichos*, or rewards, were themselves descendants of slaves who for decades had been characterised by members of the elite as 'lazy or ambivalent' towards work.[12]

Furthermore, the diligence that footballers displayed in perfecting their craft came at the expense of formal education or acquiring other skills at trade schools. The forfeiture of long-term social mobility procured through the undertaking of formal education, was a significant price to pay for the short-term, limited social mobility accessible through football. That was especially true among the many non-whites who lacked the personal networks traditionally utilised to secure stable work.[13] This employment strategy was a common one for football players in northern suburbs. The strategy reflected a clear understanding that a player's career could also be cut short as a consequence of injury on the field or a decline in form. Thus for many players, stable employment outside the game was the ultimate goal.[14]

The awkward status of such players labouring on the behalf of the local elite nevertheless offered footballers from the working classes the prospect of greater financial stability. These genuine opportunities were pursued aggressively.[15] To the many directors already attached to private sporting clubs, membership dues guaranteed the exclusion of 'undesirables' and ensured exclusive enjoyment of leisure, recreation and social networking. Regular access to private sport clubs by players from the lower classes diminished the symbolic value of the clubs and was viewed in many instances as an intrusion. Still, others were content to permit players to compete and were even willing to reward them for their performances. The essential debate over professionalism was over how far professionalisation contradicted the class-specific meaning attributed to sportsmanship in an era when amateurism was an accepted form of high culture.

When developments in the international game are examined, one finds a more general tendency was underway to include members of the working class in top-level football. In an era in which world championships in football were decided by the Olympic Games rather than an event organized by the International Federation of Association Football (FIFA), Uruguay and Argentina made strong claims to the global superiority of Latin-American football. Their success would be critical to the changes that would take place in Brazil nearly a decade later. They engendered an early sense of pan-Americanism, and illustrated the strong currents of class, race and cultural identities attached to sport during that period.

Prior to the 1924 Olympic Games in Paris, South American teams were given little chance of being internationally competitive on account of their poor overall showing in matches with European professional teams which toured South America during earlier decades. No doubt that view was enhanced by the assumptions among the international scientific community which claimed degeneracy was the outcome of miscegenation. Successive gold medals by Uruguay in 1924 and 1928 must have caused scepticism among sporting enthusiasts who subscribed to the latest medical evidence on 'mulatto degeneracy'. Though Uruguay experienced far less racial mixing during the colonial period than its neighbours, those outside of South America would not have known that Uruguayans were perceived as a relatively white nation by its neighbours in the region.

Besides locating Uruguay on the map for many followers of the Games, the success of the national team also confirmed the possibilities of sport boosting commercial and diplomatic ties with Europe and the United States. During the Games, the Uruguayan Embassy in Paris received telegrams from Dutch, French, United States, and Yugoslav officials congratulating the country and its team on the victory. The contents of these telegrams were highly celebrated and forwarded by Uruguayan officials to the diplomatic offices in capital cities throughout South America.[16] Brazil's neighbours, sporting rivals and commercial and diplomatic competitors were already well-aware of the potential that international sporting events could provide, as an Argentine observer commented:

Uruguay will derive a good deal of indirect benefits from the prominent position into which she has suddenly been brought in the football world. It is a curious but undeniable trait in human nature that a great amount of interest is often aroused on account of what seems an accidental and inconsequential circumstance than by a wealth of essential facts. The success of the Uruguayan team will probably succeed in making more impression than reams of historical, geographical and statistical information proving beyond all doubt the advance state of progress which has been attained by Argentina's neighbor. Thousands of people all over the world will be scouting the map of South America to discover the where abouts [sic.] of this country which has produced a football eleven which bid fair to make quite a name for itself, and the psychological effect of knowing ever so little about the country is easy to underestimate.[17]

The success of the Uruguayan national football team from 1924 to 1930 undoubtedly had a significant influence on the development of Brazilian football and its place in society.

Just as race and national identity were flexible social categories, so too was the meaning associated with labour in Brazil. The arrival of the game a few short years removed from the abolition of slavery meant that dark-skinned Brazilians who participated as clandestine professionals in an amateur game intended to reflect high culture were often viewed as unwanted reminders of the region's alleged determinist albatross. The policy of informal exclusions of dark-skinned Brazilians from selection to regional and national sides competing against domestic and international rivals varied depending on the venue and opponent. On more than one occasion Brazilian directors chose all-white teams composed of players from the upper classes when traveling to Argentina or Uruguay while fielding multi-ethnic teams at home. On other occasions prestigious club sides like Paulistano included the mixed-race Arthur Friedenreich on a team that toured Europe in 1925. Just a few short years earlier in 1921, the same player was allegedly excluded from the national side that went to Buenos Aires in 1921 at the insistence of then president of the Republic, Epitácio Pessoa.[18]

Tabbed in Brazilian sporting journals as '*El Tigre*' for his ferocious pace of play, Friedenreich's style conformed to and broke from ethnic stereotypes associated with athletes of the era. Journalists sought to attribute characteristics to players based on assumed racial or ethnic essentialisms, but personality traits such as tenacity or discipline were also captured in nicknames and description of players in daily journals. The styles and attributes of working-class players from southern Europe, the Middle East and the Brazilian interior were all imagined to possess qualities particular to those imagined identities in the minds of a generation of Brazilian writers. In disciplines as diverse as sociology, literature and sporting journalism, Gilberto Freyre, José Lins do Rego and Mário Filho each respectively promoted the idea of the Brazilian race through their published interpretations of the game. Friedenreich's subjectivity as a worker and Brazilian of mixed ethnicity was dependent on social context. As a boy growing up in São Paulo he could play in both private clubs frequented by the elite and the street games of children of working-class and immigrant parents.[19] The ambiguity regarding the player's identity is magnified over time as the cultural habitus of players' lives fade from living memory.

Most players from the working classes whose ethnic identity and social condition was less ambiguous than Friedenreich were judged harshly by traditionalists, who saw the increased frequency of their presence in top-flight amateur football as a competitive threat. In that way the labour of professional players paid for the aggrandisement of clubs to which they were not members; working for the personal enjoyment of elites who fetishised their athletic gifts but were frequently indifferent to the social circumstances under which they were cultivated represented an infinitely complex social dynamic at work. Professionalisation reconfigured relations of power similar to that of masters over slaves while liberating aspects of the lives of each under new terms of co-dependency.

Though financial stability was greater for professional players, their bodies increasingly came under the control of club directors and physicians. Their on-field behaviour and off-field habits became the subject of journalists who claimed to speak for the infinite fans who adored them and scrutinised their every action, inaction and impulse.

With regards to the era of false amateurism, the offering and acceptance of *bicho* was symbolically a descendant of power relations within the slave system. Like the myth associated with the writings of Gilberto Freyre regarding the banality of slavery that locates affection in coercive sex acts, or the notion of cordial racism in Brazil that asserts good relations existed between workers and employers because 'blacks are treated like family in many white homes and therefore we do not need to pay them', the bonus system was fully at the discretion of wealthy.[20] Club members, who without exception were well educated members of the elite, frequently saw bonuses as a form of charity to assist the 'poor black from the industrial suburbs'. The dynamic of power between white and non-white in early Brazilian football is a clear vestige of the slave system that controlled black labour for more than three centuries. Even though Leônidas da Silva and Domingos da Guia were among the few who were able to renegotiate relations of power, their leverage was limited when confronting elite directors. Players attempting to retain control over their bodies and the labour they offered clubs were met with severe consequences.

An example of this can be seen in the career of star player Fausto dos Santos. Of recent African ancestry, Fausto was nevertheless chosen for the 1930 Brazilian national team that travelled to Montevideo, Uruguay for the inaugural FIFA World Cup. Though clearly black, the sublime skills of the player and his tremendous work-rate and leadership as a central midfielder, in particular, seems to have whitened his candidacy in the eyes of the *cartolas*—who were extremely sensitive to class rank and skin colour in their selection process. Known in South America as the *marvilla negra*, in 1931 Fausto would 'defect' from the then amateur club Vasco da Gama to sign a professional contract with Barcelona.[21] The midfielder was a critical component of the team that engaged in a multi-country tour of Europe. Brazilians followed the team with great excitement, celebrating their victories in the Old World as a source of national pride, just as Club Athletico Paulistano had been celebrated as 'national' heroes in 1925 when the team was the first Brazilian side to go to Europe.[22]

PROFESSIONALISATION, 1930–1950

In 1931, Fausto stayed behind in Europe to play professionally in Catalonia but due to the prejudice he experienced in games or perhaps in daily life while at Barcelona, soon moved on to Switzerland so that he could continue playing professionally. Some months later in early 1932, he returned to Rio as a prodigal son and was enthusiastically welcomed back by Vasco. All descriptions about his experience illustrate the social capital that highly skilled players generated, as well as its limits, amongst elite club directors on both sides of the Atlantic. Even though many directors were sensitive to challenges to their honour, particularly by players who they considered as social inferiors, highly prized footballers held some leverage with directors despite the social- and race-based hierarchies that persisted in society. Still, some directors had expectations of amateur players more akin to discipline towards an employee rather than recreational competition.

Even in their leisure pursuits, the interests of Rio de Janeiro's social elite conflicted with the lives of working-class Brazilians. The informal and unregulated *bicho* system left many players unwilling to play on the basis of sliding-scale bonuses if it threatened their regular work. Likewise, once professionalism was instituted for the start of the 1933 season in Rio de Janeiro, *socios, cartolas* and the press had a more forceful language at their disposal to critique player performance. With football recognised as a genuine trade under Vargas, players were held to more rigid standards of discipline. Players were paid employees. Some, like Leônidas and Domingos, would earn more than the directors themselves. This was a constant point of tension between both groups. It is within this context that the preservation of social rank through subtle cues (such as how players were identified in the press) is significant. Players who participated in false amateurism were treated in a manner consistent with social norms that existed between elite Brazilians and other members of the informal economy working as laundresses and day labourers throughout the country. They were highly sought after and deemed necessary, but were left vulnerable to a patron system that created bonds of dependency.[23]

An incident that received considerable publicity in the *Jornal dos Sports* illustrates the difficult circumstances players faced within the clandestine system. In an article entitled 'The Suspension of Aragão', we have a rare instance in which a player himself responded to the punitive measure that had been levied upon him by directors for 'indiscipline'.

For readers of sports dailies, this article would have stood out for the formality by which the player in question, Jośe Pinto de Aragão, was identified by his full given name, rather than a nickname that was usually used to identify players. The article on Aragão is significant for content as well as form. The *JDS* provided a long and detailed account of what had transpired leading up to his 150-day suspension:

Even as we speak, I do not financially need the directory of Andaraí. Nor do I wait to receive the condition to which I may enter the football field. I am a poor and *honorable working man* I am a bottle maker in a large factory and as such I earn eighteen, twenty, twenty five and up to as much as thirty reis per day. They [the club directors] don't pay me a cent while I am marked by the fire with calloused hands in the quotidian fight to sustain my three innocent little girls. Thus I cannot attend to orders by the doctors under the threat of fines to miss work that places daily bread on the table. I am sure they do not toss aside their interests among others who we can consider welthy for the sake of sport. Likewise I also am not going to subject myself to the impositions of these doctors.

The refined language used to frame the protest of 'a poor and honorable working man' such as Jośe Pinto de Aragão, raises the suspicion that the *JDS* reporter may have 'coached' him so his grievances better resonated with the paper's readership. Less cynically, the language used in this appeal is an illustration of how working-class Brazilians appropriated the language of the Vargas regime where the classic discourse of 'honour' and 'work' so often prefaced appeals.[24] The issues raised in Aragão's protest certainly illustrate genuine obstacles faced by Brazilian workers to participate in amateur sport:

On the eve of the team's training session I received a telephone call from Doctor Jansen Müller saying he had selected me to compete in the game on Sunday at the field in Fluminense. I explained to him that I could not compete on that date because it was the only free day I had to enjoy myself with my family as I had to work the rest of the week. You could imagine my surprise when I read in the *Jornal dos Sports* that I had been suspended for one hundred and fifty days! I was really irritated with this and that is why I sought you out [the *JDS* reporter] to raise my protest; to a decision that was taken outside the regular session of the directors and until now I have not had the opportunity to reveal the truth of what happened with the directors Andaraí.[25]

The absence of free time, stable work and a traditional Monday to Friday pattern of employment highlights the contradictions in expecting worker-discipline in recreational activities that were staged for the pleasure of *socios* prior to the professionalism of the sport. Anyone at the time with any awareness of the workings of football knew that players of humble origins playing for big clubs already received rewards for play. Thus to delay formalising professionalism any longer was both hypocritical and potentially catastrophic for the state of the game. The *JDS* reporter went on:

> The heroic patriots [who played at the Copa Rio Branco in] Montevideo may have resisted professional offers from Uruguayan and Argentine clubs for now, but for how long will they be able to resist? The platinese do not grow tired and soon our players may be boarding the *Atlantique* back to the Rio de la Plata [...]²⁶ if we leave our football like this we will eventually come to the painful realization of losing our cracks that are between a rock and a hard place.²⁷

The sham of amateurism rewarded players, but it stopped short of contracting workers on a permanent basis, creating a number of problems. The players in Rio de Janeiro who acquiesced locally to this arrangement were predominately from the poor northern suburbs of the city. In nearly all circumstances, they lacked adequate schooling or personal networks to compete for jobs elsewhere. Many viewed football as a route to social mobility. The *JDS* strategically attached the issue of professionalism in Brazil to sporting nationalism and evolving national culture. It appears that journalists did so in the hope of opening the door for talented players who could at once climb the social ladder as well as glorify Brazil abroad.

The Copa Rio Branco, Montevideo, 1932: the catalyst for professionalism

In Mário Filho's account of the 1932 Copa Rio Branco (a diplomatic cup contested between Brazil and Uruguay in honour of the Brazilian diplomat José Maria da Silva Paranhos, Jr, Baron of Rio Branco), recent political tensions on the national stage are said to have complicated the team's selection process. Hostilities between São Paulo directors at the Associação Paulista de Esportes Atléticos (APEA), and those at the Confederação Brasileira de Desportos (CBD) and Associação Metropolitana de Esportes Athleticos (AMEA) in Rio de Janeiro, replicated the larger social drama that had recently unfolded during the separatist movement earlier that year. Those events made holding the 1932 Brazilian football championship untenable.²⁸ With football authorities from São Paulo unwilling (or unable) to partake in the championship, each regional federation, as well as the CBD, stood to lose valuable income. At the same time, the pressures to field an Olympic delegation had increased as a result of the earlier successes of the Uruguayan and Argentine teams. Thus the CBD, which was then also partly responsible for Olympic delegations, was spread incredibly thin. When forced to choose between organising a team for the Copa Rio Branco involving only Brazil and Uruguay and preparing a delegation for the 1932 Los Angeles Olympic Games, the world's most prestigious sporting event, it was really no choice at all.

For Vargas, the international exposure generated by sending a sporting delegation to the United States took political precedence over a football match that had only very limited regional appeal. Consequently, the CBD focused its finances and energies on the Olympic Games. In addition to not contesting a Brazilian championship in 1932, this meant the CBD would not be able to send its own representatives with the AMEA delegation that travelled to Montevideo on behalf of Brazil for the Copa Rio Branco.[29] According to Mário Filho, Dr Rivadávia (the president of the AMEA in 1932) explicitly evoked the inspirational success story of the underdogs from Latin America at the 1924 Paris Olympic Games as a model for the Brazilian *seleção* to emulate. If the *carioca* team now representing all of Brazil in December of 1932 was successful in winning and filling the stadium, the revenue they could generate would satisfy all interested parties at the AMEA and the CBD.[30]

Since the 1920s, South American football championships had attracted professional scouts from Europe. Professionalism in both Argentina and Uruguay by 1932 made the trip especially stressful for Brazilian sporting directors. The success of working-class teams in the 1920s, which made up the national sides of both Uruguay and Argentina in the 1928 Olympic Games, had eased the transition to professionalism in those countries.[31] The Afro-Uruguayan star from the 1924 and 1928 gold medal winning teams, José Leandro Andrade, had played professionally for the country's two most prestigious sides, Peñerol and Nacional de Montevideo by 1932. Working-class hero and gold medal teammate José Nasazzi who starred for Nacional was another example of that trend. Professional European scouts aggressively sought to sign the best available footballers but thought twice about signing dark-skinned Brazilians to play for European clubs. Unlike their Brazilian countrymen as well as Argentines and Uruguayan players of Italian and Spanish origins, dark-skinned Brazilians were only able to find professional work in the game if they plied their skills in South America.[32]

By 1932, when Brazil set sail in late November, the prospect of players defecting for professionalism was serious enough that each player selected to compete was obliged to sign a loyalty oath while on the voyage to Montevideo.[33] The two most sought after players, Leônidas and Domingos, were the special focus of talent scouts from both Argentina and Uruguay who flocked to see the Brazilian players compete in the match against the Uruguayan national team, and a match apiece against club squads Peñerol and Nacional, featuring nearly all the players from the Uruguayan national side. After three straight victories against the Uruguayans, the headlines of sporting journals and the regular press watched with great anticipation to see if the nation's newest national heroes, Leônidas and Domingos, would go abroad for professional careers or remain at home as 'amateurs' in Brazil.[34]

The Copa Rio Branco would be the first step towards Brazilian football reflecting the ideal of a racial democracy.[35] Professionalism ensured the durability of that image. Not only did it offer a positive image of a new Brazil, but it also attracted new groups of fans who would passionately support players from similar social and ethnic backgrounds. Professionalism would keep images of emerging icons such as Leônidas, Domingos and 'playboy' Heleno de Frietas in the headlines and the topic of daily conversation. Their bodies and their habits would be both a source of inspiration and critique.[36]

In the preface to Mário Filho's account of events in his *Copa Rio Branco 1932*, Lins do Rego promotes the advantages of the new Brazilian man, as embodied in football. In so doing, he virtually offered a point-for-point rejection of the determinist critiques cast on prospects for modern development made a few decades earlier:

The boys who won in Montevideo are a prime example of our social democracy where a Paulinho from a good and important family unites with a black like Leônidas or the mulatto Oscarino or the white Martins. All are an example of the Brazilian style of the most wonderful improvisations. Reading this book on football, gives credence in Brazil to the eugenic qualities that lie within our *mestiços*, the energy and intelligence of men throughout the vast Brazilian territory that are filled with diverse bloods that generate an originality that one day will be the hope of the world.[37]

The multi-ethnic, cross-class teams sent by Brazilian football authorities to Montevideo reflected a discursive shift signalled by the Vargas government of the period, and highlighted the increasing role of ordinary Brazilians in national development. These players were trailblazers for the Brazilian game. Not only were they sublimely skilled, but they were also the first to understand the capital that their skills could afford them should they accept offers to play professionally abroad. In early 1933 both Leônidas and Domingos accepted contracts for Peñerol and Nacional, respectively. In doing so, they boldly challenged the limits of the white establishment in Brazil that sought to appropriate their talents for their own gain. Their skills had tremendous symbolic value amidst the paradigm shift in Brazilian culture. Thus their departures conflicted with that emerging narrative.

Retaining players from the suburban, working-class talent pools throughout Brazil meant the *seleção* also stood to benefit—one more reason why football in Brazil garnered the attention of the state. But multicultural football in Brazil also meant opportunities for social cohesion. Fandom and the formation of *torcidas organizadas* (organised fan groups) became ways in which football culture had become national culture. The state together with the press guided the aesthetic of fandom. Stadium security was an example of the state's most blunt instrument of force over expressions of fandom, but contests which offered material rewards to go with prestige of winning equally shaped fandom in stadiums of the period.[38]

During the Vargas era from 1930 to 1945, the groundwork was laid for footballing institutions to oversee the 'whitening' of the population through reforms aimed at rehabilitating the eugenic and cultural deficiencies believed to be omnipresent among the poor of all shades of skin since the turn of the twentieth century. Under Vargas, the players and the fans that cheered them were the targets for bio-controls and cultural literacy campaigns which sought to funnel their skills and attitudes towards the glorification of race and nation. Success in football was a useful measure of work-culture among Brazilian professionals and their capacity to scientifically enhance the body, while fandom was analogous to citizenship. Those lofty expectations nevertheless had tangible material outcomes for *cartolas* and the Vargas regime. After 1933, players would represent one more commodity that could be bought and sold to further the interests of *cartolas*. The notoriety generated by Brazilian athletes created opportunities for government and commercial agents to explicitly draw connections between the discipline, fitness and dedication associated with championship-quality play and the ideal outlook and productivity of citizen workers in a new Brazil. Sporting journals did their part to encourage Brazilian players to ply their trade domestically rather than abroad in the service of another nation underscoring the patriotic duty players and fans had to Brazil.

The pacification of sport and cultural nationalism

In December 1932, the shift towards professionalism that followed the return of players from Montevideo did not seem to be the result of direct state intervention. Football stars from Rio's poor suburbs had forced the hand of the *cartolas*. The competitive leagues organised as healthy forms of recreation for drivers throughout cities like Rio de Janeiro all the way through the professional ranks would, by 6 June 1934, become the focus of Vargas's government through a process known as the 'pacification of sport'.[39] Those reforms, together with the literary efforts of journalists and scholars of the era, worked to marry a new emphasis on the body with a vision of national culture which confirmed the value of *mestiçagem*.

As early as June 1934, and more aggressively in late 1936 and early 1937, the Vargas government set the foundations for the modernisation of the national game and its governing institutions. Social tensions associated with skin colour, ethnicity, class and social condition all connect to questions of national identity emerging alongside the evolution of the game since the establishment of the First Republic in 1889. Brazil's slave past and unique history of miscegenation would, in the 1930s, become a strength rather than a weakness according to the dynamic interpretation advanced by the young Brazilian scholar Gilberto Freyre. A recent graduate at Columbia University where he was a student of the anthropologist Franz Boas, Freyre built upon the positivist tradition of the Republic, seeing balance and harmony as the Brazilian bio-cultural type. Not only did the Brazilian offer the best of Amerindian, African, and Portuguese peoples, but the long history of intimacy between the groups had obliterated the tensions of the previous epoch associated with bio-cultural amalgamation.[40] The optimistic views of Freyre were advanced in more popular prose through Mário Filho, the majestic sports journalist of the era.[41] Both found in Getúlio Vargas's rule from 1930–45 a receptive political and cultural climate to expand and popularise their views on Brazilian history and prospects for a positive future.

Professionalism was one of many changes which imagined the development of Brazil through sporting and cultural nationalism.[42] Reforms were envisioned to galvanise a new physical manifestation of the Brazilian man as well as a national ethos of equality and inclusivity. The body, mind and spirit of Brazilians of that era were to be readied together for a difficult march towards the modernity desired by elites for decades.[43] On the surface, professionalism put to rest the divisive debates over who had the right to represent Brazil abroad. It offered members of the lower classes cultural citizenship and cultural equality, even where material and political equality lagged behind. Professionalism made possible the construction of national institutions to oversee the development of Brazilian sport.

Professionalism prevented a perpetual exodus of players from Brazil. The retention of players at home reduced the prospect of players of Italian and Spanish birth or ancestry from returning to Europe.[44] For players such as Leônidas and Domingos, they were able to leverage their value in Brazil precisely by playing abroad in Uruguay and Argentina. The question of Domingos's release from Nacional de Montevideo on the eve of the 1934 World Cup was significant enough to enlist Getúlio Vargas directly in negotiations with the president of Uruguay.[45] But the release never came.

It was precisely that fear of losing native Brazilians that motivated directors and the state to modernise Brazilian sporting institutions and accept professionalism. Ironically, members of groups who were previously marginalised became the focus of the highest office in the land, the presidency. Professionalism was a decisive step: it offered the national team the greatest opportunities to generate positive notoriety for Brazil abroad. After 1934, sport became a focus of Brazilian foreign and domestic policy. Football under Vargas occupied a highly visible space in Brazil during the nation's most transformative period of the modern era. His ministries directly attempted to shape an image of Vargas as a man of the people through his affiliation with stadium spectacles associated with football culture.[46]

But the reach of the government in football culture went far beyond traditional propaganda that attempts to associate sport with any particular idea of the nation or identity. After 1934, Vargas and his ministers took control of the game, and the increased focus on football by ordinary Brazilians of all ethnic backgrounds and social classes meant that that new participants, both players and fans, were exposed to ideas related to eugenics—a particular understanding of the Brazilian race as essentially multi-ethnic and inclusive, and the values and disciplines imagined necessary in making the 'new Brazilian man'. Football represented one intersection between the private sector (*cartolas*), government ministries such as the Ministry of Education and Health, and the military. Each collaborated in their attempts to remake the national sport and through it Brazilian bodies and the nation as a whole.[47]

Together with the use of radio and the print media, as well as popular entertainers and intellectuals, football redefined how Brazilians viewed themselves and how the world viewed Brazilians. The football team and the institutions which organised the highly detailed plans for preparation and on-field success during World War II, made arguments of mulatto degeneracy and tropical decay impossible to sustain. Brazilian players of all shades were eventually highly sought after 'commodities' in a global market for player talent.

Nevertheless the promotion of football as authentically Brazilian, in part due to its multi-ethnic component, complicated the ability of ordinary Brazilians to perceive inequalities in Brazil as structural. The population in public spaces such as football terraces and the football field differed dramatically from the amateur white and elite era that preceded the professional game so closely associated with white supremacy and class based discriminations. In that way the game and culture of football presented a trope for critiques of Brazil's alleged racial democracy.

Craques, cartolas and limits to social capital

In his 1947 book *O negro no futebol brasileiro*, Mário Filho offers a version of professionalism which is certainly uplifting and edifying, but also perhaps an overly optimistic account of professionalisation. The transition from amateur to professional football is an example of player agency, but also one for dignity and equality in an aspect of social life that was tangible to ordinary Brazilians. For players identified as non-white and professional, the victory was two-fold. On the one hand their penetration into the amateur game and role in establishing professionalism in 1933, as a group, legitimised their labour as honourable and their skills as valuable. At the same time, professionalism meant the prospect of social mobility—regardless of whether that mobility was limited and long-term financial stability as a consequence of their play infrequent.

Additionally, the presence of non-white, non-elite players in domestic leagues and international football was a decisive blow against determinist logics which saw *mestiçagem* and origins among the lower classes as perpetual obstacles for the development of the Brazilian race. Nevertheless clear limits to player agency existed. Beyond the obvious, that the peak performance by athletes was finite, so too was the ability of players to challenge the structures of power which governed the sport.

According to Mário Filho, Leônidas and Domingos 'had cast open the gates to *Gávea* (the headquarters of one Rio de Janeiro's most important football teams [Flamengo]) to forever welcome blacks'.[48] Filho, like many of his era, may have lacked the sensitivity to perceive less overt forms of racism which persisted in the game well after 1933. One such example is a showdown in 1940–1 between the national hero, Leônidas, and the long-time president of Flamengo, Gustavo de Carvalho. A prolonged public feud in the sporting journals between the *craque* and *cartola* quantified the limits to and value of capital accumulated by players through on-field and commercial success when compared to that of *cartolas*.

The term *craque* describes any star player who dominated the football headlines of the era. Just as the term *amadorismo marrom* (yellow amateurism) typically identified working-class players as non-white to followers of the game in the press, readers of the period understood that both terms *craque* and *cartola* evoked specific class and racial images that revealed a coded discourse. Newspaper articles that chronicled the sport deliberately distinguished between both groups of people involved in the production of the game by the inclusion of full names for directors and *socios* and nicknames only for players. Dark-skinned players seemed to have been given nicknames, such as 'Congo', based on their appearance or on qualities attributed to the groups which white journalists had assigned them. Unlike directors and *socios* who rarely were referred to by a nickname, presumably out of respect for their social rank, players were not afforded that level of respect. It is for that reason that the Aragão incident is so unique—the voice of a black, working-class player is heard properly. Together with photos which regularly pictured players as gruff and rustic in their appearance, 'true' amateurs, club members and other members of the elite were rarely pictured without formal wear including a jacket and bowtie.

Leônidas and Domingos once more were the exception to the rule and were featured in formal attire on a number of occasions breaking sharply with the norms associated with the class and racial groups to which they were assigned by journalists. In 1940, Leônidas, a trailblazer of professionalism, was also a symbolically potent figure. As a descendant of a slave, he offered tangible evidence as to the far-reaching transformations that had taken place in Brazil throughout the 1930s and which were at the core of the Vargas reforms. The player was tremendously visible in public life and extraordinarily wealthy for his time. Reasonably, he came to believe he had acquired autonomy over his person to control the terms of his labour. He was wrong. That miscalculation transformed his life.

Leônidas had suffered a significant injury prior to the start of the 1940 season, but he played anyway at a record-setting pace. When the club cancelled holidays so that they could 'balance the books' with a group of friendly matches—this time in Argentina—he sought a medical exemption. Unknown to Leônidas, however, the clubs involved in negotiations had already pledged his participation to ensure a high turnout. Injured or not, for *cartolas* at Flamengo, Leônidas was considered a mere employee and they believed he was contractually obligated to play. Leônidas saw it otherwise, particularly due to the fact he was still recovering from injury and because of his past contributions to the club.

When Leônidas's pleas for exemption from the Argentine tour were turned down by directors, the player took indirect actions to evade what was being demanded of him. At first he resolved to simply avoid boarding the vessel carrying the team to Argentina. However, it became clear that absenteeism still placed much of the responsibility on the player and he risked the press tearing him to shreds. Wise to this fact, he chose another form of evasion by failing to secure the visa necessary for travel.

According to his biographer, Andrés Ribeiro, when the player presented himself to the club's head of the delegation, Dr Hilton Santos, several hours after the appointed time, Leônidas was presented his passport complete with the necessary travel visa and 'obliged to board the vessel wearing only the clothes on his back'.[49] Leônidas was in a lose-lose situation. If he went onto the field and attempted to play in his condition, he faced the very real prospect of further injuring himself or prematurely ending his career entirely. The 'black diamond' was far too savvy for that. A decade earlier, in 1931, he had clearly understood that his star was on the rise.[50] In 1940 it was still yet to fully ascend. If a player's body was the means of production to generate glory for club and country, it is significant that he refused to acquiesce. Here too, Leônidas read the writing on the wall. He was an expendable resource to enrich the club—little more than a commodity in the new economy of bodies that was emerging in international football. Understanding that playing poorly damaged his evolving brand-name the player was shrewd to protect his assets without having to enter the field of play.

The Argentines suspected that Leônidas was indeed injured, and suggested he be examined by a doctor at the Argentine Footballing Association (AFA). The club declined, but the player surreptitiously visited Dr Augusto Covaro, a surgeon and the head of the AFA medical team. He confirmed the diagnosis that was given prior to the start of the 1940 season and he went further in also diagnosing a double tear to the meniscus in the right knee which called for immediate surgery. Leônidas presented the medical documents to his club's hierarchy in Buenos Aires, expecting to finally be exonerated from any suspicion of feigning injury.

The response of the club's directors to Leônidas is suggestive of social tensions associated with the ethnic amalgamation of Brazilian workers and those that managed their labour in a post-slave society. Having been outflanked by an individual who they considered their inferior, they took decisive steps to remind the player of his limited agency within that sphere. The club accepted his unwillingness to take to the field but cited him for 'indiscipline' and revoked all financial support and lodging while abroad.

In the coming weeks, a series of letters that Leônidas wrote to Flamengo's president, Gustavo Carvalho, would reveal the extent to which he sought control over his own person and labour. In one letter, Leônidas asserted that 'professionals were not slaves'.[51] Such an action must have infuriated Carvalho. According to Leônidas's biographer, the star player articulated a deep understanding of how the actions of the club—which climaxed in withholding his passport and visa—harked back to the era of slavery. Leônidas was indeed a footballer and he did play for money, but like other honourable workers throughout Brazil, he refused to be a slave.[52]

Conclusion

Over the following six months, Flamengo's response to one of their player's very public acts of insubordination was as harsh as it was swift.

Leônidas's expenses in Uruguay were not reimbursed, he was suspended by Flamengo without pay and the club invoked the censorship clause in the player's contract. Additionally, Leônidas was fined several thousand réis—the precise amount remaining on his contract following the trip to Buenos Aires in 1941. As if this pressure to break his will was not forceful enough, the Justiça Militar condemned Leônidas to eight months in prison when the informal deferment of military service that he had been granted in 1934 mysteriously resurfaced, an example of the *cartolas'* far-reaching influence. Despite his high public profile as a national hero and wealthy dark-skinned footballer, Leônidas seemed to have fallen victim to a cycle of prejudice. As such it was widely considered as plausible that he was capable of moral and spiritual shortcomings such as the abandonment of his team and, by extension, his country.

Neglected by headlines during this entire period was the serious injury of the player. Finally, in August 1941, Leônidas and Flamengo mutually agreed to the surgery that he had always insisted was necessary, and he was sent to convalesce at the Vila Militar in Copacabana where he was sequestered for his non-performance of national service. There he endeared himself to rank-and-file servicemen and charmed the officers who eagerly sought access to 'war stories from the pitch'.[53] In return, he received and accepted special treatment, developing warm relations with all around him.

Despite, or perhaps in retaliation for, spending several months in a military prison, Leônidas still refused to temper his demands for justice and redemption. Prior to his release from the Vila Militar, Leônidas conducted a series of clandestine interviews through a good friend, the journalist Geraldo Romualdo da Silva. As the date of Leônidas's release became imminent, public opinion began to sway in his favour. He swore 'never to play again' for Flamengo. The pressure was now on the club to reach a resolution. Selling the most popular player in Brazil was not without its perils.

Fearful that transfer discussions would leak out to the press and compromise the deal before it could be completed, the club made tight military security arrangements before presenting an offer to Leônidas. In the same military prison where Leônidas had been held while he convalesced from surgery, the player was presented a suitcase full of cash and accepted a transfer to São Paulo. Since 1931, the *Jornal dos Sports* had capitalised on the exploits of the player. In 1942 they ran headlines that called the transfer 'a swindle of 200 contos'.[54]

Even upon his departure from Flamengo, the paper suggested that the player had exhibited a quality of *maladragem* (cheekiness or guile) from which he had handsomely benefited.[55] After so much energy had been spent libelling Leônidas and questioning his honour, Flamengo wanted to retain the financial value of the player as a commodity up for sale—altogether not an easy project for the club. Here too the *cartolas*, with the help of the sporting press, held the upper hand.

In sum, football offered cultural citizenship for those who wanted it, while retaining many of the power relationships between masters and slaves that characterised pre-emancipation Brazilian society. As the story of Leônidas da Silva's confrontation with Flamengo's board of directors demonstrated from 1940 to 1942, players were commodities who were expected to sacrifice their bodies for the club, with little recourse to resist. Leônidas made numerous attempts to outmanoeuvre the *cartolas* who valued his footballing skills but did not respect his wider person, not least for being a black, working-class Brazilian. Even clear confirmation from doctors of injury could not excuse the worker-player from his duties.

Unlike other labourers of the period who, if injured in the workplace, could look to the new social security programmes for assistance, Leônidas's employers staunchly demanded that he returned directly to the field. When he failed to do so in Buenos Aires, the limits to a player's agency were revealed. In such light, professionalism must be viewed as an opening for workers but also as a means by which the elite were able to maintain some continuity from the past epoch. In the early days of professionalism in Brazil, *cartolas* had deep connections with the epicentres of power in Brazil. This was especially true from 1934 with the interventions by the Vargas government into football's governance, and its interest in the symbolic role of the sport for the promotion of its vision of Brazil.

3

Football in the Rio Grande Do Sul Coal Mines[1]

Marta Cioccari

This chapter explores the social importance and symbolism of working-class football as expressed in the lives of coal miners and former coal miners in the municipality of Minas do Leão in Rio Grande do Sul, Brazil's southern-most state. Here, as in company-dominated communities in other parts of the world, the coal companies allowed football teams and players to develop. The 'spirit of the game' permeated social ties and there was a multiplication of sporting disputes. From September 2006 to February 2007 I lived in Minas do Leão to carry out ethnographic research on the social construction of honour among coal miners.[2] In addition, between 2002 and 2004 I had carried out research in the same community, and in the late 1990s I also produced some journalistic reports there.

Studies of the appreciation of sport among poorer groups and of the actual practice of working-class football highlight aspects such as boldness, cunning, and the use of the body—values stressed by those I spoke with. Among investigations carried out in other contexts, references were recorded to the form in which the practice of football in factory clubs led to the emergence of a type of 'working-class elite', composed of worker-players.[3]

In the narratives of those to whom I spoke, the football field existed as a canvas for the exhibition of abilities and corporal knowledge—the 'intelligence' in creating a move, the 'brilliance' of a goal so beautiful it was 'a painting', something 'which not even a professional would do', irreverence and physical resistance—the memory of performances, but also of integration and confrontation, the stage for striking episodes of bravery. In this universe, Bromberger's definitions are perfectly apt, namely that a game exalts merit, competition, but also teamwork and solidarity—principles which are affirmed on a daily basis in an underground mine. Working-class football is thus fertile terrain for the affirmation of identities and antagonisms, with the feeling of belonging being constructed in opposition to the nearby adversary—whether it is a neighbouring town or a district from the same town built around distinct mines—or a distant one, exacerbating social, political, and ethnic differences.[4]

Interviews about football allowed access to an intimate place, where the objects of the miner-player—such as photos, certificates, champion's sashes, club membership cards—are kept. These items are held in all kinds of ways. They may be kept in an apparently disorderly manner inside an old wallet—but considering that wallets serve to hold documents, they are also documents of identity and identification. They are sometimes stored in cardboard boxes, where the memory of games and teams is mixed with family history—a succession of births, birthdays, and marriages. Sometimes they are positioned to decorate bookshelves and living room walls, alongside portraits of children and grandchildren, as souvenirs from the mine and the tributes received from followers of the football team or the coal company to the 'model miner'. The reports both mark the hierarchy of merits and demerits, prestige and lack of prestige, honour and dishonour, as well as outlining reputations,[5] and how much is revealed by the performances, both those of football and those of the art of narration.

The relationship between football and forms of honour initially emerged in my research in Minas do Leão. After the closing of the last underground mine in 2002, I noticed that alongside the notion of belonging to a mining world, a fundamental element of miners' dignity, and the feeding of a public image of the heroism of the workers underground—the 'great honour' of the profession—there were concomitant elements, related to sport, the family and rural origins among others, which anchored the feeling of pride. Here I call them modalities of a molecular nature, created in the tension between prestige and lack of prestige, between recognition and disregard, 'small honour'.[6]

The rivalry between workers' teams in Minas do Leão

When I arrived in Minas do Leão—a small town with around 8,000 inhabitants located in the interior of Rio Grande do Sul, some 90 kilometres west of the state capital, Porto Alegre—to do the ethnography for my doctorate, I found some clues that football had a singular importance in its daily life. It was possible to identify metaphors which showed that the universe of the mine was intimately related to football. The affirmation of the conditions necessary to be a miner was expressed through football jargon. One of my informants told me that to be a miner it was necessary 'to be a man with a capital M, because a glass shin won't last'. While football is commonly defined as a 'box of surprises', the underground mine appears, a little more dramatically, to be a 'box of secrets'. In the daily experiences of miners, the centrality of sports emerged.

In the Rio Grande do Sul coal-mining region of Baixo Jacuí, the history of *varzeanos* and amateur football clubs finds a parallel in the history of the mining companies.[7] In the late 1940s and the early 1950s the first football teams organised in Minas do Leão emerged; teams created by workers around the mines, on whose boards there were foremen and engineers, with sponsorship directly provided by the companies in some cases. In comparison with the other mining towns in the region, such as Arroio dos Ratos, Charqueadas and Butiá, the development of football occurred relatively late, accompanying the expansion of the workers' town—Minas do Leão was reborn in the 1940s, after an initial period of existence and subsequent disappearance.

In the 1920s and 1930s many of the neighbouring districts, all part of the São Jerônimo municipality,[8] already had *varzeano* teams: Butiá Futebol Clube had been founded in 1926 with the encouragement of the chief engineer of the private company Consórcio Administrador de Empresas de Mineração (CADEM), which had also encouraged the emergence of Grêmio Atlético Jeromina in the then district of Charqueadasin in 1931. In the central district of the municipality of São Jerônimo, Grêmio Esportivo São Jerônimo was created in 1935, and Grêmio Esportivo Riograndense, whose pitch was donated by local councillors, in 1938. In 1937 Conde Futebol Clube emerged in Porto do Conde, while in the 1940s other football teams were created in the then district of Arroio dos Ratos, such as Brasil, Guarani and Estrela. At the height of coal mining in the region during the 1960s, there were nine amateur teams in São Jerônimo registered with the Gaúcha Football Federation, not to mention the many *varzeano* teams functioning irregularly.

In Minas do Leão the principal rivalry—which still causes heated disputes and disagreements—is between Atlético Mineiro Futebol Clube and Olaria Futebol Clube. The former, which would eventually become an amateur team, was founded in July 1950 after the merger of Itaúna Futebol Clube and DACM Futebol Clube. The latter was named after the company which employed the players, Departamento Autônomo de Carvão Mineral (DACM), created in 1947, changing its name to Companhia Riograndense de Mineração (CRM) in 1969. One of Atlético's principal achievements as an amateur club was winning the title of 'Campeão do Centenário' (Centenary Champion) of São Jerônimo in the early 1960s, beating another nine teams linked to the mines. Later, the club was also the state amateur vice-champion for two consecutive years.

Atlético's fiercest local rival, Olaria, emerged in the Recreio neighbourhood in December 1956, bringing together players who worked in the São Vicente Mine, owned by the Alencastro family, and in a brick factory belonging to the same company, which inspired the name of the team. The former miners Eraldo and Antônio Geret (or Butiá, as he is usually called) were the founders of the team. Butiá remembered that at the beginning:[9]

Look, I was sixteen almost seventeen when we began to create Olaria. In the first games we even put the kit on own backs [paid for it themselves]. There were adversaries here and up there was another, so we started that way, playing. […] Until we got the team together. Our bosses always gave us support, gave us strength. What we needed […] there was no problem. Kit too, when we needed it, we would go there: 'Sir, we need…' He always found a way.[10]

A son of a longstanding worker in the São Vicente mine, Butiá was born in the then district of Butiá,[11] in a family of seven children, of whom all five male children would become miners in the same company. One of the brothers, Bernardo, also played football in the Olaria team. Butiá always worked as an underground miner, exercising the functions of electrician, crane operator and car operator, until his retirement in 1973. Eraldo, another founder of Olaria, was born in Taquari, in a family with eleven children—six girls and five boys. Four boys became miners, entering the São Vicente mine or Copelmi. Eraldo always worked on the surface, first on the coal sieves and afterwards as a crane operator.

The Olaria players began training on a pitch close to the mine, with goals posts made from eucalyptus beams and a ball donated by the employer. Butiá remembered that the ball 'was pieces of leather, so it had a fold, like a belly button. It was filled there and afterwards tied with string', and remained a little 'beaked'. After the team had been formed, the company gave them their first kit: 'They gave us t-shirts, shorts, and boots'. When the group had become used to the grass pitch, they were surprised by the news that BR-290, a federal highway that was being built, was going to pass through the area. The solution was to rent the property of a rancher, with a foreman from the mine acting as an intermediary. In the 1960s the field—which still houses Sociedade Recreativa Olaria Futebol Clube—was sold to the workers, with the payment being deducted from the wages of sixteen miners over a period of two years. The last miner to become involved with organising the club was Eraldo:

I worked with weighing the coal at the time […] and Butiá was an underground miner. They [underground miners] always passed there because they drove the cars underground. He came to talk with me, and involved me in the group, because they were missing one guy to buy the pitch, and this was to be me because they had no other choice. […] We did not earn much at the time. Some really were not able to; others were not very linked to the club […] So I had to postpone my marriage for a year to be able to help buy the pitch.[12]

Olaria was thus born out of the dedication and sacrifice of the workers, and this would continue throughout its history. The benefits conceded by the smaller private company, Mina São Vicente, were considered meagre in comparison with the investments of the state company DACM (afterwards CRM) in support of its team, Atlético. Butiá reaffirmed this difference: 'This field was bought with our sweat, our work'. This does not mean that Carbonífera Alencastro, owner of Mina São Vicente, did not help the team. The first director of football was a company engineer. At a certain time even the owner, known as Doutor Alencastro, was on its board. Nevertheless, Olaria remained a *varzeano* club, while Atlético was lifted to the category of amateur. There was a difference of scale: Mina São Vicente never had more than 200 workers, while CRM reached approximately 1,500 workers.

Opposing teams were derived from the social and geographic space occupied by each club. The rivalry involved two areas of Minas do Leão, as if they were two separate towns, and until the present day these areas maintain distinct traits in footballing disputes. The town is divided by the federal highway: on the left of BR-290 is the neighbourhood of Recreio, considered one of the poorest parts of Minas do Leão, its dark soil indicating that it originated as an irregular settlement built on coal slag. This urban concentration emerged around the oldest and most precarious mines, such as São Vicente, São José and Coréia. On the right are the neighbourhoods which end up in the town centre, the old workers' district and Vila dos Engenheiros, situated near the CRM extraction shafts.

Between the 1940s and the 1980s there were armed fights involving the two areas: on one side, men from Recreio; on the other, men from Leão (also referred to as Centro or Baixada). The 'toughs' faced each other in street fights, each bearing a knife or a dagger. Violence could affect social interactions in bars, brothels, recreational clubs, and at football matches. As one worker reported at the time, 'knowing how to handle the knife was a question of honour'. Some members of these gangs of toughs would replace the street fights with the possibility of being a miner-player. This only reinforced the rivalry between Olaria and Atlético, the former considered a 'more popular' club, and the latter as belonging to a 'working-class elite'.[13] According to Butiá, who was involved with both clubs, each corresponded to a social layer:

Atlético is CRM, and Olaria, the grassroots of Olaria, are the employees, the workers. Olaria emerged from the sweat of each worker. If the rivalry continues today, it is because the sweat of the miners of Carbonífera São Vicente is buried here.[14]

These attributes have been perpetuated in the current veterans' teams. Some of these players mentioned the differences but preferred not to emphasise them, as in the case of Chicão, a member of the Olaria veterans team: 'It is said that Atlético is a team of the rich, of cushions, of people full of la-de-da and Olaria here is more working class, those more simple, more humble people'. Even the veterans of Atlético mentioned this: 'They say we are from the elite because we go by car and not by bus to games, but many of our players have gone through difficult times and the club has come together to help them', stated Beto Balão, son of the former miner-player Carlitos and a veteran player of Atlético.

Various other teams developed around DACM and CRM in the 1960s, such as Esporte Clube Poço 1 (or P1, as it is often called) and Ponte Preta, which were breakaways of Atlético. The motivation for the creation of new teams was generally differences and feuds with the established club. It was common to hold friendly games between workers who performed different duties, with, for example, car operators teamed against lumbermen (*madeireiros*) or against shaft-builders (*trilheiros*). At one point Recreio also housed the Mina São José, which had its own corresponding team, Favorito Futebol Clube.

Atlético Mineiro FC and the hiring of worker-players

For three decades, from the late 1940s to the mid-1970s, CRM encouraged the organisation of Atlético Mineiro Futebol Clube, maintaining the practice of hiring good players to be part of the team and to work in the company. These workers had privileges, such as working solely on the surface in less arduous activities, and being released for training, physical preparation, and matches. They received daily allowances when they travelled to take part in championships. In a study I carried out about the career trajectories of miner-players in the 1960s and 1970s, I noted that almost all rose to become foremen or supervisors while still young. Furthermore, the honour of football provided them with not only prestige in the company, but also popularity in the wider community, favouring political careers and matrimonial alliances.

'When I discovered a guy who played well, I brought him to work', emphasised João Francisco, a manager in the administrative area of CRM and aged forty-eight at the time of the interview. It was he who kept relics such as photos and minutes which recorded part of the club's history, rare documents about the memory of football in the city, in drawers in the company office. He was too young to have been involved in Atlético 'in the good times'. His office colleague, former section chief Volmar Cunda, fifty-nine at the time of the interview, said that he started to play football at the age of fourteen and was in the club's second team. Both the first team and the reserves participated in rigorous physical preparation, led by a coach who was a captain in the *polícia militar* (the state police).

Most of the players in Atlético were CRM workers who were reserved certain advantages, such as permission to participate in training and games: 'While the normal workday ended at 5pm, we left at 4pm to train', Volmar says. Training was held on Tuesdays and Thursdays. If necessary the miner-players swapped shifts with colleagues to cover day shifts. Volmar reported that 'if there were a good player who was unemployed, I would certainly arrange a place in the company'. Depending on the talent of the player, doors could open. These selection criteria could provide space for criticism: 'Some were better as players than as miners', another informant told me. However, it does seem that among their colleagues the miner-players attracted more admiration than rivalry.

The first miner-player hired by a coal mining company in Minas do Leão was Leotilde Braga (or Leo, as he is generally called), aged seventy-eight at the time of our final interview. A goalkeeper who made history in the amateur football of the region, he only felt committed to a club when he went to play for Atlético in 1949, and for this reason he became an employee of the then DACM. Before that he had been a 'much in demand' athlete. He remembered that at the time there were approximately fourteen *varzeano* teams around Minas do Leão and Butiá, and that he had played for almost all of them. Payment was symbolic—a ticket to the cinema or formal clothing. Since local transport was unreliable, Leo sometimes had to walk thirty kilometres on foot to play a game in another district. From then on he worked in the state company and played in the company team:

Due to my actions here [in football], the people, the directors here of Itaúna [FC] were very interested in investing in me to go there in one way or another, if I arranged a job, if they paid, anything. 'Does he have a profession?' 'He does, he is a bricklayer, a carpenter.' 'OK, so if he has two good professions and is a good goalkeeper, let us hire him.' It was then I got myself a job. I stayed working in the company. [...] Later, the director authorised the hiring of players to play in the team, because it would represent the district in the federation. With the permission of the directors, so then those players who interested the team would be hired. So they all came.

Entering the company in 1949, Leo spent nineteen years employed in the workshop sector, an above-ground activity—a condition extended to other miner-players, since they were to be preserved from overexerting themselves within the mines themselves, in potentially dangerous and unhealthy conditions. As a young man he went to live in a building with three rooms in a communal housing area. Soon after he moved in, his mother and three of his four sisters did so too, who he helped support with his wages. In 1957, Leo had to undergo several knee operations, and although he never totally recovered, he continued to play.

Exactly ten years after Leo joined the company, Ademar was also hired. Living in Porto do Conde, he had been told by a friend that a team, Atlético Mineiro Futebol Clube, was starting in Minas do Leão. A son of a 'single mother', Ademar first asked the opinion of his mother since, at that time, he was 'very subject to his family', and there had been rumours where he lived that Minas do Leão had become a violent place. With his mother's agreement, he moved, in December 1959, to the mining town. In 1960 he started in the team as centre-half and at the same time started to work in the company. He thought about turning professional. He was tried out by Grêmio Esportivo Brasil in Pelotas, a city in the far-south of Rio Grande do Sul, but because he was disappointed with the treatment he received there, he gave up on his project and remained at Atlético.

By the beginning of the 1960s, Atlético had players who had emerged from within the company. One of these was Antônio Manoel, the penultimate of fifteen children of the carter José Antônio Freitas, twice a widower, who had moved from Rio Pardo to Minas do Leão in 1946 to work with the transport of coal, and who had five wagons and around eighty oxen. The family plan was that the children would help their father in the transport business with their ox-drawn carts, but the family's survival strategy was frustrated by the modernisation of road transport. In May 1954, fourteen-year-old Antônio Manoel began work with DACM as an apprentice in the mechanical maintenance area. Shortly afterwards he joined Atlético's first team. His boss, Cândido Francisco de Oliveira, responsible for general services (and his eventual father-in-law) was the president of Atlético.

In 1959 the player Butiá, one of the founders of Olaria, joined Atlético. Butiá's recognised talent made him a significant asset in the exchange of favours between the two mining companies: São Vicente and DACM. It was at this time that DACM provided favours for São Vicente by transporting in its trucks raw materials purchased in the state capital, such as wooden rails. To repay the favour, Doutor Alencastro, of Mina São Vicente, came up with the idea of loaning Olaria's best players to strengthen Atlético. As Butiá summed it up, 'My boss told us to play there', stating that other teammates after him, such as Eraldo and Tibúrcio, were given the mission of bringing glory to their rival team. Butiá says that a director of DACM (which he calls CRM, the name the company would adopt later) came to look for his boss: 'Look, we need this boy here...'

They arrived here to see my boss, Doutor Alencastro, they went up there. And the director of CRM arrived. [...] I was down below in the mine and they sent for me. 'Go call him, have him come up here to the office.' I went there, I left what I was doing. When I arrived up on top, the bosses of Atlético were there with my boss... I felt the badness... [he laughed] Today will be the day... Me: 'Ah, *doutor*, I am training and you know best...' 'No, you will have full freedom. If you want to play you will be at their disposition, at the time they need you, they will come here, you will have full autonomy.' So when they needed me to train, they would come, tell me and I could be freed from work at 3pm.

As a result of this, between 1959 and 1969, Butiá played with Atlético, although he continued to meet with Olaria. However, the link with Atlético had its advantages. The team had become amateur: joining it was an excellent opportunity to improve the abilities of players. Thus, Butiá saw his prestige grow in football, in the company, and in the community. His financial condition also improved a little due to a daily transportation allowance.

The hiring of Ademar and the loan of Butiá were part of Atlético's preparations for its launch as an amateur side. Carlitos and Antônio Manoel, recruited the previous year, were part of the team, as well as the centre forward Zoely and five of his brothers, who were recruited by DACM and joined the football club, aided by their father. Making up almost half the team, the brothers Zoely, Elói, Anzen, Valdir, Aloísio and Danilo were the sons of a longstanding mine employee, respected for his experience, his position as manager of general services, and his authority—he was a former police chief and had a violent temperament, closely identified with the local model of masculinity. Cândido Francisco de Oliveira, or Seu Candinho as he was usually called, was also the first president of Atlético Mineiro Football Clube.[15] Seu Candinho's six sons played on the football team and at least five of them appeared in team photographs. The youngest, Danilo, even played as a professional in

Clube Esportivo, in Bento Gonçalves, a town in the northeast of Rio Grande do Sul.[16] This group of brothers/players already had a prestigious place in local society, but football, initially, and professional paths, afterwards, allowed the individualisation of their trajectories.

Outside of football, Zoely carved out a successful career in politics. He started to work at DACM in 1952, at the age of fourteen, as an office-boy. The same year, he debuted on the first team of Atlético, playing as a centre forward, a position he held for fifteen years. 'I was the captain of the team, so I rose greatly in the company', he reported. In this position he helped to scout talents to be recruited by the company. After working for six years in the administrative sector, he moved to Porto Alegre where he was employed by a fireworks factory.

His aim was to play football professionally. Parallel to his daily work routine, he did trials for Sport Club Internacional, Esporte Clube Cruzeiro, and Esporte Clube São José, all in Porto Alegre. But his dreams of a footballing career were not fulfilled. Instead, when he received an offer from DACM to return to Minas do Leão, he went back to playing football with Atlético and worked in the administrative section of the company. At that time Zoely was twenty and thinking about marrying. As an encouragement for his return, he was offered a job in the central office and help in building a new home. Zoely accepted the proposal and his presence in the team helped Atlético win the principal amateur titles in 1960, 1961 and 1962. Later he held the position of company store clerk, a job he held until his retirement in 1991.

He was a player desired by other teams—in 1962 he received an offer from Butiá FC to play with them and work at Copelmi, a private mining company that was a competitor of DACM, and whose club was one of the principal adversaries of Atlético. Before making a decision, Zoely looked for the president of Atlético and explained that he was preparing to get married. 'He gave me an oven. We were paid by the club, not in money but in goods'. With this encouragement he remained in the team. It was a time when the amateur champions of the region attracted a substantial crowd to their stadium.

Zoely inherited from his father not just a taste for football, but also for politics. When I met him in 2003, he was in his second term as mayor of Minas do Leão; the first had been when the municipality was formed in 1992. He attributed his early popularity to sport: 'Since I was a leader in football, they convinced me to run as a candidate for councillor'. He was a councillor for Butiá for three terms, beginning when he was twenty-six and still playing football for Atlético. In September 2008, when I met him again at the end of my research, his wife was running for councillor and he was her main asset.

The taste for football was not limited only to the men of the Oliveira family, who took turns playing for Atlético. Geni and Gedi, the daughters of Seu Candinho, exercised a peculiar type of kinship ritual in the club: they were the 'godmothers' of Atlético and circulated with the 'gold book,' asking for donations for the teams. The godmothers were elected by the voters of the community, as stated in the club's minutes. At least one of them, Geni, appeared in an official photo of the official team. The Oliveira family was at the centre of Minas do Leão's lively social life. The other sister, Gedi, was queen of Clube Duque de Caxias. These sisters later married two members of the Atlético team: Geni married the goalkeeper Antônio Manoel, while Gedi married Zé Custódio, a former winger in the old Leão FC team, who would go on to coach Atlético. Zé Custódio and his brother Osvaldo were the children of one of the first bakers in the mining town. Antônio Manoel belonged to the large and united Freitas family, whose names were given to streets, squares and even an entire working-class district, Vila dos Freitas.

Zoely's activism intensified after 1963. He was a member of the youth wing of the Partido Trabalhista Brasileiro (PTB) and was invited to be one of the orators in the visit to Butiá of the then governor of Rio Grande do Sul, Leonel Brizola. At the time, Brizola was traveling throughout the state in an attempt to get the population to organise in groups of eleven—like football teams—which became known as the *grupo dos onze* (group of eleven), an objective being to pressurise the president of Brazil, João Goulart, to urgently carry out 'basic reforms'[17], but also defended armed actions.[18] When the *grupos dos onze* were still being organised, the military coup of 31 March 1964 took place and their members were persecuted and arrested.[19] I often heard references to this organisation in Minas do Leão. One of these occasions was remembering players and coaches from the past. My interlocutor pointed to a photo of Zé Custódio, stating that 'he was arrested after the 1964 coup' having been one of the members of the *grupo dos onze* in that region.

This group of Atlético players had a certain amount of political cohesion, involving political affiliations in the Movimento Democrático

Brasileiro (MDB), then the PTB, and most often ending up in the Partido Democrático Trabalhista (PDT), attracted by the ideals of Leonel Brizola. Among these were Zoely, Leo, Carlitos, Butiá, Eraldo, Antônio Manoel and Zé Cabeça, the youngest of them. In the case of Carlitos, his interest in politics predated the military regime. After the 1964 coup, he worried about what would happen to him:

Agents came from the Department of Social and Political Order (Departamento de Ordem Política e Social)[20] to the [company] workshops [...] From here they took away Zé Custódio under arrest, they took Procópio Farinha from Butiá, and two more [...] They did not take me because I had not signed the form. At that time there was the *grupo dos onze* [...] Then they went to verify in the municipal archives if I was a member of the party. If I had been I would have been arrested as well. After that, I never wanted to know anything about politics.

Ademar followed another path, far from the passions of politics. In the 1970s, under his wife's influence, he converted to the Jehovah's Witnesses, in which he is still a preacher—a decision which had a profound impact on his work relations. He had to face prejudice and mockery for being a *crente* (religious believer) miner in a community in which the miner is identified as a rascal. In the company, after a many years as a heralded football player, Ademar was noted for his sense of discipline and his dedication to work. His employment records registered praise for his 'exemplary' behaviour and promotions 'for merit'. When in 1963 he stopped playing football, he went to work underground.

By the time he retired in 1986, Ademar had risen from being a team boss to being a supervisor. His case, like practically all those of the group linked to DACM, seems to confirm the contribution of football to a successful career in the company. Raised by his mother—without ever knowing his father—in a strikingly masculine universe, he had to overcome numerous obstacles until he found a job that would allow him to support his family. His four children have now finished secondary school—of his three sons, one is a metallurgical technician and the other two are mechanics.

In relation to family origins, Ademar's background is similar to that of Leo, a son of a laundress who was abandoned by her husband and left with five children. Leo—the oldest son—began working at a very young age to help his mother with the expenses. These two cases configured a type of moral commitment of sons to their mothers, as mentioned by

Tânia Salem in her study of 'popular' classes.[21] She says that in the absence of husbands or partners, it was not rare for there to be a transfer to the son of the masculine support normally attributed to partners. Two of my sources precociously assumed the role of providers.

When Leo went to work underground, he had already achieved the position of foreman. In his case there are also elements to suppose that his path as a miner-player contributed to the increase of his professional prestige. In his employment records, to which I had access in the company's office, there is praise of the 'relevant service provided' by him to the company. His popularity among his fellow workers had been measured when he won a local contest for the model miner, something which depended on the vote of the mine's workers. In recent decades Leo has become a type of local authority, frequently put forward for interviews on the mine, football, and the emergence of the mining town. At the end of 2008, he told me in good humour that after having been interviewed in a documentary about the miner-players,[22] he had become the 'greatest goalkeeper of all times in the region', because he continued receiving trophies and tributes from amateur teams and municipal authorities.

One of his three sons, Adalberto, also a former miner, continued to play for Atlético following his father's example as a goalkeeper. 'At that time our doctrine was to replace the father. I was an outfield player and when my father stopped playing, I moved into goal', says his fifty year-old son, who at the time of the interview held the presidency of the Municipal Sports Council. In turn, the son of Adalberto, Orieuglas (his grandfather's surname, Salgueiro, backwards), tried to build a career as a player at Sport Club Internacional, a first division team in Porto Alegre, but he believed that he was not chosen 'due to the lack of a sponsor'. The young man played well in second division teams, but preferred to invest in his technical education instead of following the uncertain career of a football player. A little more than twenty years of age, he found employment in a metallurgical plant in Porto Alegre as a specialised worker.

Antônio Manoel, like Ademar, was also touched by religion. But the former Atlético goalkeeper converted to an evangelical church only after retirement. From an episode as a boy when he was expelled from school, escaping under the legs of the teacher who was standing at the door, to a series of warnings for 'insubordination' and 'indiscipline' in his company work records, Antônio Manoel's story is full of anthological episodes. In his case, it was not the discipline exercised over the football team linked to the company that changed his rebellious disposition, nor his marriage, nor his successful career in the company as the foreman of the workshops and maintenance. It was much later, after his conversion to the charismatic evangelical church Sara Nossa Terra. It all started when his son discovered the church in Porto Alegre, when he was going to Sport Club Internacional for trials as a player. After this first contact, family conversions occurred in a chain. Antônio Manoel and his wife were baptised together, his two daughters becoming deacons, and his son is a pastor. In the company his career had lasted forty-three years— he carried on work for sixteen years after formally retiring. His career and personal trajectory contributed to increase the tolerance of episodes of 'indiscipline' and 'insubordination'. Especially under the military regime, the mine was administered by engineers with dictatorial bents, and an episode of resistance could result in persecution. In 1981 Antônio Manoel became the foreman of Iruí mine, six years later returning to Minas do Leão.

Like Zoely, Eraldo, a former Olaria defender, also had a political career. He was a councillor in Butiá for sixteen years, a period of which part was parallel to his football career, his work in the mine, and union activities. His father was a railway worker and in the 1940s and 1950s he took part in strikes alongside the communist leader Procópio Farinha.[23] Both Butiá and Eraldo were supporters of Leonel Brizola, drawing on family tradition which had supported the 'workerist' ideas of the former Brazilian president Getúlio Vargas. In turn, Butiá was on the margins of one of the *grupos dos onze*, in which a foreman from São Vicente had participated, the same one who had helped purchase the Olaria pitch:

Butiá: Here we had the *grupo dos onze*. So we barely escaped being seized [by the military]. One of our leaders […] when this 1964 revolution occurred was Pedro Lima, who was the [… mine foreman]. So, he had contact with others, I don't remember if they were from Butiá [the municipality]. They knew about weapons. So, we had weapons available, because if we had had to fight we would have. It had not been so long since we had done our military service. But we were also liable to be persecuted every moment, to be arrested. If they had arrested me they would have done with me what they did with Zé Custódio. They really let him have it. Zé was beaten a lot.

Author: And did you participate in the *grupo dos onze*?

Butiá: We had two members in the *grupo dos onze* at the time. One was Pedro Lima and the other was Zé Luiz. They were brothers. So they coordinated this, in the town of Butiá. The *grupo dos onze* was in favour of fighting for Brizola [...] But when it really began, the Army came...

Other former Atlético players also mentioned the trajectory of Zé Custódio, also known as Zé Padeiro, who had died some years previously, referring to both his football skills and his political activities. Little by little, I noticed that various threads linked these worlds. On one occasion I heard: 'The documents of this *grupo dos onze* stayed here in the Atlético office'. They did not just have football and the mine in common: they were linked by political affinities and ties of kinship.

I tried to discover more about the path of Zé Padeiro through his brother, Osvaldo, and his widow, Gedi. 'Zé played a lot, he was like Garrincha, he dribbled loads and left people on the ground. Zé was Garrincha in his dribble', his brother Oswaldo Custódio told me, also a former baker and player.[24] As a winger in Minas Leão Futebol Clube (one of the teams which gave rise to Atlético Mineiro), in the 1940s, Zé Padeiro tried-out for Sport Club Internacional in Porto Alegre. Unsuccessful, Zé Padeiro gave up his hopes for a career in professional football and returned to play with Minas do Leão, later becoming the trainer of Atlético. When Oswaldo talked about the creativity and irreverence of his brother, he said: 'Zé would have put Garrincha in his pocket!'

Zé Custódio's real passion was actually Grêmio Foot-Ball Porto-Alegrense, one of Brazil's first—and long one of its best—football clubs. When Grêmio won a national championship, Zé Custódio drove around the streets of Minas do Leão, honking the horn of his truck and handing out sweets to children. According to Osvaldo, after abandoning his hopes of becoming a professional player, Zé Padeiro did his military service during which time he contracted a dermatological complaint which made him lose his hair. He started to use a cap, but this prevented him from exhibiting all the acrobatics he was capable of with the ball, as he was concerned about showing his incipient baldness. He thus lost popularity in football.

The comparison of his irreverence and ability in football is only one of the facets by which Zé Padeiro can be compared with the famous player Garrincha, leaving aside the differences between the amateur status of the former and the international professional career of the latter. Both had poor origins—one was a baker by profession and the other had been a worker in a textile factory—[25] and they also shared the charisma of trickery, talent as seductive as it was provocative, and the ability to attract women and make friends and enemies. Zé Padeiro was given to excesses, even in the consumption of alcohol. According to his widow, Gedi, in Zé Padeiro's final years he was drinking more and more, which led to cirrhosis of the liver and an untimely death—like that of Garrincha's—caused by the effects of alcoholism.

As passionate about politics as he was football, Zé Padeiro was an obstinate activist and an advocate of the 'workerist' ideas of Leonel Brizola. Oswaldo never knew for certain if his brother had really been part of a *grupo dos onze*, because this information was kept secret by the family. However, the suspicion of being a member of the organisation hovered over Zé Custódio, and at the start of the military regime in 1964 he was arrested. He spent some twenty days in prison with Gerino Lucas (a miner and communist activist) and Procópio Farinha Vieira (a railway worker and also a militant communist). Zoely remembered that his brother-in-law Zé Custódio was living in São Jerônimo when he joined a group linked to Leonel Brizola, then the executive secretary of the PTB. He also remembered that when the 1964 military coup occurred, 'he was arrested for belonging to the *grupo dos onze*'. When he recounted episodes from his brother's life, Oswaldo, in turn, explained that that charismatic man was also the target of adversaries:

My father was an admirer of Getúlio Vargas, from the PTB, and Zé followed the same path of being a follower of Brizola. He was very fanatical. He would speak on Radio Butiá […] He created many enemies because of football and politics. First, because of politics and afterwards football.

Zé Custódio was provocative, exuberant. In a context in which provocation and strangeness easily became sources of enmities, his political positions against the military government were denounced by a supplier to the family bakery, who afterwards publically justified his gesture:

The person who denounced my brother sold yeast to the bakery. 'I denounced Zé Custódio, he deserved it!' He told this to the others like a great advantage… He was the Fleischman [company] representative. And in the end he died shortly afterwards, much before my brother.

Among the miner-players of this generation, as mentioned, some participated in unions, others entered politics, became religious leaders, or symbolically overcame the difficulties of access to education which their early entrance into the world of work represented, received a title and were treated as 'teacher', as in the case of Butiá in his time as a trainer of both Atlético and Olaria. In his case, his victories were more symbolic that economic. Football allowed Butiá, having been raised in the poor and often tough neighbourhood of Recreio, to comfortably mix among the superior social classes from Centro, and to be respected and chased after by the directors of CRM and the command of Atlético—and like other players to be remembered for his abilities and talents.

Miners' sons and the dream of becoming a professional footballer

Like their fathers before them, many children of coalminers in Rio Grande do Sul aimed at building professional careers. Some of them, having left locations where football was encouraged by coal companies, gained national and international renown, as in the case of Daniel da Costa Franco who, in the late 1980s and early 1990s, was a right back for Sport Club Internacional in Porto Alegre before going on to play with, amongst others, the Brazilian clubs Corinthians (in São Paulo), Bahia (in Bahia), and Atlético (in Minas Gerais), as well as the German club FC St Pauli (in Hamburg).

Daniel is one of four sons of Bega (a former miner) and Maria (a former factory worker), residents in Minas do Leão. I met Bega and Maria in 2003. Bega had worked in precarious conditions in the old Coréia Mine in the 1950s and 1960s. He started mining at the age of nine, at a time when coal was pulled to the surface by horses. At the age of fourteen, Bega began to work in the mineshafts. After retiring as a miner, he drove his own truck transporting coal from the mines. The old man's entertainment was horse racing, but he always proudly followed the career of his football-player son. Considered at one time to be Brazil's best right back, Daniel was even mentioned as possibly playing for his country in the 1994 World Cup. After a successful career as a football player, he left the sport for a while to do a business studies degree. By 2007, Daniel had returned to the world of football, this time as an assistant manager for a youth team back at Sport Club Internacional in Porto Alegre where he had originally made his name as a player.

Daniel's career path inspired other youths in Minas do Leão, such as André who, encouraged by an agent, tried his luck in Argentina. There he had the possibility of trying out for Club Atlético Boca Juniors. Due to a rule that imposed a limit of four foreigners in the team and the competition, André was not selected. However, he experienced unforgettable moments in the club: he particularly enjoyed telling the story of the goal he scored from a pass by the Argentine star Riquelme. After this, André had some trials with Club Atlético River Plate. Having been turned down, he returned to Minas do Leão in 2001 and continued to play in local teams. Two years later, after the birth of his daughter, André gave up his ambition of becoming a professional athlete.

In 2008 he received an offer from a mining subcontractor to play on their football team and to work preparing mineshafts—to a certain extent reproducing the situation of earlier generations of miner-players. Nevertheless, as his father, the former miner Alírio, noted, these 'new miners', hired by outsourced companies faced painful and precarious working conditions. Some key employment rights, such as working a maximum of six hours underground, do not exist, while wages are lower than those of the state company, CRM, for which Alírio once worked. With the gradual closure of underground mines in the region, André's footballing talent, opened doors—as it would have done half a century before—for employment, but it has not given him the prestige and possibility of career or social ascension of the old miner-players in Minas do Leão.

4

Futebol De Várzea and the Working Class

Amateur Football Clubs in São Paulo, 1940s–1960s[1]

Paulo Fontes

The essence of Brazilian football

São Paulo, Brazil, 13 November 2011. Thousands of fans drive to a humble suburban football stadium in what seems to be a very common scene every Sunday in this vast metropolis. After all, football is known worldwide as the most popular sport in the country. Brazilians are proud to have won the World Cup five times, to have produced Pelé, Garrincha, Didi, Zico, Sócrates, Romário, Ronaldo and many other skilful players who earned Brazil the epithet as the land of the kings of the 'beautiful game'.

However, the scene that Sunday seemed far from a glorious football kingdom. It was not a match involving Corinthians, São Paulo FC or Palmeiras, the best-known professional football clubs in the city. Distant from the glamorous, rich and commercial world of top professional players, two modest neighbourhood clubs were disputing the final round of the municipal amateur championship, considered to be the largest in Brazil. Despite the modesty, both enthusiasm and spirits were high. For many, the fervour of the fans and the sense of attachment between the local clubs and their communities make amateur football, 'real' football, the heir of the best of Brazilian football traditions.[2]

In the last decades, the scarcity of pitches due to state speculation, changes in popular leisure patterns and even urban violence have made amateur football less visible in the major cities. Nevertheless, after many years of decline and ostracism, amateur football seems to be back in fashion again. Popular major championships, films on the topic, as well as internet and television coverage are helping to recover the lost prestige of this form of leisure, especially in São Paulo.[3]

During the golden age of Brazilian football, between the 1950s and 1970s, the widespread practice of the sport by amateurs in the main cities of the country spread the familiar idea that amateur football was the cradle of the sport in Brazilian. As the former coach of the national team, Mano Menezes, recently stated, 'amateur football is the essence of Brazilian football. It is the reason why we are five times world champions'.[4] In fact, the majority of professional players started their careers in humble local clubs. In places such as Rio de Janeiro and São Paulo, experts from professional clubs used to pick the best amateurs and hire them in a constant flow from the city suburbs to fame. Since the professionalisation of the sport in the 1920s and 1930s, football has been one of the forms of upward mobility for working-class youngsters in Brazil.[5]

This chapter focuses on the amateur football clubs in the workers' districts of the city, mainly during the 1940s and 1950s. Widespread in São Paulo during this period, these clubs are fascinating examples of the connections between popular leisure and political and social organisation. They were often associated with local political forces, companies or other institutions, such as trade unions, and frequently played an important role in the creation and support of neighbourhood and householders' associations.

These clubs also served as spaces of popular entertainment and recreation. Beyond the matches themselves, the clubs organised picnics, parties, dances and other activities which included not only the sportsmen, but also women, children and whole families. Additionally, the study of such associations can provide interesting clues to understanding the lines of identity and diversity within the working class in São Paulo in this period. Different neighbourhoods and districts, racial and ethnic divisions, regional origins, diverse professions and workplaces—all these factors were important in the organisation and routine of these football clubs.

An extraordinary urban and industrial expansion

Between the 1940s and 1970s, the city of São Paulo underwent an extraordinary urban and industrial expansion, matched by very few cities in the world. From a population of 1.3 million people in 1940 to around 8.5 million people in 1980, São Paulo became the largest city in Brazil and one of the largest in the world. It is certainly one of the best international examples of urban growth in an era marked by import substitution industrialisation and policies of national developmentalism. This expansion posed various challenges to the workers, both at the workplace and in their everyday lives in the neighbourhoods of the city.

The pattern of urbanisation of São Paulo during this period, often termed the 'centre-periphery model', primarily constituted strong class segregation within the urban space. The middle and upper classes lived in central and well-equipped districts, while the working classes lived in the poor and mostly illegal periphery.[6] Alongside real estate speculation, the workers had to face frequent problems related to the absence of urban infrastructure in the city. Lack of transportation, street pavements and sanitation, as well as the absence of educational and health facilities, were part of the experience of the vast majority of the workers and their families in the new outskirts of the city.

During the 1940s and 1950s, the metropolitan region of São Paulo city was the scene of an accelerated and diversified industrialisation and urbanisation process. The region was the main centre for the country's high rate of industrial growth. From 1945 to 1960, Brazil's secondary sector grew at an average rate of 9.5 per cent a year, making it one of the most outstanding industrialisation processes in the world for that period. In 1959 almost 50 per cent of all factory employment in the country was concentrated in the state of São Paulo.[7] Furthermore, São Paulo's industrial growth stimulated a huge expansion of the service sector in the region, thus opening up even more employment opportunities.

The transformations and intensification of the industrialisation process and the diversification of the service sector significantly changed the labour market. At the same time, an intense process of migration from rural areas also took place, profoundly altering the social and cultural composition of the working class. The great workers' migration from rural areas to the cities is one of the most important events of Brazilian social history in the second half of the twentieth century. Between 1950 and 1980 more than 38 million people left the countryside, profoundly changing many features of Brazilian society and its economy.

The metropolitan region of São Paulo and the Northeast Region of Brazil played a special role in this process—São Paulo became the place of residence and work for millions of migrants from the Northeast. Between 1950 and 1970, the city grew three times in size, while the Northeastern population in São Paulo increased ten times. The 1950s were the period of most intense migration and Northeasterners formed the majority of the workers in the city's new factories.[8]

Politically, this period—particularly between 1945 and 1964—was marked by new a form of relationship between the workers and the state, generally termed 'populism', which established a field of conflicts and reciprocities in a dynamic system of alliances and disputes between these social actors. In the city of São Paulo, such a political system was based not only on the traditional *trabalhismo* of Getúlio Vargas,[9] but also around the powerful local leadership of politicians like Adhemar de Barros and Jânio Quadros.[10] Moreover, the Communist Party, although illegal most of the time, remained active and relatively influential among workers and their institutions.[11] After the 1964 military coup, and especially during the 1970s, the presence of the Catholic Church's social activism on the outskirts of São Paulo had a vigorous impact on both working-class political discourse and organisation, with decisive influence on the general process of the re-democratisation of the country in the late 1970s and beginning of the 1980s.[12]

The workers expressed and faced the challenges of this era through a series of different strategies. Their social networks, based mostly on informal relationships among family, friends and members of the community, were essential for the formation of a class identity. These networks, for instance, directed the migrants to specific cities and neighbourhoods and, often, also to jobs in particular factories and companies. Frequently, these informal relationships with relatives and friends remained the basis for solidarity and mutual help among the workers, with important consequences for social struggles and for local political life.[13]

These networks and informal relationship also established one of the main bases for a true 'associational fever' that the workers of São Paulo experienced in this period. They formed the political and cultural organisations capable of structuring and articulating collective movements. In this sense, the connections between popular culture and political culture are of particular interest. The diversity and heterogeneity of these organisations clearly expressed the formative process of a multi-faceted class, with different cultural and communitarian values. However, in spite of this organisational multiplicity, it is possible to frequently find spaces of articulation and integration, not only in critical moments such as strikes and protests, but also in the everyday life of the working-class neighbourhoods.

Neighbourhoods, identities and amateur football

Amateur football in São Paulo has a long history that goes far beyond the history of the sport itself and strongly merges with the trajectory of civil society organisation and working-class activism. Introduced through the interaction of the British community with the local population, and cultivated in fashionable sporting clubs of the Brazilian and British elites, football quickly spread through the city's neighbourhoods. The working class soon mastered the sport and increasingly included football in its recreational menu. The move to professionalism in the early 1930s even boosted the popularity of football, both as a spectator sport and as a leisure activity. Analysts conservatively estimate that there were around 3,000 popular amateur football clubs in São Paulo, involving a very significant part of the working-class population during that decade.[14]

Many of these clubs were related to the new factories and workplaces of the city. Indeed, many industrialists, particularly in the textile sector, promoted the creation of company clubs as part of a broader policy of paternalistic industrial relations, seeking to discipline and control the leisure time of the workers.[15] The historian Barbara Weinstein demonstrated how industrialists' organisations such as SESI (Industry Social Service) were also interested, during the 1950s, in disciplining amateur football. By offering technical and financial support to the companies' clubs, SESI sought to boost 'a climate of [...] good relations between the footballers and the management', taking care to avoid the 'excessive enthusiasm', which was considered a 'negative aspect of the amateur sport'.[16]

Industrialists and management in general indeed took the practice of football in the factories seriously. Beginning in 1947, SESI started to organise the Jogos Esportivos Operários (Workers' Sports Games) every year. Football was the most important and prestigious sport in the event and the organisers generally scheduled the final competitions to take place on 1 May, Labour Day. Even the president of the FIESP, the powerful Federation of Industrialists of São Paulo, used to attend the games. In 1955 for instance, Antonio Devisate, president of FIESP, gave a speech at the opening of the games before 'the governor of São Paulo, many politicians from different political parties and thousands of workers gathered in a great sportive party'. Devisate stimulated the formation of football clubs in the industrial plants and stressed the importance of the games and the sport for social peace and harmonious relationships between industrialists and workers.[17]

Despite the importance of factories and workplaces for amateur sports, the workers shaped more informal and autonomous spaces (in relation to the employers) for their recreational and sporting practices. Working-class neighbourhoods became the locus par excellence for the practice and creation of popular football clubs. An observation from some of the founders of the Associação Esportiva Jardim Bélém, created in 1955 in the industrial district of Ermelino Matarazzo, underlines their views about the differences between the factory and neighbourhood clubs in that region:

These factory teams weren't like the neighbourhood teams rooted in the communities, such as the Jardim Belém and the Boturussú clubs. The community, through the residents of the neighbourhood, created these teams. Keralux, Matarazzo and Cisper were company clubs. The industries used these teams to try to establish connections with the social context of the neighbourhood. The neighbourhood teams aggregated the community, unlike the factories' teams that were more dedicated to disputing tournaments.[18]

In the first half of the twentieth century, thousands of neighbourhood clubs were created in the industrial districts of the city, such as Brás, Mooca, Belenzinho, Bom Retiro and Lapa, among others. This first industrial belt of São Paulo was located near the main rivers and rail lines of the city where there was plenty of low and flat land alongside the watercourses. It was in these spaces that the working-class practice of football proliferated. These peculiar conditions helped to popularise the term *futebol de várzea* (lea or floodplain football) for the amateur practice of the sport.[19]

Frequently stigmatised by the ruling classes and the police as a space for disorder and violence, this *futebol de várzea* became the most popular leisure practice in the districts of the city and had, by the 1930s and 1940s, gained some recognition and legitimacy. Until the 1970s, the popular and sporting press reported extensively on amateur football. Many of these amateur games drew impressive crowds. As Eclea Bosi showed in the 1970s, *futebol de várzea* remained one of the most common memories of leisure practices for older São Paulo residents.[20]

After World War II, amateur football accompanied the growth of the city, spreading out around the new working-class districts on its outskirts. In every neighbourhood, dozens of different clubs and teams appeared and came to constitute a fundamental aspect of working-class leisure and associational practice. As a contemporary observer stated: 'football is the recreational and leisure form par excellence and more accessible for [...] the people of São Paulo'.[21] This phenomenon was by no means restricted to São Paulo and became common in many other newly industrialised Brazilian cities that were undergoing an accelerated process of urbanisation at the time. Interesting parallels can also be found with other major cities in Latin America.[22]

The large number of football pitches in São Paulo during the 1950s clearly indicates how widespread the sport had become. In the original industrial belt of the city, however, the dense new construction, real estate speculation and the canalisation and straightening of the main central rivers of the period destroyed hundreds of pitches. In 1954, for instance, a reader wrote a letter to the communist newspaper *Notícias de Hoje* demanding more news 'on the amateur football clubs that currently are facing the problem of finding pitches to play'.[23] Complaints like that, stressing the lack of spaces to play football in the most central areas became common in the newspapers of the period.

Nevertheless, the new areas on the outskirts of the city had plenty of space for the practice of football. As Afonso José da Silva, an old resident of one peripheral district of the city, recalls, 'every new neighbourhood had to leave a space, a specific area for a football pitch'.[24] Progressively, a geographical dislocation of working-class sociability took place, altering the social conformation of the older and more central industrial areas. *Futebol de várzea* increasingly became a leisure activity restricted to the peripheral zones of the city. Nowadays, the lack of football pitches is a common problem throughout the city and the main demand of amateur clubs in the periphery of São Paulo. A survey in 2013 counted around 300 football fields for the practice of amateur football in the entire city. The great majority are concentrated on the extreme outskirts, while the former traditional working-class districts such as Brás or Belenzinho have almost no pitches anymore.[25]

Although football was a predominantly male recreation, women could also take advantage of the clubs as a space for leisure. Only men played the sport, but women became eager spectators, sometimes bringing along the whole family for picnics and parties on the sides of the fields. Moreover, the clubs often expanded their activities beyond football itself by promoting balls, parties and beauty contests. As the authors of a commemorative book narrating the history of the Lausanne Paulista Futebol Clube, from the Cantareira district, proudly state:

> In the 1940s, the club inaugurated its own headquarters through the efforts of the whole community, particularly Francisco Gaboni, who provided the first bricks for construction. After that, the Lausanne Paulista started to become the most important recreational space for social and leisure activities in the region, initiating a tradition of huge balls, beauty contests, communitarian events and other festivities.[26]

A series of more inclusive activities in terms of gender and generation could take place around the practice of football and were often promoted. At the Associação Atlética Anhanguera, as an old club member recalls, 'there wasn't only football. There was table tennis, there were dances, and there were birthday parties, parties in general, the traditional feast of Saint John in June'. In 1948, the Esporte Clube Silva Telles created a Women's Department in order to 'organise activities such as beauty contests, bingos, balls in general, dancing Sundays, Christmas parties for the poor kids of the region'. The clubs could function as important centres of working-class leisure and integration, but this did not exclude varied forms of divergence and antagonism. In the same Anhanguera club, for instance, conflicts around gender roles in public events such as parties and Carnival balls (in particular, supposed disrespect towards young ladies) were quite common and divisive among the club members.[27]

The creation and existence of these clubs were strongly associated with the informal groups, particularly male, that got together in their districts and places of residence. In his memoirs, Walter Scott Vicentini provides a good example of the informal and casual ambience surrounding the foundation of a club in a popular neighbourhood of the city:

The Bar of Nai was in the Simão Borges Street [Vila Maria district], former Street One. There was the famous sin corner. During the 1940s and 1950s, there were few houses and the folks got together in the bar. It was a party place, where friends could talk, play cards, dominos and listen to some guitar players. Nai was the nickname of Naife, the real name of the bar owner. In this bar, a football team was formed...[28]

Almost every district and new concentration of people had their own club and football team. They were important in reinforcing a local identity. The residents frequently considered the teams a sort of representation of their 'space', their 'area', a representation of the place where they lived and shared difficulties but also solidarity with their neighbours and friends. Therefore, the clubs served as important spaces for the constitution and reinforcement of ties and bonds among specific working-class communities.[29] Not by chance were references to the names of streets and neighbourhoods quite common in the denominations of the clubs.

However, the sense of identity with a specific locality also played a major role in building up parochialism and rivalry between the clubs from different districts. It is not surprising, for instance, to note the huge participation and enthusiasm of the fans and supporters (including women and children) during local tournaments. Maria José Jensen, for example, remembers that when the team from her district, the União Esportiva Paulista from Vila Curuça in the district of São Miguel where Northeastern migrants predominated, played against its main rival, Santa Cruz, from the neighbouring district of Guainazes: 'it was a real party, a lot of lorries full of fans' went to the pitch.[30] In the sometimes partisan general climate, violence and conflicts could frequently break out.

Dino Sani, former football player and world champion in 1958, initiated his career in the 1940s as an amateur player in the neighbourhood of Pompéia, near the textile factory where his parents worked. In his memoirs, he emphasises the high technical quality of the matches at that period, but also the 'fierce rivalries between the clubs and districts. Sometimes, because of these rivalries disturbances and fights took place. Bust-ups and quarrels happened very often. Sometimes we had to run away very fast'.[31]

In addition to local identities, the clubs could express ethnic and racial characteristics or other working-class cleavages. There is much evidence of specific amateur football clubs for African descendants, ethnic migrant groups such as Italians, Spaniards, Hungarians or Portuguese, or internal migrants from different areas of Brazil. Clubs could be composed of individuals from specific cities or regions within these different countries and states of Brazil. The Marítimo Futebol Clube, for instance was created by Portuguese migrants who worked in the canalisation of the Pinheiros river in 1928. They named the team after the homonymous club that existed on the island of Madeira where they come from. The Grêmio Esportivo Canto do Rio was formed in 1941 and only black players could play on the team until the mid-1950s. The previously mentioned Associação Atlética Anhanguera, from the Italian-dominated district of Barra Funda, was created in the 1920s as a club of Italian-Brazilians, reflecting a supposed desire for integration in São Paulo society. During the 1950s, in the multi-ethnic neighbourhood of Mooca, one long-standing resident recalled:

There were the Portuguesa, the Vasco da Gama, the Lituânia, the Suábia… The Spaniards had the Madrid… All clubs promoted football and balls. And all of them had their own headquarters, even if it was in the back of a residence… or behind a little pub.[32]

Some of these ethnic and racial cleavages continue to the present day. Since the 1970s, for example, the residents of the Heliópolis favela organise a lea football match every year in the weekend prior to Christmas called 'black people vs white people'.[33]

The different identities of internal migrant groups were reflected by some clubs, too. The Bahia Futebol Clube, from the Vila Nitro Operária in São Miguel Paulista, was a good example. The *baiano* (a person originally from the Northeastern state of Bahia) Antonio Xavier dos Santos affirms that the team was named after the state of Bahia as an 'homage to the Northeasterners from Bahia. There were a lot of *baianos* there [at Vila Nitro Operária]'.[34] However, the exclusiveness of a club's identity could vary considerably. In the case of Bahia of Vila Nitro Operária, for example, it wasn't necessary to have been born in the state of Bahia to play on the team. Thus neighbourhood and friendship relations seemed to be more important for club association than other criteria. In this sense, the clubs were important forms of popular organisation to integrate residents of the same locality. However, they achieved more than that.

The numerous tournaments and championships among amateur clubs integrated residents from different neighbourhoods, allowed them to get to know the city space and landscape, and also stimulated exchanges of experience. Neighbourhood tournaments were taking place as early as 1921. The District Championship, for instance, gathered together teams representing the main neighbourhoods of São Paulo.[35] Although from the 1940s onwards sports newspapers, such as *A Gazeta Esportiva*, or the municipality sponsored many of these tournaments, the clubs' members still had a great deal of autonomy and a vital role in the successes of the championships. Moreover, many tournaments still took place in a very informal manner, taking advantage of an extensive network of contacts and relations in the city.

Particularly important in this regard were the so-called football festivals, a sort of championship tournament in which clubs from various districts could play against each other during a whole day of festivities. Diana Mendes Machado da Silva argues that the football festivals originated from the traditional neighbourhood parties promoted by the Catholic Church. This kind of festivity was also a common practice of anarchist militants and groups throughout the city in the early twentieth century. However, according to Silva, by the 1930s the neighbourhood festivals had become an almost exclusive preserve of the local football clubs.[36] In the 1950s, the sports pages of newspapers were full of festival announcements. Celebrations such as the anniversary of a club or a neighbourhood, as well as the inauguration of a headquarters, were propitious occasions for the festivals, which generally also included picnics, barbecues and balls. The club and festival tournaments helped to integrate the São Paulo working class in a communication network that connected the different areas and spaces of the popular zones of the city.[37] Alongside leisure, workers also shared, debated and contested experiences and worldviews. The *futebol de várzea* brought together residents from diverse localities and 'introduced' the city to many of them.

Popular associations, football and politics

The amateur football clubs are very interesting examples of a network of local and voluntary associations that proliferated in the working-class districts of São Paulo in the decades following World War II. The neighbourhood organisations called *sociedades amigos de bairro* (neighbourhood friends societies), for instance, were the most vocal in demanding infrastructural improvements, as well as social facilities such as schools and hospitals, for the deprived new working-class districts.[38] This neighbourhood associativity was a fundamental feature of working-class culture and political action in São Paulo. These organisations frequently crossed the supposed borders, created by academics and some political activists, between the world of labour and the world of residence and leisure, reflecting an inclusive class perspective, which took into consideration the diverse dimensions of the workers' lives.

Based on informal relations and on diverse social networks, these local associations were not necessarily permanent entities. Actually, organisational discontinuity was one of the features of these social movements, although this rarely meant the absence of struggles for rights. Leisure activities could often be the basis for movements based on specific demands, and amateur clubs also served as key spaces for the discussion of 'neighbourhood problems'. The long-time trade unionist Waldomiro Macedo, for instance, affirms that 'many recreational associations themselves used to claim benefits for their neighbourhoods'. At the football clubs, recalls Nelson Bernardo, an amateur footballer in the district of São Miguel, 'it was common that the lads started talking about politics and the neighbourhoods' problems'. Isidoro Del Vechio, an old resident of the Mooca district who got involved in local politics in the 1950s summarises these connections very well. According to him:

The *sociedades amigos de bairro* in that period [...] to be honest, the people were all the same. There was a web. Amateur football clubs, dance clubs, *sociedades amigos de bairro*. All of them were a web.[39]

In certain specific conjunctures this 'web' could become very political and radicalised. In the late 1950s and early 1960s, neighbourhood associations, trade unions and popular political parties joined forces in demands against inflation, agitating for urban improvements and deep social reforms. During the 1950s, trade unions and neighbourhood organisations grew increasingly close, often to the point of joint participation of local sports clubs. Trade unions also used the popularity of football to recruit support from its working-class audience. They promoted championships and trade union clubs. During a generalised strike in the city in 1957, for instance, many meetings and picket lines were organised at the amateur football clubs in the neighbourhoods.[40]

On some occasions, the web could be so interconnected that the club leaders also functioned as organisers and agitators. Such was the case, for instance, during a political rally in 1960 in São Miguel Paulista, a distant district of São Paulo, which gathered trade unionists, local politicians and other local leaders. As the political police agent covering the event reported, one of the most vociferous speeches was made by Vavá, the president of Olaria, a local football club, who complained about work conditions at the local factory, the bad salaries and the high cost of living.[41]

The adhesive quality of *futebol de várzea* and its multiple possibilities of connections with the everyday life of the residents of the city's popular districts did not go unnoticed by political forces, particularly those close to working-class demands. Different political parties and leaders became involved and supported the amateur clubs during the period. The former communist militant Eduardo Dias provides a good example, albeit probably a romanticized one. He recalls how the communists from the Mooca district decided, just after World War II, to:

Create a sport society where we could unite the youth, with no ideological restrictions. We founded the Clube Esportivo Dínamo Paulista [...] at the same time we named it after a Russian club and we could please the Slavic community, which was large in the neighbourhood. Everybody lived for football at that period [...] the club was a powerful way to organise militants. After a month, we already had a headquarters, furniture, table tennis [...] From the point of view of football, the team was pretty good. Multitudes watched the matches. In the headquarters, we had talks. The club also participated in the political rallies. The women taught how to sew. All of these were new. Women did not go to the clubs only for the dances. They also went to participate in the meetings [...] Sport and politics lived together. One could help the other [...] This kind of organisation, the common people understood.[42]

João Louzada, a trade unionist from the construction sector and city council member in São Paulo during the 1950s, also highlighted the political potential of amateur football clubs. Louzada remembered the Progresso Paulista, a club where he was 'a founder, a player and president. We were even vice-champions in the municipal *futebol de várzea* tournament on a certain occasion. In the last match, Flor do Ipiranga beat us by 4 to 2, here at the pitch of Silveira Bueno Street'. During the elections, he recalled:

I had contact with a lot of politicians. So we arranged microphones and on Sundays [after the matches] the candidates could talk to people. It was such a beautiful thing. It was always crowded and after that there was a ball in the headquarters. So I used to bring people to get to know the candidates. At election time people already came to me and asked who was my candidate.[43]

Politicians, such as Jânio Quadros and Ademar de Barros, who structured their political careers to a large extent toward these neighbourhood demands and toward creating local connections, also devoted enormous attention to amateur football. The Partido Social Progressita (PSP), Barros's political party, even had its own team to contest local tournaments in the different regions of the city. The party also organised championships and invited the most talented amateur clubs to participate. It was like that in 1955, when the 'Bandeira Paulista participated in the PSP tournament, promoted by the party branch of Vila Maria district'.[44]

Jânio Quadros commonly initiated his political campaigns with a tour through the amateur clubs. It was on one of these visits that Eduardo Rosmarinho, a community leader from the Mooca district, met Quadros for the first time. In 1952, months before his victory in the election for mayor, Quadros attended the festival promoted by the Cruzeiro Paulista Futebol Clube and impressed Rosmarinho. 'Jânio watched the whole match. He sat on the edge of the field and at the end he drank *pinga* [a popular Brazilian sugarcane spirit] in the trophy with us'. As mayor, Quadros gave a lot of attention to the local clubs, creating municipal tournaments and a special division for amateur sports in the Municipal Secretariat of Sports.

Tarcilio Bernardo, another council member in São Paulo during the 1950s with close links to Jânio Quadros, depended very much on the local football clubs to create his large political base in the district of São Miguel. Through these clubs, Bernardo received information about the residents and their problems, thus establishing a fundamental contact network for the electoral period.[45] He was by no means the only politician to do so. Local politicians from different parties also established similar connections with the clubs. This helped them to reinforce their claims of belonging to specific localities, communities or even to the working class as whole. It also created a long tradition of political patronage. Many clubs' leaders based their control of the teams on tightening their connections and alliances with local politicians. Pitches, uniforms and resources for barbecues or parties served as common bargaining chips. Walter Scott Vicentini remembers, for instance, the case of 'Nove de Julho Futebol Clube, which came to have fifteen different new uniforms. The reason was that Mr Chiquinho, the club's president got them through close friendship with politicians and important people'.[46]

Amateur football clubs were key elements of working-class culture and political action in those years. They were deeply connected with the process of rapid industrialisation and urbanisation in São Paulo and interacted with both the formal and informal world of the workers during that period, helping us to understand the varied facets of working-class lives, their solidarity and conflictive aspects. The creation of new football clubs and teams by informal groups in the different districts and streets of the city also opened a space for workers' relative autonomy as they faced control by the companies, the employers' organisations concerned with working-class leisure and the state. Football as a leisure practice was very much part of a dispute over different meanings and values among social classes in Brazilian society—a representational struggle—which helps us to understand not only working-class culture, its sociability and cleavages, but also class relations at a vital moment in the history of the city and country.

5

The 'People's Joy' Vanishes

Meditations on the Death of Garrincha[1]

José Sergio Leite Lopes

Ethnography of a Funeral

At the end of his life, Garrincha was living in a house that the Brazilian Football Federation (Confederação Brasileira de Futebol) had rented for him five years earlier on Rua dos Estampadores in Bangu, a working-class suburb of Rio de Janeiro—a neighbourhood where employees of the Companhia Progresso Industrial were housed.

The fact that Garrincha's last years were spent on a housing development built for textile workers went unnoticed by the press, which gave in-depth coverage to the somewhat bizarre events that followed the death of the former football star. Curiously enough, Garrincha died in a place quite similar to the one where he was born and lived until he became a famous sportsman: the Pau Grande housing development for workers built by América Fabril, a textile mill in a rural setting outside Rio. Garrincha did not spend his last years in Pau Grande, but it seems that Bangu was congenial enough to serve him as a refuge for his twilight years. Death would take him back to Pau Grande. This apparent coincidence points to the decisive impact of the relations that are part and parcel of social configurations—such as some workers' neighbourhoods—on Garrincha's entire life.

From Sunday, 16 January 1983 to the following Wednesday, Garrincha drank nonstop at local bars. He was forty-nine years old. He had started his professional football career thirty years earlier, had reached the height of his fame twenty years before, and had officially retired—somewhat belatedly—a decade before he died. When Garrincha finally went home, already feeling ill, his wife (the third) sought help from one of his friends, a former private secretary of his second wife, the internationally acclaimed singer Elza Soares. This man's presence was the only link with Elza in Garrincha's final moments. But Elza had played a key role in his footballing career after 1962.[2] Garrincha's first wife, Nair, who had been a fellow worker at América Fabril, had died before him, but her family would later be present at the funeral—as was seemingly the entire population of Pau Grande.

An ambulance was called from the Bangu outpatient clinic. Garrincha was given a tranquiliser and taken to Sanatório Dr Eiras, a psychiatric hospital in Botafogo, where he had been admitted three times before. This medical routine seems to have definitively transformed the famous champion into a nameless drunkard: his record card, filled out at the Bangu clinic, read 'Manuel da Silva'—quite close to 'José da Silva', the Portuguese equivalent of 'John Smith'—instead of Garrincha's real name, Manuel Francisco dos Santos. This telling slip only reinforces Garrincha's own self-destructive tendencies. He was indeed at the nadir of his existence, the low point in a long process of deterioration that began after the 1958 and 1962 World Cups, when Garrincha became famous as the greatest Brazilian football player, side by side with Pelé. So it was as an anonymous 'Manuel da Silva' that he was admitted to the hospital, at 8pm, in an alcoholic coma. He was not given any special medical treatment, and was found dead at 6am the following morning.

As soon as his death was reported, children in Botafogo, who were on their summer holiday, began to converge on the hospital's chapel, together with the nurses and other hospital personnel. At 10am, the body was taken to the Instituto Médico-Legal (Forensic-Medicine Institute) for an autopsy. The press reported the names of the mourners present: Garrincha's last wife; Agnaldo Timóteo, a schmaltzy pop singer who had been elected to the Federal Chamber of Deputies only two months earlier and was actively associated with Botafogo, Garrincha's football team; a CBF official; the producer of *Garrincha, alegria do povo* (*Garrincha, the people's joy*), a documentary feature; and two famous retired footballers. One of these, Ademir Menezes—the centre-forward in the 1950 Brazilian World Cup team and the head of the Professional Athletes Association— proposed that Garrincha be the first player to be buried at the Association's recently-built mausoleum in Jardim da Saudade, a fashionable new cemetery. But Nilton Santos—who played left half for Botafogo and for the Brazilian team in Garrincha's time, was the godfather of one of Garrincha's children, and, most importantly, had sponsored his entry in professional football—insisted that the deceased be buried in the Pau Grande cemetery, in accordance with his last wishes. Santos's authority as Garrincha's friend and protector proved decisive.

Around noon, the body was transferred to the Maracanã stadium in a deluxe coffin—it is not clear whether it was paid for by the CBF or by Deputy Timóteo. The fire engine carrying the body found it difficult to make its way through the dense crowd that had gathered in front of the Instituto;[3] it was forced to stop for a few minutes while the crowd applauded. Apparently the decision to hold the wake in the Maracanã Stadium was uncontested, unlike that concerning the place of the burial. It was generally felt to be necessary to rehabilitate Garrincha, to undo, if only symbolically, the tragedy of his fate, thus celebrating certain traditions and interests that are part of the world of football, even if such interests are quite unevenly divided between the various participants in the ceremony. Club officials, retired players and fans of different teams were all present at the wake, and rivalries between clubs gave way to a harmonious tribute. People queued up to venerate the body.

However, two notable incidents occurred on this day. In the first, Garrincha's family clashed with his third wife, accusing her of having been partly responsible for his death. This was a revival of the conflicts that had erupted in 1965, when his family's opposition to his second marriage led Garrincha to move out of Pau Grande in order to live with Elza Soares, with whom he had been having a love affair since the 1962 World Cup. The dramatic eruption of a family quarrel in full view of the assembled mourners was the natural sequel to the permanent spotlight that the press had kept focused on Garrincha's life throughout his final years. The police had to interfere to restore the peace.

The second incident occurred when a Botafogo fan covered the coffin with the flag of his team, with which Garrincha had played for more than ten years when he was at the height of his sporting powers. One of Garrincha's nephews objected to this, arguing that the deceased would have preferred a Brazilian flag. This was clearly an expression of the resentment that Garrincha's family—as well as Elza Soares—felt in relation to the team that had exploited the player, through unfair contracts that took no account of his fame and which imposed on him an excessive number of appearances at matches, which had the effect of forcing him to resort to repeated injections in his ailing knees. Once again Nilton Santos solved the problem, and finally managed, by rather emotional means, to persuade Garrincha's family to drape both flags on the coffin, symbolising two glorious phases in his career. At this moment, Nilton Santos was the common link between Garrincha's fellow World Cup champions in 1958 and 1962 on the one hand, and an earlier tradition represented by certain players who had been members of the Brazilian team in the 1950 World Cup, such as Ademir Menezes and Barbosa, the black goalkeeper on whose shoulders the burden of Brazil's defeat rested. Their presence at Garrincha's wake only made the absences of other great soccer stars of the past, such as Pelé, or of the time, such as Zico or Sócrates—who were then active in devising new forms of association for professional players that would ensure them their rights—more evident.[4]

At 8.30am on 21 January, Garrincha's body was taken to Pau Grande on the fire engine that had transported it to the Maracanã. It was on such vehicles that the 1958 World Champions had been cheered by the population of Rio. Cheers from organised supporters of the major football teams accompanied the cortege. Everywhere along the route Brazilian flags or the flags of various clubs were flown from windows, as commonly occurs when there are important national championship or World Cup matches. This style of popular show of support for club and country started to be the norm in 1950, when Brazil hosted the World Cup. With Brazil's 1958 and 1962 World Cup victories, football became even more popular, reaching its acme when Brazil beat Italy in the 1970 World Cup tournament in Mexico. This was the first World Cup final to be broadcast live on Brazilian television, reaching an audience of millions, who took time off work to watch the games. In June 1982 there was a huge popular mobilisation—streets were decorated and murals painted—during the World Cup in Spain, which Brazil failed to win. Garrincha's funeral, however, was very different, both because the crowds were predominantly working class, and because of the unlikely destination of the funeral cortege for such a nationally celebrated figure. Most celebrities from Rio de Janeiro—even those of humble origins—including politicians, pop singers and songwriters, radio and television stars, are buried in the city's prominent cemeteries. Garrincha, however, was laid to rest in a cemetery located in an outlying working-class suburb, a place highly unlikely to ever attract such a huge, admiring crowd.

On Avenida Brasil—Rio's major exit route, a thoroughfare lined with warehouses, industrial plants, housing projects and favelas—a compact mass of mourners, with flags in their hands, could be seen on pedestrian crossings and overpasses. Traffic was completely halted, and drivers were forced to watch the progress of the funeral parade. The crowd thickened as the cortege came closer to the municipality of Magé, whose population felt that Garrincha and they had common roots.[5] When news of the funeral began to be aired by the media early in the morning, thousands of people set off for Pau Grande, by train, bus or car, as well as on foot in the case of those who lived in the neighbourhood. From the town of Imbariê (twenty kilometres from Pau Grande), the traffic flowed very slowly due to the large number of cars and pedestrians. Many abandoned their vehicles and walked the rest of the way, holding their transistor radios close to their ears, much as they did when they went to the stadium to see a game. Additional trains were put on, which stopped and blew whistles when they arrived at the station closest to the cemetery. At the entrance of a factory near Pau Grande, a sign was fixed to a tree: 'Garrincha, you made the world smile and now you make it cry'. It took the procession two hours to cover the 65 kilometres between the Maracanã and Pau Grande.

The first stop was at the local church, where a funeral service was held. The church—built in 1910 by América Fabril, the textile mill—seated no more than 500 people, and was entirely overwhelmed by a crowd of about 3,000. By the time the coffin was brought into the nave, the tension was such that the priest decided it would be impossible to say Mass, as originally scheduled, and instead simply blessed the body.

Garrincha's family and his Pau Grande friends were pushed into the background by this vast, anonymous, crowd, made up of people from all over Greater Rio. Even so, some of them took a more active part in the ceremony: it was Garrincha's old department head at the factory who made the formal arrangements with the cemetery administration for the burial.

In the cemetery, the situation was as chaotic as it had been in the church. Here, about 8,000 more people had been waiting since early morning, standing on graves, perched up trees, some even standing on the roofs of neighbouring houses. The grave—where one of Garrincha's brothers already lay buried—had been opened in haste; no tombstone marked it. Botafogo fans stood guard, determined not to let any 'outsiders' get in, even if they were family members. When the fire engine finally arrived, the coffin was carried by persons unknown—probably fans—to the place of burial. But just then, it became clear that the grave was too small for the deluxe coffin. All the adversities typical of a working-class funeral were evident in this improvised ceremony, with far too many attendants for such a humble cemetery: there was not enough earth to cover the coffin completely; the flowers—by then wilted—flung into the grave were supplemented with tall grass cut by the local population from neighbouring lots, something of a tradition at Brazilian funerals. The Botafogo fans began to sing the national anthem, and the rest of the mourners soon joined in; this was followed by the official Botafogo anthem, sung by fewer voices. It was 1.30pm by the time the crowd and the press left. The cemetery was left half destroyed.[6]

A media-age chanson de geste

Clearly these popular manifestations were generated by the media, which brought the news of Garrincha's death to the public as soon as it occurred and invested it with a strong emotional charge. Thus the media was largely responsible for the strong mobilisation of football aficionados. Even so, the intensity of the popular response went far beyond what was expected and became itself a major news event. Its utterly strange and unprecedented character was documented by the press and underscored the need to explain Garrincha's life.

In fact, Garrincha's death proved a drastic reversal in the slow descending curve of his existence—which had reached its lowest point, a veritable social death, in its last phase—by suddenly highlighting once again his past triumphs and his status as a legendary figure in Brazilian football. It was as if some sectors of the press, from the best-known sportswriters to major political columnists, had decided to treat Garrincha's life as the raw material for a modern *chanson de geste*, using the media to explain his heroic deeds[7] In the week, the major Rio and São Paulo dailies published long articles on Garrincha on prominent pages. The most famous sportswriters wrote about him or unearthed old articles. Armando Nogueira, a former sportswriter who at the time was news director of the Globo television station in Rio, republished in the Rio *Jornal do Brasil* his 'favourite column', in which he proposed that a farewell match be arranged for Garrincha as 'a tribute to and in acknowledgment of the feats of a hero'.

Such a tribute seemed particularly necessary because—unlike most famous names in the spheres of politics, the economy, culture, or even athletes like Pelé (through multiple biographies translated into several languages), who regularly speak or write about themselves—Garrincha was a man of few words, who spoke only, as it were, with his own body, when playing football. Precisely because he was characterised by a peculiar playing style, by his love of football for football's sake, by an apparent lack of any strategy in his professional career—things that made him seem 'pure' or 'naïve'—Garrincha had never made a public statement on any subject, not even football. On 23 January 1983, when a large number of articles about him were published, *Jornal do Brasil* printed extracts from one of his rare radio interviews, in which several sportswriters took part: his comments were of a personal nature, but did not dispel the mystery that surrounded his life. *O Globo*, Rio's other major daily newspaper, preferred to accept Garrincha's silence and publish, on the same day, a lengthy 'exclusive' interview with his 'authorised spokesman', Nilton Santos who, unlike his deceased friend, had much to say. Out of Garrincha's silence arose an abundant interpretive literature, texts not only by journalists but also by serious writers dabbling in sports writing, such as the playwright and novelist Nelson Rodrigues, and major poets and *cronistas* like Carlos Drummond de Andrade, Vinícius de Moraes and Paulo Mendes Campos.[8] The most famous work focusing on Garrincha is still the feature film *Garrincha, alegria do povo*, a title clearly alluding to the common Portuguese name for J.S. Bach's well-known cantata chorale known in English as 'Jesu, Joy of Men's Desiring'. This phrase has ever since become associated with Garrincha, and was widely quoted by newspapers upon the occasion of his death.

In the various newspaper accounts of Garrincha's familiar but mysterious life, certain issues were repeatedly brought up. One of these was Garrincha's stature in the history of football. Another was how he had been able to rise to glory in such unfavourable circumstances. The questions concerning the originality of his playing style and his behaviour off the field in the world of professional football always lead to discussions regarding his social background, to which Araujo Netto, a political journalist and correspondent of *Jornal do Brasil* in Rome, once famously referred as Garrincha's 'peasant' character. He was once compared to Chaplin's little tramp in a laudatory *crônica* by Carlos Drummond de Andrade because of the comic effect of his style; and indeed Garrincha, like Chaplin's character, seemed to display a 'simple-mindedness' often attributed to his humble origins. Such observations were in many cases full of the sort of class ethnocentrism that is so common in journalistic descriptions of events involving the Brazilian working classes. As a player, Garrincha was portrayed as a charismatic champion, a unique football star; as a social symbol, he was reduced to his roots, an uncouth peasant who had become a professional player by mere chance, and whose behaviour was at best that of a simpleton, at worst a case of mental retardation. Although hinted at, the nexus between his playing style and his social background was never explicitly discussed, and the question remains an open one: just how does Garrincha's way of playing betray or evoke—more in his case than in that of his fellow players—the popular roots to which he was constantly ascribed as a part of a generation when most football players came from the same background?

An unpredictable and disconcerting playing style

Garrincha became a professional football player in 1953, at the age of nineteen. He had been playing in the América Fabril factory's major amateur team for four years. In a championship series involving factories and other companies in the interior of the state of Rio de Janeiro, he was spotted by a scout, a former Botafogo player, who gave him a letter of recommendation allowing him to train in Botafogo. Thus Garrincha followed the usual path of young workers or working-class children who would eventually become professional players. At first there are the informal barefoot games in the neighbourhood, on any kind of patch of land and using any type of ball. Then the budding sportsman plays in an organised team until his superior talent or the patronage of an influential person wins him an opportunity to try his luck or train with a first-division team.[9] Before coming to Botafogo, Garrincha had knocked on the doors of two other major Rio clubs: Vasco da Gama and Fluminense. Both had rejected him for medical reasons and for his 'peasant' demeanour. Indeed, Garrincha's legs were deformed—they looked like parallel arcs curved to the right, as if a strong gust of wind had bent them out of shape. Perhaps because of this double rejection, or perhaps—as he later argued—because his working day at the factory made it impossible for him to train at a distant club on weekdays, it was only a full year after he was given his letter of recommendation that Garrincha went to Botafogo.

There the recommendation was taken seriously, and Garrincha was submitted to the initiation rite that all prospective players had to undergo: a game played with members of the club's first team. The story of Garrincha's performance in this test is part of his myth of origin. Placed at outside-right, he faced Nilton Santos, the left-half player of Brazil's 1950 World Cup team, of whose renown he was entirely unaware. He not only dribbled past the famous player several times but successfully aimed a kick right between his legs. Nilton Santos immediately asked the coach to have the newcomer hired, since he did not want ever to have to face him as an opponent in any other team. Garrincha's first professional match confirmed his talent: he entered the game only in the second half, when his team was losing, scored two goals and secured a victory for Botafogo. He then began to play a major role in his club's rise, culminating in winning the 1957 Carioca Championship. Garrincha was elected the best player in the competition, and in the following year became a member of Brazil's national team at the World Cup, which was to take place in Sweden.

The most notable characteristic of Garrincha's playing style was his reinvention of the role of the outside-right. Traditionally, the outside-right (or right-wing) is positioned near the touchline, where he receives passes from the central players; he then runs toward the goal line, trying to outrun the other team's left-half or any other opponent and to kick the ball to a teammate in the centre of the field. Garrincha, however, often carried the ball from the midfield all the way to the goal. In addition, he had an unchanging way of dribbling to the right, which was entirely predictable but no less manageable for that. He attracted the opponent and dribbled past him, often several times in a row, in a series of duels most, of which he won. The public was delighted, and—more importantly—the opposing team was disorganised and demoralised. Later, one sports journalist reflected on Garrincha's playing style:

With those bowlegs, both curving in the same direction, legs that were nearly crippled, it should not have been possible for him even to walk properly. His entire body was unbalanced, bent to the right, so that logically he ought to fall every time he tried to run. And yet this anti-athlete, this man who challenged physiology, was straight like a plumb line, and fell only when toppled. On the contrary, it was he who unbalanced other players. How to explain this phenomenon?[10]

The effectiveness of Garrincha's dribble seems to have been related to his odd physical constitution, but also to his enormous ability to accelerate. The most amazing thing was the way he carried the ball forward slowly, his way of suddenly stopping before his opponent and, thanks to his superb thrust, breaking out of an apparently precarious balance into a fast race that disconcerted the other player, then halting again, with his foot on the ball, while the opponent kept on running, propelled by inertia. Other players then attacked, and Garrincha immediately made use of the gap opened in the opposing team's defence. Sportswriters resorted to military analogies, and spoke of Garrincha's 'guerrilla' style:[11]

He came into the opposing team's field and caught the ball: he froze. A second later came the sudden spurt, and a meter ahead he tensed his muscles and soared, light as a bird…. Then he would stop dead, again rush to the right, and in this way would destabilize the outside defenders. Mathematicians will find it interesting to hear that at times he seemed to shed his own center of gravity along the way and glide on, smooth as a waterfall. When he dribbled he was transfigured: he was like Chaplin, sculpturing in air a wonderful succession of comical gestures: he was a bullfighter, devising veronicas that elicited olés from the audience; he was Francis of Assisi, ennobled by the humility with which he suffered the kicks of desperate opponents…. He reached the goal line, the backs circling the penalty area, closing in on him—one meter, half a meter, the opponent thinks: "Well, he's finished, I'll spring on him now." No way: Garrincha could dribble out of a corner no bigger than a handkerchief. And then, from middle range, with a low or a high kick, he would land the ball right on the feet of his teammate placed in front of the goal.[12]

What is typical of Garrincha is this informal style, with its disregard for the unwritten rules and for the tension of the competition, although these resources were placed in the service of a highly competitive game. Unlike Didi, Botafogo's great black midfield player, or Pelé, or Zizinho, or Zico years later—all of them brilliant stylists—Garrincha performed outstandingly while giving the impression that he was merely having fun.[13] But with his relentless penetration of the opposing team's defence, always using the same dribbling strategy, he gave a new importance to the position of outside-forward at a time when it was seen as secondary to that of inside-forward. In Sweden in 1958, Garrincha made a brilliant debut in international football in the match against the Soviet Union: from the very beginning of the game he used his usual dribble to advance and retreat, always with deadpan seriousness, even though fans laughed, before running toward the goal line, and from there he either passed the ball to a central player or kicked straight at the goal, at a very dangerous angle from the viewpoint of the Soviet goalkeeper.[14] In the final match against Sweden, the Brazilian team's first two goals, which offset Sweden's earlier advantage, both resulted from Garrincha's dribbles along the right touchline, followed by perfect passes to the centre-forward Vavá.

But this debut is just as telling of the obstacles Garrincha encountered along his career: for, though he was a key player, he had not yet earned the trust of the coach and of the Brazilian team's managers. The world of football knew how indifferent he was to these people's attempts to subject him to their tactical schemes. It was only in the third match, after a tie with England, that a committee of seasoned players (Nilton Santos and Didi among them) managed to convince them to let Garrincha and Pelé (whose lack of experience was a concern at only seventeen) play. Thus, once again Garrincha was subjected to a test, as in 1953 when he became a professional player; once again he had to prove his competitiveness, the effectiveness of a playing style that seemed amateurish, and his own ability to develop an original style.

Racism in football in the 1950s

Behind the expressions of concern over Garrincha's unpredictability and Pelé's inexperience, there seemed to lurk old fears as to the weakness of black players in international matches. What began to happen during the 1958 World Cup, however, was a gradual 'blackening' of the Brazilian team, first in the attack, and then in the defence, with the inclusion of Djalma Santos, who had already played as right-half in the 1954 World Cup. Garrincha's contribution to the 1958 victory and to the 1962 one (in which Pelé had only a minor participation following an injury in the second match of the tournament) clearly underscores the achievement of this handful of great players: the two preceding Brazilian defeats in international football were forgotten, and the racist explanations that had been offered then were discredited. It was surely no coincidence that so many veterans of the 1950 World Cup were present at Garrincha's funeral, whereas many of his contemporaries and players active at the time of his death were absent.

As Guedes, DaMatta and Vogel show, the final of the 1950 World Cup, held in Brazil—when the Brazilian team, which had performed brilliantly throughout the tournament and was the clear favourite, was defeated by a mediocre Uruguayan team—was the occasion for covertly racist evaluations of the left-half Bigode and the goalkeeper Barbosa, two black players who became the unfortunate scapegoats for happening to have contributed to Uruguay's two goals. This defeat—which was felt to be 'one of the greatest tragedies in contemporary Brazilian history' according to DaMatta, as it was collectively perceived as the loss of a historical chance to finally escape destitution—acted as a metaphor for other defeats of Brazilian society, and brought to the fore once again the old racist theories about the causes of the nation's backwardness.[15] It even provided a point of departure and an empirical basis for studies treating football as a 'laboratory' where the major characteristics of the Brazilian people could be immediately seen at work.[16] The best example is provided by João Lyra Filho's two books. The author—a self-described 'social scientist', a former member of the Audit Tribunal, a professor and former rector of the Universidade do Estado do Rio de Janeiro—was a sports director and the head of the Brazilian delegation at the 1954 World Cup. In his first book, *Taça do Mundo de 1954* (*The 1954 World Cup*), published that year, Lyra Filho expanded the report he had submitted to the CBF in response to criticisms by the press. His second book, published in 1973, titled *Introdução à sociologia dos esportes* (*Introduction to the Sociology of Sport*), was clearly aimed at a different public but it was essentially a reformulation of the theses presented in his earlier work. His empirical evidence consisted of his observations as head of the Brazilian delegation and a number of documents, among them the notes scribbled by players and sent to him during the competition, which were full of spelling mistakes. Lyra Filho made a comparison between Brazilian players and the members of the Hungarian team, which had beaten Brazil 4–2 in the quarter-finals. Seeing the Hungarians as quintessential Europeans, the author argued that the Brazilian players were always guided by their instincts rather than reason, and their behaviour was marked by immaturity and nervous instability as opposed to maturity and self-control. These defects, he stated, were a consequence of miscegenation and the heritage of the black race.

It was, then, in a context where such explanations were taken seriously by football authorities that Garrincha appeared. But his practical sense of the game testified against these analyses and the facts on which they were supposedly founded. This bow-legged man displayed in his physique and bearing all the stereotypical characteristics of the Brazilian working classes and of the Brazilian poor, which were noticed even by his own teammates who came from a similar background. But just as he turned his supposed physical handicap into a physical asset, he also capitalised on certain socially stigmatised traits, drawing from them to develop an unpredictable and disconcerting grasp of the game. He embodied, almost as a caricature, the traits and marks that provided a basis for racist ideologies and class ethnocentrism, and out of them he created the indispensable elements of the success of his style of football.

Sense of the game and class habitus

After Garrincha's death, the mystery remained unsolved by the press, which had always reduced the virtues of this player to a single fact, an individual gift, a kind of genius, or simply a figure of 'nature'. However, we can see the unique excellence of Garrincha's style as a successful recasting of an amateur style in the context of professional football. Garrincha was the product of a working-class tradition of amateur football, encouraged and practiced by sport institutions managed by factories and companies.

It seems that companies, particularly factories, played a major role in the popularisation of football in Brazil. Historians say that the Anglo-Brazilian Charles Miller introduced to Brazil a formal version of the game in 1894. After attending school in England, Miller returned to Brazil and promoted the game among the members of the British clubs in São Paulo. The São Paulo Athletic Club created the country's first soccer team, involving managers of the local gas utility company, the São Paulo Railway and other British interests. Another source of Brazilian football was the Mackenzie College, a school for sons of the upper-classes in São Paulo. Soon a number of elite clubs adopted football; other teams were created after the turn of the century, such as the Fluminense Football Club in Rio. Up to the 1940s many clubs, Fluminense included, refused to accept black players, a situation that remained unchanged even after the rise of professional football. Other clubs, however, such as the Bangu Atlético Clube, founded in 1904 by British employees of the Bangu textile mill, quickly turned to working-class players because there were not enough British to go around. So it was that Brazilian employees, most of them labourers, began to train in Bangu, and opportunities were offered to worker-athletes for the first time. Other clubs then began to find it necessary to resort to the working-class areas, where football was increasingly popular, to recruit new players in neighbourhood, factory or company teams. In Pau Grande, since 1919 the Companhia América Fabril—the local textile mill which operated four other plants in Rio alone—had been creating football teams through the workers' association, in close cooperation with the administration.

The loose network of football leagues that had been developing since the turn of the century began to come under state control in 1941, although opinions diverged as to whether the sport should remain an amateur pastime or whether, on the contrary, it ought to be further professionalised. The centralisation of the sport's organisation is one more aspect of the creation of a specialised football sector. Association football was to become Brazil's first mass sport, largely thanks to the introduction of radio in the 1930s. From then on, football could be professionalised without external support, and with its new autonomous status it would be able to generate extraordinary, if exceptional, careers such as that of Pelé—a world champion player in 1958 at the age of seventeen.[17]

Though Garrincha's public image is less that of a proletarian than a peasant or a (lovable) tramp, in his youth he was a factory-mill worker, and his family lived in a workers' housing development in a rural setting.[18] Such corrections seem important for an explanation of the 'mysteries' of Garrincha's free and unexpected style. Ultimately they can be effectively related to the mysteries of the everyday social existence of the workers' community from which he came, for one of the intriguing characteristics of workers living in these 'paternalistic' towns, which have something of the 'total institution' about them, is that, seen at closer range, these workers turn out to have a certain degree of mobility, license, and 'freedom' within an environment under strict company control exerted not only on industrial production but also on workers' entire social lives. Even inside the factory a certain indiscipline and 'floor culture' can develop; indeed, they seem to be almost a requirement of good production management.[19] In addition, thanks to the autonomous exploration of the resources offered by the company—such as the concession to workers of plots of land for cultivation, or the use of woodland for material exploitation (firewood) or leisure (hunting, particularly of game birds)—these workers, most of whom had a peasant background, had living conditions somewhat more favourable than their industrial jobs might lead one to suppose. There were yet other resources at their disposal, such as medical assistance, religious associations, folk groups, and the urban institution par excellence, the football club.

Thus Garrincha followed the same course as many other employees of factories that provided housing to workers. Born into a family entirely dependent on a factory, Garrincha even changed his name when he was hired. Originally named Manuel dos Santos, he became Manuel Francisco dos Santos, adding part of his father's name (Amaro Francisco dos Santos) to his own in order to avoid confusion with the other men named Manuel dos Santos in his section.[20] According to some biographical notes published by the press, as well as the movie *Garrincha, alegria do povo*, it was thanks to his performance as a football player that Garrincha was not fired. Indeed, his ability as a sportsman was quickly noted, and it became possible for him to follow a sort of informal career as an athlete-worker that was allowed by factories, a career that was protected from conflicts with department heads and foremen and therefore from the succession of dismissals and rehirings that characterised the lives of young textile-mill workers.[21] So it was that Garrincha's undisciplined behaviour and his frequent absenteeism, his habit of pushing the recreational side of a worker's life to its utmost limits, were tolerated because of his promising beginnings as a football player, while other young men had no other option but to submit to the disciplined training routine that might give them access to a foreman's post in the future.

Manuel Francisco dos Santos was nicknamed 'Garrincha', after a species of bird, because from an early age he had shown an interest in hunting birds and raising them in cages.[22]

Unlike peasant families, which tend to instil in their children a sense of responsibility concerning farm work, working-class families are usually quite permissive as to their children's leisure time, as if in anticipation of the excessive load of industrial work that awaits them. In factories located in rural areas, children's play centres around the exploitation of the 'natural resources' offered by the company. In adult life, this leeway might be expressed as engagement in more 'productive' activities variously allowed or encouraged by the factory, such as individual or family cultivation of vacant lots or workers' plots, odd jobs or craftsmanship—in short, all kinds of work supplementary to salaried work.[23] Thus Garrincha belonged to a subset of workers who invested much time and endeavour in activities over which the company exerted less control, as opposed not only to factory work but also to study in the company school or to participation in the various forms of social work promoted by the company.

Workers today speak nostalgically of the relative freedom that ended in many factories around the 1960s, when employers lost all interest in anything not directly related to industrial production and cancelled the non-financial advantages they had previously granted their workers. This led to protest and resistance movements that had the effect of undermining the legitimacy of their paternalistic domination.[24] The strength of such nostalgic narratives brings out the ambiguity of this relation between employers' concessions and workers' practices: one perceives here all sorts of crevices, gaps, or contradictions in the system of domination, allowing working-class families the 'recovery' of some paternalistic institutions; alternatively, one may see this illusion of recovery and the retrospective satisfaction experienced by workers as the ultimate success of a social policy that aims to minimise frustrations and conflicts even as it organises an effective form of overexploitation. Be that as it may, in his youth Garrincha seems to have struck a balance, first as an apprentice and later as a worker in the factory, capitalising on the ambiguity between a minimum of discipline and diligence in his work and a maximum of extracurricular activities, particularly soccer, which—as a sport encouraged by the company—conferred on Garrincha the accepted status of worker-athlete.

Some sportswriters, as we have seen, perceived Garrincha's style of play and his behaviour as typical of a peasant, so that his working-class background was suppressed in favour of a vague rural landscape. Other observers seem to see in him the miracle of inspiration spontaneously arising in an underprivileged boy.[25] Yet another view is Mário Filho's:

according to him, there was a connection between Garrincha's soccer style and his social background, but his emphasis is on the player's childhood hunting habits, totally unrelated to the social universe of the workers' housing development. He writes:

One can understand Garrincha only by identifying him with the figure of the hunter—or rather, with that of the hunted animal. What is best in his style was taught to him by the birds, the pacas, the opossums. Garrincha dribbles the way a bird or beast flees the hunter.[26]

Now, in addition to immediate evidence of a natural talent for sport that apparently reveals no more than a personality well-known and admired for a style of dribble that mimics the instinctive movements of a fleeing animal, would it not be possible as well to perceive more covert aspects of a social identity[27]—that is, the presence of such an ambiguous identity as Garrincha's in the context of a workers' housing development? Might one not indeed identify in his footballing style—which affirmed the effectiveness of a certain degree of amateurishness in professional sport, revolutionised dribbling technique, stressed the importance of the attack launched from the outside position, demolished tactical schemes previously established by trainers and their schools, demoralised the opposing team's defence and made the public laugh, while at the same time preserving the seriousness and humility of the craftsman who sticks to his work—some of the proclivities activated by a worker's creativity, however limited and inclined toward disobedience, and necessarily ambiguous and circumscribed to certain autonomous and marginal activities offered by the workers' community?

Garrincha was never quite at home as a professional athlete. To football aficionados, the awkwardness he displayed in his career only went to underscore the purity of his playing. If Garrincha was indeed the people's joy, it was because he was perceived less as putting on a show produced by professional means, through training and discipline, than as displaying an innate sense of 'sport for sport's sake', which we might qualify as a habitus materialised as a physical body and a style of play, and in a manner quite different from that of other players. Garrincha's finest phase of playing lasted only ten years, from 1953 to 1963. The high points of his career were the 1962 World Cup—where, in the absence of Pelé, he was the star of the Brazilian team, and was considered the best player in the world by sports journalists—and the 1962 Rio de Janeiro championship, which was won by Botafogo thanks to his extraordinary performance. Soon after began Garrincha's painfully drawn-out decline, marked by Brazil's defeat in the 1966 World Cup and the former star's relegation to second and third division teams. Worn out by medical attempts to mitigate the problems with his legs, he desperately sought an afterlife in a career that, from its very beginning, had had no other purpose than 'sport for sport's sake'.

Now the tables were turned on Garrincha: he was exploited by the world of professional football, which reduced him to the condition of a prematurely burned-out labourer of sport who did not quite know what to do with his retirement. It was as if the paternalistic mode of domination that had allowed Garrincha to develop his creative habitus, associated with the culture of working-class communities, now avenged itself on a subject that had been able to attain a certain amount of freedom through football. It must be stressed that what companies encouraged was sport of a strictly amateur nature, a leisure activity that was not supposed to replace work in the factory; that Garrincha himself had assimilated this view to such a degree that it took him more than a year to take a test at Botafogo after he had been invited; and that even after he became a great professional player he went on developing his creativity without ever realising that it might lead to a long-term project, as though he believed it remained subject to the will of his employers. At each turning point in his professional career, Garrincha was lucky enough to be able to count on the support of other players, particularly Nilton Santos. The deference and respect he always showed for this man—who in his life played the part of a *padrinho* (godfather) though he was actually his *compadre* (godfather to his child)—is reminiscent of the role some department heads had played in Garrincha's career in the factory, men who had the power to change his name and to determine whether or not he was to be allowed to play in the factory team. Garrincha's utter lack of control over his own professional life led him to accept outrageous contracts with Botafogo, contracts that took no account of his fame.[28] Indeed, the parallel between his passivity in relation to his club and the situation of the Pau Grande workers, who had no means to contest company decisions concerning wages or work conditions, is reinforced by the fact that up to 1963 Garrincha still belonged to the world of Pau Grande, where he lived with his wife and his seven daughters. His glory was shared by his neighbours, who told the press, on the occasion of his funeral, how he used to come from the Maracanã

Stadium on the same truck that brought his fans and celebrate Botafogo's victories with them in the bars of Pau Grande.

After the 1962 World Cup, Garrincha's love affair with the singer Elza Soares distanced him from Pau Grande and put him in contact with the world of show business, but it gave him no help in getting a stronger grip on his own career. The eye-opening comments made by Elza, who had signed enough contracts with nightclubs and recording companies to realise how shamelessly he was being exploited by Botafogo, came too late: by the time he finally secured a decent contract, Garrincha had developed arthrosis in both legs. Suffering acute pain, he refused to play, and as much as 50 per cent of his salary was withheld. After an operation that had not been recommended by the Botafogo physicians, he recovered very slowly and was unable to return to the club's main team. In 1966 he was sold to Corinthians, a São Paulo club, but his ability on the pitch was no longer what it had been. He played in the 1966 World Cup in England, in which Brazil were eliminated in the first round. Dismissed by Corinthians, Garrincha moved to a succession of clubs between 1966 and 1973, each weaker than the previous one. In 1973 an international match was held in the Maracanã to mark Garrincha's official retirement—an event that was known as 'The Thank-You Game'. Nevertheless, this Sisyphus of soccer went on playing in veterans' teams until his death without ever becoming a coach or turning to any other football-related activity.

Thus Garrincha's professional and private life after 1962 was a series of defeats. In 1967 and 1968 he was rejected by a number of clubs. Late in 1968 he was indicted for failing to pay alimony to his first wife for six months, and escaped jail only because a banker paid off his debts. In April 1969 he was involved in an automobile accident that killed Elza Soares's mother and, later in the same year, he had to flee to Italy with his wife to avoid another brush with the law. In Italy, however, though Elza had no trouble finding work as a singer, Garrincha's attempts to play football failed dismally, and he was forced to accept an advertising job offered by a Brazilian coffee-exporting agency. In December 1973, the farewell match in his honour was a public manifestation of his defeat. His ex-wife died two years later, and he had to take in five of his unmarried daughters.

Nevertheless, 1976 brought him a belated victory: after having another daughter with Elza Soares, at long last the son he had always hoped for was born. But the publicity surrounding the birth of the boy immediately led to trouble: a former girlfriend in Pau Grande publicly presented a putative son of his, aged fifteen. In 1977, Garrincha finally separated from Elza, after a year of very strained relations.

In 1978, the former player was hospitalised for the first time, a victim of hypertension. In the same year he got married once again, this time to Vanderléia, the widow of another retired football player. In July 1979 he was again in hospital, this time suffering from cirrhosis of the liver. In the 1980 Carnival, Garrincha took part in the samba-school parade on a float built in his honour by the Mangueira School. He cut a rather sorry figure in the midst of the merrymaking, still showing signs of depression and apathy—he had only come out of hospital in the preceding month. Although he was clearly in physical and psychological decline, Garrincha carried on as before: in 1981, yet another daughter was born; and on Christmas 1982 he went to Brasília for a friendly match. Soon after, he succumbed to deep alcoholic depression and died.

The king and the people

In the early 1960s, the two top names of Brazilian football were in their prime: Garrincha and Pelé. But while Garrincha's career soon fell apart, as we have seen, Pelé played professional soccer up to 1974 and was wholly successful in reshaping his career, so that to this day he remains immensely famous in Brazil and abroad. This calls for a comparative study, one that attempts more than—as is often done—simply to put down the different fates of these two sportsmen, whose class origin was similar, to mere chance.

Pelé, whose international career also had a spectacular start in 1958, was able to ensure his continued success, although his participation was slight both in the 1962 victory and in the 1966 defeat, due to injuries. Twice a champion in the world interclub championship, in 1962 and 1963, playing for Santos, he quickly consolidated his international status, culminating in his participation in the 1970 World Cup in Mexico, won by Brazil. After this, Pelé left both the national team and Santos to explore a market that, though technically less demanding, was of fundamental importance for the growth of football and for the reshaping of his own career: the United States and the New York Cosmos.

Pelé also came from a working-class background. But unlike Garrincha, who always stressed his deep-rooted attachment to his origins, in public

Pelé emphasised only his relation to his immediate family—father, mother, siblings, and grandmother. The more the press attempted to focus on Garrincha's private life, the less was found about his family. Concerning his father, who always held menial jobs such as sweeper, night-watchman, or farmhand working for the textile mill, little more is known than that he died of cirrhosis of the liver. There is no information about his other close relatives. In short, information about Garrincha's origins—mostly of an apocryphal nature—involves his social milieu rather than his actual family. The case of Pelé is precisely the opposite: we know much about each individual in his family; his parents were often publicly presented early in his career; but his private life was kept out of the limelight.

Pelé was the oldest child of a little-known football player from Bauru, São Paulo State, who at an early stage of his career was deprived of an opportunity to join better teams because he injured both his knees while playing with Atlético, a team in Belo Horizonte, the capital of the state of Minas Gerais. Since boyhood, Pelé was determined to achieve the success his father had missed. But such local fame as Dondinho—the nickname Pelé's father was known by—had managed to attain allowed him to complement his salary as a football player with his earnings from a job as a minor official at a neighbourhood outpatient clinic. It also gave him a chance to persuade his team's coach—Valdemar de Brito, a retired player of international renown who had also been forced to discontinue his career prematurely because of injuries—to take an active interest in the junior team in which his son was already showing his exceptional talent.

Pelé had joined this team after playing street football and trying to create a real team of his own, with what little money he managed to earn from odd jobs. As can be seen, the material conditions necessary for the practice of football were a major concern of this boy who was obsessed with his father's failure and with the untimely end of his coach's career. While Garrincha originally intended to become a labourer and became an athlete thanks to the factory's social initiatives, Pelé, who had always planned on being a professional player, did only a brief stint as a worker, at a shoe factory at the age of thirteen, to help out his family and prove his sense of responsibility to his mother, who—made sceptical by her husband's failure—only then allowed him to go on playing football with local teams.

It was thanks to Valdemar de Brito that Pelé was accepted by Santos, a major club that had twice won the São Paulo state championship. Brito, a football coach and a labour secretariat inspector in Bauru, wanted to move to the city of São Paulo. For this reason he asked his former teammate, Deputy Athiê Curi, who at that time was president of Santos, to ask Governor Jânio Quadros to transfer him to the São Paulo branch of his department. In exchange for this favour—asked of a governor who was an unpredictable man and who was generally averse to using political office for private purposes—Brito introduced a very young player who had all the makings of an exceptional athlete. Brito, a friend of Pelé's family, was finally able to persuade his mother—for it was her opinion that really mattered—to let the boy go to Santos by himself. Since he had no relatives there and was only fifteen, Pelé was to live on a permanent basis in the 'total institution' that characterised football in the period—the *concentração*, the boarding-house where players were kept in seclusion immediately before a game. There Pelé led a self-imposed ascetic life, going beyond his father's strictures against tobacco, alcohol, and nightlife, to concentrate solely on his athletic training.

With a professional discipline that amounted to a precocious internalisation of his father's frustrations, relying on the social connections in the world of soccer he had inherited from Dondinho, Pelé was able to develop his technical abilities, as exceptional as they were manifold, as well as an extreme sensibility to the material problems of a professional football player.[29] While Garrincha owed the essence of his talent to amateur sport, Pelé's gifts were fully developed in professional sport only. His twelve years of success have allowed him to preserve to this day an aura of prestige that he can now bring to bear on other sectors of activity related to sport, such as advertising and entrepreneurship.

'King Pelé's'[30] extreme professionalism thus stands in sharp contrast with Garrincha's strong links to working-class culture: during his rise to fame Garrincha was the perfect example of what Richard Hoggart has called the Epicureanism of everyday life.[31] Garrincha's Epicureanism, expressed in sport as 'sport for sport's sake' and outside it as a taste for irresponsible sex and for the humble forms of entertainment indulged in by workers,[32] kept him permanently in that short period of condoned license that is adolescence, so that he was mostly indifferent to and only occasionally concerned about his professional career. Had he remained a worker, his relation with football would probably have been smoother, for informal football games among forty-year-olds is, in working-class districts, a common form of leisure that naturally rounds off a life dedicated to the sport.[33] What is tragic about Garrincha's fate is precisely the contrast between his early brilliance, as he managed to raise the purity of his amateur style to the ultimate heights of professional competition, and his inability to act in accordance with his status as a professional athlete.

Death of the 'people's joy'

Garrincha's tragedy, brought to light by the circumstances of his death, fascinated the public, particularly the working-class crowds that turned out to mourn him. These crowds were in some ways similar to those shown in the movie *Garrincha, alegria do povo*, when Garrincha and his brilliant generation of Brazilian football players were at their best.

The film was shot at a time when many filmmakers in the Brazilian Cinema Novo movement were focusing on the country's impoverished, largely rural northeast to capture the specificity of the Brazilian social drama: examples are Gláuber Rocha's *The Black God and the White Devil* and Nelson Pereira dos Santos's *Dry Lives*. But Joaquim Pedro de Andrade was mostly concerned with the urban masses. He began with a short subject set in a Rio favela ('Couro de gato', an episode in the collective movie *Cinco vezes favela*), then turned to football, a less dramatic and political subject but one that was strongly associated with the working-class urban population, adopting a neorealist outlook. Andrade's film on Garrincha concentrates on the part of the public in the *gerais*—the cheapest section of a stadium, on a level with the field, providing low visibility. Here an essentially male crowd stands, pressed close together, and the difficulty in following the action of the game is compensated by the proximity to the players when they celebrate their goals and victories. Their pathetic faces, tense with anguish or joy, faces of working men, atoms in a huge multitude, are singled out by a camera in search of 'the people', whose hopes were exalted by intellectuals in the early 1960s.[34] The film's closing sequences show a throng of workers rushing off the trains and running toward the stadium on the day of a major match; these are the people who will watch the game from the *gerais*.

The film is much less interested in the spectators crowded in the stands, the organised cheering groups who are the majority and are also the most vocal forces in the stadium. It should be noted, however, that these groups greatly developed since the late 1960s, when different factions of fans of the same club competed against each other by making themselves quite visible and audible in the stands, setting off firecrackers, waving giant flags, chanting slogans, and so on. In addition, these groups encouraged the growth of a flourishing trade in merchandise and match-day logistics.

These same workers' faces can be seen on the crowded trains blowing their whistles as a final tribute to the dead football star, a multitude that grows ever denser, now including women and children, as it approaches Pau Grande. Throughout the ceremony, however, one notices the conspicuous presence of the organised cheering groups; particularly evident are the Botafogo fans, who try to capitalise on this tragic moment in order to celebrate the faded glories of their club, which at the time of Garrincha's death in 1983 had not won a championship for fifteen years. One might see in the appropriation of Garrincha's funeral by these new organised groups a sign of professional soccer's increasing autonomisation, its tendency to turn into a world apart, with its own rules and tropes.[35] But it can also be seen as the ultimate proof—if such proof were necessary—of the utter misery to which Garrincha was reduced; for it was his own and his friends' desire to be buried with his family in peace and quiet.

Though the public's intrusion on Garrincha's burial unintentionally added a final tragic note to his life, we can also interpret the public fervour as a tribute and a redress to a player who had fallen so low after a period of glory, and whose end illustrated so vividly the miserable lot that typifies the existence of the poor. Upon his death, even the 'sins' that had made him unpopular seem to have been forgiven. His marvellous football style, his indifference to professional competition and the ascent in social status it might confer on him, his strong links with his social background and the sacrifice this forced on him were some of the factors that contributed to the collective grief over his death.

The feeling of loss, however, was brought about not just by the awareness that a great age in Brazilian football was closing, but also by the sense that the social conditions which had made possible the rise of a player like Garrincha, with the particular sort of style that had made him famous, no longer existed. Gone with them were a brand of worker, the sort who lived in the traditional housing developments built by factories.

On a more general plane, his death symbolised the end of a certain style of working-class life, the memory of which was the only remnant of it that had survived the growth of the difficulties of the present. The 'euphoria' of the years 1950 to 1964—a period relatively favourable to workers not only on the economic plane but also as regards politics and civil freedoms[36]—was followed by a certain degree of sadness and of wild violence that one is tempted to associate with the intensification of economic exploitation and political oppression since the military coup—a kind of violence that was particularly common in the 1970s, especially manifested as riots in the urban centres of Rio and São Paulo. Garrincha's miserable death was the ultimate symbol of the end of the 'people's joy' generated by the successes of the 1950s, in particular by the victory in the 1958 World Cup, when Brazil at long last made a mark abroad, even if only through soccer—that is, through its working classes.

6

Football as a Profession

Origins, Social Mobility and the World of Work of Brazilian Footballers, 1950s–1980s[1]

Clément Astruc

The stakes of the history of Brazilian footballers

In a documentary from 1998 called *Futebol*, João Moreira Salles and Arthur Fontes portrayed the daily life of Fabrizio, a young and talented footballer who wanted to become a professional. As he was interviewed in front of his humble house, located in the Rio de Janeiro favela of Morro do Alemão, his father stated:

With the job I have it's not possible, it's not possible to get out of this *morro*.[2] So I depend only on him. With the football I think he can play [...] Every father sees this in his son, right? And I hope that he will spend this money getting us out of this *morro*, out of this area where we live.[3]

Ever since football became a professional sport in 1933 in the states of São Paulo and Rio de Janeiro, the game has appeared in Brazil as an opportunity for social mobility, especially for people of colour. In 1947, the journalist Mário Filho, in his book *O negro no futebol brasileiro*,[4] related how professionalisation has enabled black and mixed-race people such as Leônidas da Silva and Domingos da Guia to reach the status of idols and improve their standard of living in the Brazilian post-slavery society.[5]

Indeed, the end of amateurism must be linked to a change in the sociological composition of the main teams. In the first decade of the twentieth century the elites of Brazil's two main cities adopted football as an English and sophisticated novelty. They promoted an aristocratic conception of the sport, formed socially homogenous associations and organised restrictive leagues.[6] But soon enough, the game started becoming popular among mixed-race working classes and some of their members created new teams in the suburbs. During the 1910s and 1920s, the progressive apparition of teams whose players were manual workers or black (including mixed-race) people in the main city leagues—which subverted the elitist practice of the sport—created numerous conflicts. These conflicts were further compounded when some clubs started practicing a form of 'shamateurism': to attract the best working-class players, they gave their footballers gifts based on their performances or appointed them to fictitious jobs in order for them to have more time to train. For instance, the victory of Vasco da Gama—the club most closely associated with the Portuguese community of Rio—in the metropolitan championship of 1923, with a team mainly composed of black and mixed-race players who were paid unofficially, created considerable controversy and the club was excluded from the 1924 competition. In this context, according to Pereira, the adoption of professionalism appeared as a solution to growing racial, and also social, tensions.[7] As a matter of fact, it introduced a difference of status between the *socios* (the members) and the employees of the club—this difference helped in the selection of the best players but did not require the end of discrimination and prejudice. It also led to the creation of a new profession: the footballer.

As this short description suggests, a study of this peculiar job not only concerns football but also Brazilian society at large, and especially its working classes. Composing a history of the profession means asking how and why some young people chose this risky job and if this option was related to an individual or family strategy or hope of social mobility. To do so, the social origins of the footballers, their perspectives of inclusion in Brazilian society and the image of the profession at the time must be considered. But it is also useful to stress the specific nature of this occupation and of the working experience of these sportsmen. Firstly, footballers are hardly considered as *trabalhadores* (workers) and their working status is specific.[8] For most people, football has been, since its introduction to Brazil, a hobby. Moreover, the football community can be described as a 'universe structured by work's denial'—one where the idea of work is rejected or absent.[9] During the twentieth century, footballers had been employees of clubs whose managers—the *cartolas*—were volunteers. As a consequence, amateur ideology continued to influence their working experiences.[10] Secondly, they have a double condition. They are salaried employees but also goods that can be 'bought', 'sold' or 'loaned' by their club. This observation helps to understand the specificity of football's labour market, based until 1998 on the *passe*—the Brazilian version of the retain-and-transfer system—which prevented players from disposing of their own labour. Finally, the inner diversity of footballers makes it difficult for social scientists to study them as a group. Their short careers are usually described as individual trajectories and they are frequently compared with artists. Furthermore, due to the competition to attract the best players, the differences in the standard of living between two sportsmen can be spectacular even if their job is exactly the same. In a word, the unity of this socio-professional group appears as a major issue. As a consequence, not only should the condition of footballers and their status be considered, but one should also look into their relationship with their employers and colleagues.

This chapter mainly relies on a study involving the testimonies and the individual trajectories of forty-three players who represented Brazil at World Cup tournaments between 1954 and 1978. So far there appears to be no research based on a collection of careers covering this period. These players, representatives of the Brazilian footballing elite, mostly started their careers in the states of Rio de Janeiro and São Paulo between 1948 and 1970,[11] when the characteristics of the profession were generally similar to those of the 1930s and 1940s.[12] The youngest amongst these footballers played until the late 1980s. It should be noted that during these four decades—a period partly corresponding to the years of the Brazilian military dictatorship (from 1964 to 1985)—the *seleção* won three World Cup tournaments and various laws were passed to regulate the footballing profession.[13]

Origins, choice of occupation and social mobility: a rational choice?

In a pioneering dissertation published in 1980, Ricardo Benzaquem de Araújo looked into why the professional players he interviewed had originally turned to football as a career.[14] He emphasised that, after being selected by an *olheiro* (a spotter), they made a rational and strategic choice by leaving behind their former outlooks of inclusion in the labour market. On the one hand, although it was risky, this peculiar job appeared to them as a unique opportunity for social mobility. They aimed at making some money quickly so that they could invest it and become self-employed or even businessmen at the end of their sporting career. On the other hand, they could fulfil themselves: not only were they passionate about football, but it also allowed them to turn what they considered a personal gift into reality.

The survey for this chapter did not exactly reach the same conclusions.[15] The informants' choice of occupation cannot be described as mature, long-term or strategic. Indeed, when money is mentioned in their interviews, it appears in a specific context. For instance, they explained how their first contract enabled them to quit their former job, to satisfy their parents' requirements to get one, to stop putting burdens on their family's tight budget or—for those in more precarious situations—to answer an immediate necessity.[16] In addition, the presence of two other discourses shows that their choice of occupation cannot be understood only by considering social interest and highlights the peculiarity of such an option. First, by becoming a professional football, some of them realised a childhood dream.[17] Then—and this is a significant feature of the way many players perceived their career—some insisted on the weight of chance and circumstances.[18] In a word, they said that they became professional footballers more than they chose to become professional players, as Ado, the former Corinthians goalkeeper, explained:

Football, for me, was a coincidence. I had no plan, no idea. I had some idols—mine was Gilmar, I loved this guy. Castilho, oh my god… [inaudible] he was a goalkeeper—I enjoyed playing as goalkeeper at school—my idols. But I'd never… I said: 'God, it must be something this field, this thing'. I did not see myself in it, ever. And then, when I started playing football, I said: 'God, that's not so difficult'. I was very daring, wasn't I? And, when I entered, so, God. But, at the beginning, I never dreamt about being a football player.[19]

FOOTBALL AS A PROFESSION

Footballers and their bad reputation

Even if the interviewees seldom brought up the social capital they could gain with football, the testimonies provide indications of how desirable or undesirable this profession was and who it could or could not attract in the post-war decades. It is to be noted that, during the 1920s and 1930s, as youth from the mixed-race working classes were replacing members of Rio de Janeiro and São Paulo's elites in the main teams, the footballers' image worsened. While they were figures of elegance in the first decades of the sport's history in Brazil, footballers started to be regarded as dropouts and suffered social prejudice.[20] This helps explain why the interviewees accepted that their profession had a bad reputation during their youth, even in some working-class families, and why some parents were reluctant to accept their son's aspiration to become involved in the sport.[21]

While they described footballers' reputation, interviewees often used words that refer to the fringes of society such as *vagabundo* (vagabond), *malandro* (a scoundrel but also a streetwise person),[22] and *safado* (lewd). As they suggest, this representation had an economic facet as well as a moral one. First of all, it seemed hard to make a living playing football, except for those who were extremely gifted. Thus, Carlos Alberto Torres used the expression '*não dava camisa pra ninguém*' (literally speaking, 'it did not provide a shirt for anyone') in explaining the poor standards of living of professional players at that time.[23] Additionally, Joel Camargo stated that they were regarded as 'semi-unemployed'.[24] Such an expression may have a double meaning. On the one hand, it stresses how risky and precarious athletes' lives could be; on the other, it implies that their occupation was hardly considered work. Pepe also explained that, in the view of his parents' generation, 'the football player is a vagabond, who does not work'.[25] At this point, economic and moral considerations are intrinsically linked. During the 1950s and the 1960s, it seems that, no matter the money it could bring in, professional football lacked respectability. Various testimonies mentioned the alleged questionable habits of players.[26] Others—such as Marinho Peres—provided indicative anecdotes that suggest that footballers had little prestige:

You know that, at that time, that's an interesting fact, because at that time being a football player, even if Brazil was the world champion and all, the image people had of you, of somebody coming from the *morro*, you were the poor guy who clung to football. You see what I mean? So, I remember that while I was playing in the Portuguesa de Desportos, I was used to going to dances there in Sorocaba, the girls would ask: 'What do you do for a living?', and I'd answer: 'I'm a student', because if I had said: 'a football player'... You know, it's not like nowadays, when it's synonym of [...] At that time it was a guy who came from the slum.[27]

The sociological profile of footballers

If Marinho Peres's words stress the social contempt footballers some-times experienced, his personal case also reveals that their common characterisation as poor youths with very little perspective of social inclusion was partly distorted. As a matter of fact, his father was a doctor. Of course, he was an exception considering only two or three individuals in the sample belonged to the Brazilian elite or upper-middle class. On the other hand, only a few players came from the most precarious and marginalised stratums of Brazilian society.[28] In fact, in their accounts, numerous players described a modest background. Thus, more than one out of three footballers interviewed had performed an unskilled or a low-skilled job such as that of an office boy or an industrial worker before becoming a professional player.[29] This was often a way to contribute to household expenses or to stop being a burden on the family's budget. Having lost his father at an early age, Jair da Costa stressed that, at the age of just fourteen, he had no choice: 'I needed to work. I had two sisters, a brother, a mother I had to take care of, there was the little one, my brother, so I started to work and play in this firm'.[30]

Furthermore, examining the occupations of the parents of interviewees sheds light on the social origins of the young men who became professional footballers in the post-war decades.[31] Generally speaking, the great majority of them were from working- and lower-middle-class backgrounds. That said the diversity of this group was greater than one might expect. Seven of the players had at least one parent working in the industry and of these some were skilled. For instance, Cabeção was the son of a mechanic from a company called Sprinter; Roberto Miranda's father was a metalworker; Alfredo Mostarda's father was a welder and his mother—like Lima's—was a weaver. Ten of them had a parent who worked in business or in the craft industry, some of whom were self-employed. For example, Pepe's father owned a grocery shop. Emerson Leão's father was tailor. Feliciano Marco Antonio's mother ran a boarding-house and his father worked in the coffee trade. Some parents had jobs in the public sector such as with the city hall, post office, prison service or police. Others worked for an electric power company, a bus company or for a railway. Tostão's father was a bank clerk. Three players each had a parent who was a teacher. Some mothers were domestic servants. Additionally, one was a washerwoman and another was a midwife. It appears that only two fathers had a job directly linked to agriculture.

Significantly, six out of forty-three fathers of those interviewed—almost 15 per cent of them—had been football players.[32] Considering the low number of football professionals in the wider Brazilian population, this ratio is striking.[33] At the very least, this partly upholds the possibility of the formation of a footballing aristocracy and contradicts the idea that succeeding in the competitive process of becoming a professional simply involves being gifted, understood as a personal, specific and innate talent, whose origin cannot be known or explained.[34] Indeed, because a gift of this sort cannot be transmitted or inherited, recruitment based on this single criterion would make the reproduction of a professional elite impossible.[35]

Several of the interviews offer indications of what the players would or could have done if they had not chosen to become professional footballers. A systematic study is impossible, especially considering that they did not all start working in the same period and that they came from different places—some grew up in the cities of São Paulo and Rio de Janeiro while others spent their youth in more rural locations with fewer potential employment opportunities—but meaningful individual cases can be described. The players in this study turned to football between 1948 and 1970, a period when Brazil was undergoing significant industrialisation.[36] The country became capable of making almost all kinds of industrial products and many new opportunities in the labour market were created. Brazil can be described at that time as a 'society on the move' in which, to at least a certain degree, almost all its levels and strata were in ascendance.[37]

In this context, the outlooks of the football players were as diverse as their social backgrounds. Some had little chance of obtaining a better standard of living. Valdomiro, whose father was a coal miner in Santa Catarina, explained that he too would probably have been a miner had he not been dismissed by the company he had worked for; soon after this, he turned to professional football.[38] He stated: 'because you know that [playing football is] the only way for a person to succeed, for the poor guy to triumph over life [...] I always say, even now, he can either sing or play football'.[39] Others could have become skilled or semi-skilled workers. Indeed, they mention an occupation they had learned or their parents wanted them to learn. Paraná started a course to be a typist. Amarildo had tailoring skills. Alfredo Mostarda, whose parents were both industrial workers, would have been a welder. He revealed that his father enrolled him in a welder and mechanic class in the Serviço Nacional de Aprendizagem Industrial (SENAI) and insisted that his son obtain a diploma before he allowed him dedicate himself to football.[40] Few of the young men had a chance of reaching respected professions that required a university education. Leão's brothers, the sons of a tailor, studied medicine while he became a sportsman. Tostão, who had considered the liberal professions, opted for football instead of taking on the *vestibular* (a university's entrance examination). José Baldocchi, whose father ran a joiner's workshop and a hardware store, also had the opportunity to take the *vestibular* to pursue medical studies, but he failed, partly because he was unable to keep up in the preparation class. His account reveals that his parents probably had a familiar strategy of social mobility based on education:

I studied. Even in my family, one of my cousins is a dentist, one is an engineer and the other a doctor; [all] are more or less my age. And my father was saying: 'Go study. Go study'. With sacrifice—we did not have a lot of resources—but... 'I work so that you can study'.[41]

The few players with greater potential to gain a valued social status were white, some of them being descendants of European immigrants. This observation illustrates Florestan Fernandes's analysis: black and mixed-race people were still discriminated against and occupied low social positions in Brazil during the post-war decades.[42] Even if their situation had been improving since 1930, they had fewer chances of ascending in the social ladder than did descendants of European immigrants. With their origins in very low social levels, they continued to occupy similar positions in the labour market, mainly being confined to secondary and routine jobs.[43] In this context, there are different meanings to the fact that a significant proportion of the interviewees were black or of mixed race.[44] On the one hand, it demonstrates that they did indeed have access to the elite of this profession and could achieve, thanks to football, a better life. On the other hand, it could go to show that most of the young men who chose football as an occupation had rather low prospects of inclusion in the labour market.

Social mobility for a restricted professional elite

The standard of living of the footballers between the 1950s and the 1980s also needs to be considered to help understand to what extent this occupation could provide social mobility. What was the lifestyle of a professional footballer? A report—published in 1975 in the Brazilian magazine *Placar*—about Ademir da Guia, a player with Palmeiras and the national team who can be seen as typical of the profession's elite, provides indications.[45] Various symbols of his place in the Brazilian elite or upper-middle classes are mentioned. At almost thirty-three years old, he lived in a large house in Vila Madalena, a wealthy São Paulo neighbourhood. He owned a car, employed a domestic servant, paid for his two children to attend a private school and was making plans to take his family on a cruise. He earned a fixed wage of 30,000 cruzeiros a month and could receive an additional 10,000 cruzeiros (an equivalent total of $5,000). The report's author also made it clear that Ademir did not need to use this money for household expenses. Indeed, investments he had made during his career guaranteed further income. He had also bought five other properties—apparently a widespread practice for the most successful players.[46] His father, the former footballer Domingos da Guia, occupied one, another was at the beach and the other three properties were rented out. Moreover, Ademir earned dividends from investments and was the main shareholder of two companies.[47] But, by comparing Ademir and a second-tier professional called Afonso, the author stressed that if football could lead to a high social status, few managed to reach those heights.

What makes any general assertion about social mobility difficult are the great disparities that existed—and still exist—between professional footballers. Thus, according to a survey conducted by *Placar*,[48] less that 1,000 out of the almost 7,000 Brazilian professional footballers registered in 1971 lived on the income from this occupation alone. Many of them had another job during part of the year or were studying. Furthermore, 77 per cent of this population earned less than 1,000 cruzeiros a month (around $200). Only approximately 500 individuals earned more than this amount and a very small elite—representing less that 0.5 per cent of the profession—made more than 10,000 cruzeiros a month (around $2,000). The elite aside, some footballers did manage to lead a comfortable life, buy a house and sometimes a car, but the great majority experienced precarious living conditions. Finally, two other issues should be explored for a fuller understanding of the opportunities of social mobility for highly paid footballers. One is their ability to deal with sudden enrichment;[49] the other is the need for premature professional retraining. These issues, however, are beyond the limits of this chapter.

Thus, only a minority of professionals managed to get a higher social status. In this sense, football could be considered as a way of social emancipation. But this required experiencing a very exacting or even alienating worker status.

Footballers' world of work: special status and dominated workers?[50]

Researcher (R.): You chose São Paulo?
Mirandinha (M.): I didn't choose. They chose me. [laughs] It was very nice.
R.: I understand. The player had little influence.
M.: He didn't, no. The player had little influence. He didn't have this option: 'I want to go here. I want to go there'.[51]

Listening to the player's testimony, one is struck by the passivity of some footballers during a process primarily concerning them: their transfer, which is to say their sale, to another club. This highlights the peculiarity of these workers who were—and still are—simultaneously both people and salaried employees, as well as objects, goods to be bought, sold or loaned out.[52] Furthermore, some of them implied that sometimes no one asked their opinion or consulted them and that they first heard of the negotiations for them only after discussions had concluded between the two clubs. In 1975, Palmeiras's president informed César Lemos that the following year he was to play for Corinthians. When he disagreed, the president answered: 'No, you need to go. Because you have already been sold'.[53] Commenting on the anecdote, Lemos said: 'At that time we were sold without knowing it, dude. First, they met each other, then they met us. We were the last to be informed that we were sold'. Once more, the footballer did not take part actively in the negotiation and his transfer appears more like the sale of goods than as a change of employer. In such cases, the athletes seem to be dominated workers who did not dispose of their own labour and could not—when it was not in their club's interest—make the best personal choice. Paraná explained for instance that, when he was playing in São Bento at the beginning of the 1960s, two clubs—São Paulo FC and Santos—were interested in recruiting him. His employer chose São Paulo FC whereas the player's personal interest lay in playing for Santos where he would be paid more.[54] The balance of power was clearly in favour of the club. Furthermore, the authorities were aware of this imbalance: the preamble to a decree about the profession of the footballer—passed in 1964—clearly identified various abuses.[55] First, in a majority of cases, athletes were sold regardless of their own will. Second, they did not receive any financial benefit from their sale, whereas their former clubs received significant indemnities. Finally, due to the prohibitive price demanded for their sale, some players remained linked to their employer against their will and this went against their aspiration for better payment for their work. These problems justified a regulation of the *passe*.

Thus, the club's control of their athletes relied on this legal device, which was the Brazilian version of the retain-and-transfer system.[56] Strictly speaking, the *passe* was a letter, a transfer certificate, which linked the player to his club.[57] When a player was transferred to another club, his new employer had to buy his *passe* from his former club, the *passe* owner. The link established between the footballer and his employer prevented him being hired by a new club without the permission of the *passe* owner. As a consequence, the *passe* gave the employer control over its athletes and their assets and the ability to secure a transfer payment even after the end of the player's contract. In this regard, the system's defenders argued that this guarantee was necessary because the clubs would stop spending money to train and identify new talent if they had no certainty of a return on their investment.[58] Both a 1964 decree and also a 1976 law had regulated the *passe*.[59] Among other aspects, it was specified that the player's agreement to the transaction was required and that he had the right to receive 15 per cent of the transfer fee. But, even if these clauses could benefit players, they did not change the root of the system, which was eventually abolished in 1998.[60]

Factors which maintained the footballer's position as a controlled worker continued: as he was the only professional who could not dispose freely of his own labour force, his status was more exacting or even alienating than that of salaried employees, above all going against the principles of Brazilian labour law.[61] In an interview with *Placar* magazine in 1971, Maria Nunes Silva Lisboa, a judge of the Regional Court of Labour of Bahia, even stated that the *passe* went against the Brazilian constitution.[62] Opponents of this much-disputed legal device did not hesitate to compare the position of football players with that of slaves.[63]

From the testimonies, however, it appears that it was not only their legal status that prevented some players from taking full advantage of their careers, but also that they were at a disadvantage for being unable to negotiate. For example, Indio, who played from the late 1940s until the 1960s, stressed his powerless position against the *cartolas*: 'I never knew how to make a contract, I have always lost, never [...] I had nobody to call on, and I had to accept what they said.'[64] This passivity is reminiscent of that of the Brazilian footballing idol Garrincha, who embodied the figure of the dominated player abused by the *cartolas*.[65] Garrincha, as Leite Lopes's chapter in this volume shows, signed contracts that bore no relation to his sporting value and was totally unable to handle his professional career because of a mind-set and background linked to his youth in a very specific context of industrial workers.[66]

Obviously, the description of these players' cases must not lead to a wholly negative vision of the footballers' condition. Indeed, in a trade in which each player had a different value with individual terms of contract, some managed to defend their interests better than others. Instead many different factors should be considered, including the athlete's role in the team, his experience, the quality of his personal support network, his conception of the activity, his ability to communicate with the media and his social background. Also, most of the transfers and contract negotiations mentioned in the testimonies were not presented as having been conflicts. Moreover, the relationship between employers and employees is not systematically presented as antagonistic. Nonetheless, a few of the players stated that they had been at loggerheads with their employers at least once in their career. Although an extreme case, one example is particularly significant for showing that conflicts of interests between employer and employee, typical of the working world, existed in Brazilian professional football, even during the 1970s when the sport was still influenced by amateur values; on the other hand, the case also demonstrates the particular nature of this labour environment.

FOOTBALL AS A PROFESSION

Baldocchi's case: an example of employer vs employee conflict

The defender José Guilherme Baldocchi was a reserve in the Brazilian team during the World Cup tournament in 1970 and played for Corinthians between 1971 and 1975. His stint with the club was ended by a tough conflict and legal proceedings against his employer. Baldocchi's account does not present this labour dispute in terms of professional issues but, instead, as being a personal disagreement with the club's president, Vicente Matheus. Baldocchi gave two examples of the *cartola's* hostility towards him. First, when he became head of the club—a position he had once occupied previously—after Baldocchi was hired, Matheus allegedly asked him if he would return to his former club Palmeiras—Corinthians's great rival in São Paulo—and told him: 'A player of Palmeiras in the Corinthians—that never works out'. This remark, which linked this professional to a team he no longer represented and referred to a traditional rivalry, suggests that amateur conceptions were still influencing the work ethic of footballers. Secondly, Baldocchi also blamed Matheus for his removal from the team for the 1974 final of the Paulista Championship. This personal choice—based on the president wanting to get rid of the player rather than a sporting criterion, according to Baldocchi—further deteriorated their relationship. However, even if Baldocchi did not insist on the differing interests that could explain the conflict, his case provides a significant example of labour disputes surrounding the working environment of footballers.

In 1973, the renewal of Baldocchi's contract resulted in conflict between the player and the *cartola*. Corinthians offered Baldocchi the same wage—240,000 cruzeiros (about $37,000) for two years.[67] However, as Baldocchi wanted an increase in pay, he at first refused this offer. Consequently, the value of his *passe* was fixed and he was put up for sale.[68] In September, he was—as were other players on the team—without a contract as he kept on refusing the club's offer.[69] Even as he continued playing with the club, the conflict with his employer continued. In February 1974, a newspaper reported that Baldocchi and the Corinthians had been involved in litigation and that the Tribunal da Justiça Desportiva (Justice Court of Sport) of São Paulo had sided with the player.[70] This decision went against the request of contract suspension for indiscipline (due to an interview given by Baldocchi) that the club had made. Once more, Matheus decided to put Baldocchi's *passe* on sale. But the following year the most serious conflict began.

In 1975, Baldocchi was suspended from the Corinthians team and his contract was not renewed. In October, the *Diário de Notícias* reported that the player—without contract and consequently without wages—was thinking about quitting the profession.[71] No club had accepted to pay the price of his *passe* and Vicente Matheus refused to give him his *passe livre*, even though this would have helped him to find an employer more easily. It seems that in October, the São Paulo team Portuguesa had expressed an interest in signing Baldocchi, but he was still waiting for *passe livre* two months later.[72]

During the first months following his removal from the team, while he could not train with the team on the advice of a labour justice lawyer, Baldocchi went to the club every day to train separately and be seen working.[73] Baldocchi's suspension from Corinthians continued throughout 1976 (though after a few months he reported for training), only ending at the beginning of 1977 following a judicial process.[74] At the first hearing, the Labour Justice ruled in favour of the employee. At first Corinthians appealed, but then decided to make an agreement with Baldocchi: he received his *passe livre* and Corinthians agreed to give the player back-pay for the period between August 1975 and November 1976. After almost two years of exclusion, Baldocchi at last had the right to exert his professional status and he signed for Fortaleza, a mid-level club in the northeastern state of Ceará that did not take part in the national league.

This case, which exemplifies the existence of conflicts typical of employment in Brazilian professional football, set a legal precedent.[75] That said, there were parallels between Baldocchi's case and an earlier situation involving Afonsinho, which attracted a lot of media attention.[76] In conflict with Botafogo in 1970, Afonsinho was prevented from training and was excluded from the team because he refused to cut his long hair and shave his beard. This led him to the kind of impasse that Baldocchi would also experience. Afonsinho received no wages but could not offer his labour to another club until he eventually gained his *passe livre* thanks to a request at the Tribunal Superior de Justiça Desportiva (Superior Court of Sports Justice). These two examples show how in the 1970s labour conflicts relating to professional football were occasionally brought before the courts and that a player could even win his legal case.[77] They also suggest that having a *passe livre* was not as favourable as it seems: both players appear to have partially been blacklisted because they had questioned the authority of their clubs to control players.[78] But, although their situations were clearly subversive, Baldocchi's attitude was less rebellious than was Afonsinho's.[79] Another issue also made their cases similar: these were individual labour disputes, in which the players struggled alone against their employer. This observation raises the question: were footballers able to defend their interests collectively?

The footballers: a weakly mobilised professional group

In Brazil, no national professional movement of footballers existed before 1990,[80] with the first representative organisations being, instead, at state level. São Paulo's union, the Sindicato dos Atletas Profissionais do Estado de São Paulo (SAPESP), which was created at the end of the 1940s, was for a long time the only organisation of its kind. During SAPESP's first decades, it seems to have had little visibility. As an example of SAPESP's lack of influence, in an article about the *passe* that was published in *Placar* in 1971, the lawyer Werner Becker stated: 'I did not know any players' union with an active existence'.[81] Six months later, during a conversation with Afonsinho organised by the same magazine, Pelé referred to a 'very divided class', adding: 'We do not manage to bring together all the players around a common cause, a common idea. We do not even manage to bring them together around a trade union here in São Paulo'.[82] He then mentioned difficulties the president of SAPESP, Gilmar, had faced while he wanted to organise a campaign to encourage more players to enrol in the association.

Furthermore, at the beginning of the 1970s, in the context of the dictatorship but also of Brazil's third World Cup victory, part of the footballing elite could have articulated—or at least thought that they could have articulated—demands directly to the authorities. In 1970, after the Brazilian team's triumph, the players had the opportunity to discuss with the country's president, General Emílio Garrastazu Médici, a better regulation of their profession and the issue of pensions.[83] A few months later, in an interview, Gérson mentioned direct dialogue with the president as the best way to improve the players' condition as the clubs' attitude made the development of trade unions difficult.[84] Even if the possibility of direct negotiations seem unlikely, and while Gérson's opinion may not have been representative of the vision of the elite footballers, this suggests the existence of a certain amount of scepticism toward the appearance of a collective and autonomous movement at that time.

As an indication of the trade unions' development, a few figures can be mentioned. São Paulo's footballers' union gathered 560 out of the 2,500 or 3,000 players in the state at the end of the 1970s,[85] 240 out of 2,400 players in 1981,[86] and 650—less that 30 per cent of all professional players—in 1984.[87] In Rio de Janeiro, the trade union (Sindicato dos Atletas de Futebol do Estado do Rio de Janeiro),[88] created in 1979, had 500 members out of the 1,020 professional footballers of the state in 1983.[89] It is likely, however, that very few of these unions' members were active. In two interviews given to *Placar* in the 1980s while he was president of the SAPESP, Waldir Peres lamented the inertia of his professional group.[90] In a 1984 article, he attributed the inertia to a lack of class-consciousness and explained that players did not attend meetings about issues concerning general demands but only came to ask for help when they were individually affected, that is to say when they had payment problems or after suffering 'all the injustices you can imagine'. It is to be noted that Peres voiced similar views in 2011, when he stated: 'The players' trade union here in Brazil is negligible. It is not very active. The union is sought only when the players do not get paid, there is no political movement behind this union'.[91]

Conclusion

The fact that the players hardly defended their interests as a group echoes one of the main issues of the reflection upon footballers: their unity. Writing the history of these professionals implies considering to what extent the creation of a new occupation has led to the constitution of a new socio-professional group, which could share labour practices, ideas, working conditions, experiences, memories or even a common professional culture. But what appears more clearly and makes the study of footballers (or at least any generalised considerations about them) difficult is precisely the great inner diversity of this population.

This chapter shows that the professionals active between the 1950s and the 1980s did not correspond to a single sociological profile and were not just simply poor young men with very low expectations. Due to the great wage inequalities which existed among players and because of the low standard of living that most of them had, only a minority of them had the chance to experience a spectacular social mobility and join the Brazilian upper-middle class or elite. The ability of a football player to defend his own interests and to take the maximum advantage of his career varied between individuals. Nonetheless, these obstacles to the homogeneity of footballers as a socio-professional group also points to the peculiarities of this occupation. Footballers had to compete with teammates and players from other teams occupying the same position, and a different value was attributed to each worker. Moreover, the best opportunities in the labour market—in the twenty or thirty clubs at the top of the sports hierarchy—were rare. Although players' careers were very short, most of them had significant professional mobility and as a consequence successively belonged to different teams,[92] which in turn were changing and ephemeral groups. Representations linked with individualism—such as talent and self-realisation—were also central.[93] Finally, employees faced their employers individually when they had to negotiate their contracts.

Even if the unity of footballers is problematic, this chapter discusses some historical landmarks of their profession. Firstly, the choice of this occupation cannot be understood simply by considering elements of a rational social strategy because in their accounts the players stressed other decision-making factors such as passion and circumstances. Secondly, during the post-war decades, footballers had a bad reputation, at least for their parents' generation. Football as an occupation probably did not appear as financially attractive as perhaps it appears in the first decades of the twenty-first century, and offered little in the way of respectability. The great majority of the former sportsmen discussed in this chapter, then, came from the working and lower-middle classes—the analysis of their parents' occupation showed that quite diverse social backgrounds can be identified. Many of them were mixed-race or black people, which confirms that they had the opportunity to reach the elite of this professional group but also that most of the footballers had relatively low social prospects. Only a minority of them could expect to have well-respected jobs requiring higher education. Moreover, this occupation—that provided the best players with a form of social emancipation—implied the experience of an exacting or even alienating worker status. Indeed, footballers were often passive in their transfer negotiation and did not freely dispose of their own labour force due to the *passe* mechanism, which brought up their double status—as both employees and assets—in the eyes of their employers and converted them into specific workers. But this partial lack of control upon the evolution of their career was even broader: the necessity to deal with uncertainty—especially regarding injuries—was also constitutive of players' working experience. In addition, Baldocchi's case is evidence that, even if amateur values remained influential, conflicts of interests between an employee and his employer, typical of the world of work, existed, and could lead to radical opposition including legal proceedings. These conflicts were individualistic in nature and it seems that collective mobilisation was low, perhaps indicative of the weakness of the Brazilian football players' trade union movement.

7

Dictatorship, Re-Democratisation and Brazilian Football in the 1970s and 1980s

José Paulo Florenzano

Introduction

The process of the militarisation of football in Brazil involved multiple aspects, entailed many paths and transcended the mere use of the *canarinho* team ('canary team', the nickname of the Brazilian national team) for political propaganda purposes. In effect, this was a much more ambitious, diffuse and multifaceted ideological project. It unfolded on several converging lines of action. These were drawn from various instances of power with the purpose of attaching the whole of civil society to the semantic plot of exacerbated nationalism, visceral anti-communism and authoritarian conservatism, which are constitutive aspects of a Manichaeistic world-view. This world-view operated an internal division between 'those who have nothing to fear' and the 'bad Brazilians'. The former complied with the authoritarian order established with the coup. The latter insisted on questioning it, either through peaceful means, or through armed struggle.[1]

To carry forward the relentless fight against the so called 'forces of evil', and also the implacable employment of repressive apparatus, the military dictatorship (1964–85) would turn to a vast system of trenches based on the creation of the Olimpíadas do Exército (Army Olympics),[2] the resumption of the Olimpíadas dos Trabalhadores (Workers' Olympics), the promotion of football matches involving Indian communities, or even on the institution of the National Championship. These initiatives had a quite unequal weight, value and range. However, in one way or another, they were empowered by the sweeping campaign of the Brazilian national football team, either in the World Cup qualifying phase in 1969, or in the celebration of winning, for the third time, the tournament one year later.

On the other hand, the years 1978 to 1984 correspond to the most revolutionary period of Brazilian football. The 'Republic of Football', as Brazil was sometimes called, constituted not only the 7,892 professional players registered by Brazil's many federations and organised in many athletics collectives, but also by the ones who, outside the official circuit, acted as creative individuals in dusty strips, amateur teams plotting survival strategies and elaborating experiences of self-organisation.[3] Based on the principles of equality, freedom and participation, Brazil housed a deliberating nation willing to put everything into question,[4] starting with the meaning of being an athlete, passing through the link between field and stands, and including the sense which clothed the game. This chapter aims to establish a counterpoint between the 'authoritarian utopia', forges in the context of militarisation, and the Republic of Football, founded in the context of re-democratisation, highlighting some aspects involved in the historical process along which the Brazilian athlete struggled to establish himself as his own guide.

Authoritarian utopia

In early April 1970, the Clube de Regatas Flamengo, the football team with the largest number of supporters in the country, landed in Curitiba to launch the first ever Army Olympics. This was a sporting competition which had as the objective of promoting the coming together of the armed forces and grassroots classes.[5] With Brazil's 1970 World Cup victory in Mexico a few months' later, this initiative would gain further impetus as a consequence of the outpouring of nationalism that the football tournament aroused. Indeed, in the next Army Olympics, held in Belo Horizonte in 1971, the event included concerts performed by famous Brazilian singers such as Roberto Carlos. The programme also included radio, theatre and television artists, art, commerce and industry exhibitions, rodeo events and samba-school parades, among other attractions besides sports. All this transformed the event into a national version of the nineteenth- and early twentieth-century great exhibitions held in Europe that showed off the scientific developments, economic progress and political strength of imperialist nations.[6] Brazil's Crystal Palace, however, assumed the features of a football stadium; its third World Cup victory resembled the nation's cutting-edge technology. Thus, in early June 1971, the Army Olympics were opened in Mineirão Stadium by the Brazilian president, accompanied by senior members of the civilian and military authorities. On the football field, a game took place with the best players from the states of Minas Gerais and Rio de Janeiro, such as Carlos Alberto, Paulo César, Tostão and Piazza, amongst others who had helped Brazil win the World Cup the previous year. Thus, they were all involved in competing for the Emílio Garrastazu Médici Cup.[7]

The third Army Olympics, in 1972, coincided with the celebrations marking 150 years of Brazilian independence and for this reason it deserved special treatment from organisers. Taking place in Porto Alegre, the capital of Rio Grande do Sul, the program boasted an even wider range of spectacles than before. A special children's festival included circus performers and attracted some 250 thousand people, while other events included a naval parade and a display of aerobatics.[8] The military regime acted to mobilise popular support for the cause it defended and embodied. A celebration of the military government's so-called 'economic miracle', the authorities did not stint on resources and ensured that the main attraction—football—remained a central event. On 26 April, in Porto Alegre's impressive Beira-Rio Stadium, the games commenced with a football match between the Brazilian and Paraguayan national teams, much to the delight of President Médici who was in the grandstand alongside his army, navy and air force ministers.[9]

Every year the Army Olympics was held in a different location, undertaking the ideological manoeuver which had been prescribed as part of the war of positions fought by the military regime. In 1973, Recife hosted the fourth Army Olympics.[10] In the following year, it was the turn of Brasília, the federal capital, to promote the festival. Against the background of General Ernesto Geisel's new presidency, the fifth Army Olympics involved intense programming, including the four army units, the military commanders of Brasília and the state of Amazônia and students from public and private schools. The print media published a text that showed the organisers' intention of using the festival to gain support from the working classes. As was noted in the official propaganda, 'the people and the army, once more united'.[11] In effect, this was about obtaining popular support for a government that resorted to the use of brute force against political dissidents and opposition groups. Football allowed the government to show-off two distinct sides. To appeal to its supporters, it wanted to show that it was easy-going, affable and sportive; but for the opposition—the 'internal enemy'—the message was that of toughness, relentlessness and violence. In the opening of the Games, the Brazilian national team had no difficulty overcoming the amateur athletes representing Haiti with a final score of four to zero. However, the authoritarian regime's true opponent lay elsewhere.

In September 1969, in Jequitinhonha Valley, one of the poorest and most remote areas of the state of Minas Gerais, the Maxacalis Indian nation were co-opted by the military police for the Semana da Pátria—a week of patriotic celebrations commemorating Brazilian independence which included speeches, firework displays, archery exhibitions and sports competition: a match organised between 'the football team of Maxacalis' and 'a civilised team'.[12] The event would include a parade of the Indian Rural Guard (Guarda Rural)—a body formed to patrol zones of forest reserves.[13] This unusual guard formation was soon deployed in many other Indian communities, as was suggested by newspaper reports published in February 1970:

Ninety Indians take an oath to the flag and deliver headdresses to authorities, during the graduation ceremony of the first Indian Rural Guard class, in a solemnity to be held today at 11 o'clock at the Military Police Block Battalion of Minas Gerais, in the presence of the Interior Minister, Colonel Costa Cavalcanti.[14]

The first Indian Guard was divided into four battalions: thirty Carajás, twenty Xerentes, ten Maxacalis and thirty Krahô. 'The first Indian police' in Brazil's history were directed to ensure safety and maintain 'order in the villages'. The ceremony included the playing of the national anthem, pledging an oath to the flag and displays of search and arrest methods, unarmed combat and the use of firearms. During their three month training programme, military instructors also taught guard members torture techniques. At a ceremony in Belo Horizonte before the authorities and members of the public, the Indian soldiers did a march past, carrying a figure hanging on a *pau de arara* ('parrot's perch'), a favourite torture position that causes severe joint and muscle pain, headaches and psychological trauma.[15] Publically, the military government defended itself from accusations of committing genocide against the Indian population. Internally, however, it promoted the Amerindian metamorphosis of police involved in the culture of terror. Not only were they being co-opted to fight against armed left-wing resistance, they were also being integrated into the logic of war that drove the military regime. As General Bandeira de Mello, the president of the Fundação Nacional do Índio (Indian National Foundation), argued of the 'process of acculturation' that was underway in the country: 'We cannot spend five to eight years dealing with isolated Indian tribes, because that would delay the implementation of the National Integration Plan in the opening of roads such as Transamazônica and Cuiabá-Santarém'.[16] Thus, Indian culture was being violated; native forests were being destroyed, all under the mantle of national unity, economic development and the promotion of Brazilian identity. At the same time, obstacles which threatened the process of construction of a *Brasil Grande* (Great Brazil) were gradually eliminated.[17]

Football, used as a means of acculturation, seemed a cultural shortcut to gain the Indian communities' hearts and minds.[18] The repressive practices used to accelerate acculturation moved alongside games of seduction that revolved around a ball. Regarding repression, the creation of the Rural Guard resulted in predictably disastrous outcomes with beatings, arbitrary treatment and insubordination.[19] In terms of seduction, football was not without risks when it came to predicting the outcome of matches between the 'wild' and the 'civilised' teams. Neither means of acculturation was allowed to circumscribe precisely the meaning of a game which, although performed under military auspices, acquired its own unforeseen dynamic. It was also more autonomous in relation to how the human body was used, how the rules were elaborated, and how teams interacted in an intercultural field where the spirit of the game escaped the control of the military authorities.

In 1971, the Xavantes of the village of Couto Magalhães in Mato Grosso had formed a team that used to attract both spectators and income in friendly matches in the Xavantina region, located some 200 kilometres from the border of the state of Goiás. They brought to the matches their native songs and dances, wore neither football boots nor uniforms, but instead displayed their traditionally painted bodies.[20] If the opposing team came with sports equipment, the Xavantes added to their team three more players to 'compensate', as was explained by Chief Kaptuluazu de Jesus, whose body painting indicated the predominance of green. Asked about the chromatic predilection, he answered with no mystery, 'I support Palmeiras'.[21] Thereby, the Sociedade Esportiva Palmeiras—one of the most powerful teams in Brazilian football, founded by Italian immigrants in late-nineteenth-century São Paulo—inspired the leader of the Xavantes Esporte Clube. Its existence problematised the encounter between 'wild' and 'civilised'—football was no longer conceived of in terms of an acculturation process destined to eliminate all hints of difference, reducing the otherness represented by Indians in Brazilian society. Instead it existed as a playful experience, able to shelter the game amidst cultural diversity, recreating it beyond the authoritarian setting in which it unfolded.

The preceding case demonstrates how football was used to transfigure forest culture into a 'civilized' way of being, involving an increase in status, a change of identity and a symbolic border crossing of an implied rite of passage. The following case is an example of how workers were kept within the orbit of capitalistic and Western-Christian civilisation, instilling the rules of a game in which there were no losers, but only predetermined rules necessary for the cooperation between social classes. Strictly speaking, this configuration began being drafted in the first decades of the twentieth century. Indeed, in 1947, at the inauguration of the Serviço Social da Indústria, SESI (Industry Social Service), the first Jogos Esportivos Operários (Workers' Games) was held in São Paulo and became an annual event to promote the 'healthy spirit of fellowship'.[22] Scheduled for Labour Day, the Games transformed the day into one of 'fun and recreation' rather than an occasion for protests and demands. On 1 May 1969, SESI again organised the Games, claiming that the event provided invaluable 'educational, physical, moral and social services' to industrial workers in São Paulo. Converging with this initiative, in the same healthy spirit that inspired it, the mayor of São

Paulo, Paulo Maluf, promised to build clubs throughout the city as a way to bring sport to the people. The newspaper *A Gazeta Esportiva* interpreted the spirit of this idea thusly: 'Nevermore the youth gathered in gangs, loose in the streets, as a rabble of vagrants and stray dogs'.[23] Not to be outdone, the governor of the state of São Paulo, Abreu Sodré, in partnership with the newspaper, instituted the 'Worker Olympics'.[24]

Thus, the authoritarian regime took control of and reinterpreted 1 May to negate the historical significance that the day represented, erasing all traces of the struggle between capital and labour. Stripped of its original character and repressing all demands and protests, 1 May was essentially reduced to 'Football Day'. Year after year, football was deliberately used by the authorities to mobilise workers politically, attributing to the ball hypnotic properties. In 1972, Belo Horizonte was the solemn seat of such an official claim to Labour Day. In Mineirão Stadium, Rio de Janeiro's Flamengo and the local team Atlético Mineiro, competed for the Taça do Trabalho (Work Cup). However, such celebrations were not limited to Belo Horizonte alone. Throughout the country, free games were held in the spirit of 'fellowship' between government, capital and labour.[25]

1972 was a special year for the military dictatorship due to the 150th anniversary of the independence of Brazil. For this reason, on the occasion of the twenty-fifth annual 'Workers Olympics' SESI mobilised around 100,000 workers across 148 industries in the state of São Paulo.[26] Football was exhaustively used, as it was throughout the 1970s. In 1979 a wave of strikes was organised by the new metal workers' union led by Luis Inácio Lula da Silva—the future leader of the Partido dos Trabalhadores and an eventual president of Brazil. As a means to deflate a protest event that workers were due to hold in the Vila Euclides Stadium in São Bernardo do Campo, an outer suburb of São Paulo where the metal workers' union was strongest, the authorities chose the city's Pacaembu Stadium as the site for the official 1 May celebrations. 'Today is the party of the people', proclaimed the event's organisers. To prove this point, the gates were opened without an admission charge. Free snacks and soft drinks were distributed. Officiated by the chaplain of the military police, the event had the feel of an ecumenical cult, with a musical show in which several popular artists performed and, as the highlight, a match was held between two teams formed by players from the state of São Paulo.[27] The only thing expected of the public was to leave at the stadium's entrance the political consciousness that they might possess in relation to the events that were unfolding in Vila Euclides. Before analysing this new historical conjuncture, it would be useful to trace another line of action outlined by the military during the dictatorship's most repressive period.

On Wednesday, 3 June 1970 Brazil began its World Cup campaign with a match against Czechoslovakia in Jalisco Stadium in Guadalajara, Mexico. About fifteen minutes after the end of the game, the head of the Brazilian delegation, Brigadier Jêronimo Bastos, received a telephone call from the president, General Médici, telling him to congratulate the players on their 4–1 victory.[28] Médici followed every step of the national team's progress, maintaining constant contact with the team's leaders and lavishing the players with words of encouragement. Following Brazil's narrow 1–0 victory over England on Sunday, 7 June, Médici sent a telegram emphasising 'fans' embrace of their belief' towards the athletes.[29] However, the telegrams, messages and compliments were not meant for the delegation alone, but were also circulated in the Brazilian mass media, to promote the image of a president-supporter. This gave the impression that he was in tune with public sentiment, with announcements to the media explaining that it was the 'duty' of every Brazilian supporter to 'grit their teeth and stay glued to the radio'.[30] However, unforeseen actions altered the desired narrative of national unity.

On Thursday, 11 June, halfway through the World Cup tournament, news spread that guerrilla commanders of the Vanguarda Popular Revolucionária (VPR or Popular Revolutionary Vanguard) and the Ação Libertadora Nacional (ALN or National Liberation Action) had kidnapped the German ambassador to Brazil, Ehrefried von Holleben, in Rio de Janeiro. This kidnapping was one of a series of actions by urban revolutionaries beginning on 4 September 1969 with the kidnapping of the American ambassador, Charles Burke Ellbrick, ('the first operation of its kind in the world, in guerrilla history') jointly by the ALN and the Movimento Revolucionário 8 de Outubro (MR-8 or Revolutionary Movement October 8th).[31] On 12 March 1970, the Japanese consul-general, Nobuo Okuchi, was seized in São Paulo by the VPR and two other armed organisations. As the kidnapping of diplomats occurred in mounting numbers, the military responded to real or perceived opposition with the arbitrary imprisonment of political dissidents, systematic torture and murders of people, whether or not they were actually connected with urban guerrilla units.

The escalating confrontation with the armed left did not constitute the dictatorship's only source of concern. At the same time, a major drought spread across Brazil's already poor northeastern states and created a tragic scene ripe for social explosion. From February 1970, desperate groups of people seized food from shops and warehouses in several cities in the interior of the region.[32] A day before Brazil's first World Cup match, around 'two thousand starving [people]' in Quixadá, a city in the state of Ceará, 'broke down the central market doors and two warehouses, looking for food'.[33] From now on, the attention of the public was divided between Pelé's team in Mexico, the subversive actions of the armed left in Rio de Janeiro and the desperation of the victims of drought in the northeast. Official propaganda tried to unify these parallel dramas at all costs, but their image ran the risk of being shattered into a thousand pieces. The authorities tried to take control of the situation. On one hand, they reassured the wife of the German ambassador about the efforts that were being made to rescue her husband and, on the other hand, they sent the president to the scene of the drought to offer comforting words to its victims.[34] Descriptions by journalists of desperate scenes of starvation in the northeast did not tally with the military representation of the 'Great Brazil'. Instead, even the most patriotic use of the World Cup could no longer obscure the tragic reports. Just when the whole country was holding its breath to watch the semi-final against Uruguay, journalists were registering the existence of social groups that were alienated and indifferent to what was happening on a football field: 'Now, in today's match, there are people who don't know about Mexico, just as the northeasterner who asked the president who Pelé was. There are still many who would give the same answer that was given to the President: "King Pelé? He's a goalkeeper"'.[35]

There were signs of political and social revolt spreading across Brazil. While in Ceará trains carrying food needed to travel with armed police escorts to prevent seizures by gangs of hungry people, in Rio de Janeiro, under international pressure to rescue the German ambassador, the military surrendered to the kidnappers' demands. Apart from sending forty political prisoners to Algeria, the VPR-ALN command required the dissemination in the press of a manifesto addressed to the 'Brazilian people'. With no way out, after a tense meeting at Palácio das Laranjeiras, the presidential residence in Rio, with senior officers of the armed forces, Médici agreed to authorise the publication of the manifesto. The text denounced, among other things, the torture and murder of political prisoners, censorship and repression of popular organisations and the 'regime of slavery' endured by field workers in the northeast. The situation portrayed by the armed leftists aimed at exposing the true nature of dictatorship to public opinion. In a prophetic tone, the manifesto declared 'the rural guerrilla will be invincible in Brazil'.[36] However, the only invincible offering was that displayed by the *canarinho* footballers—in the World Cup final, the national squad beat Italy 4–1, apparently confirming Médici's belief in the greatness of the team… and of Brazil.[37] This presidential prophecy seemed to crown the communication strategy that was grounded in the symbolic power of football.

Amidst this collective trance, however, the full of meaning of football in this repressive period emerged. A prime example was the propaganda disseminated in the press during the sesquicentennial independence celebrations. It established the juxtaposition of various images that alluded to the supposed achievements of the dictatorship. Included were portraits of a craftsman working on the assembly line in Volkswagen, a child attending lessons in a public school and heavy vehicles paving highways in the Amazon forest. However, the photomontage was incongruous because alongside the images representing the 'economic miracle', monumental works, moral and civic education, it appropriated, with pictures, the recent World Cup, such as a photograph of the forward Tostão in action in Mexico.[38] From the standpoint of dictatorship, the football conquest and victory was not in the 'Great Brazil' mosaic as a product of somehow innate qualities of Brazilian players. It demonstrated a concrete success of the militarisation of the national team, reflected in the directives and ideological goals that guided the athletes' conduct and in the excellence of their physical preparations as developed by the technical committee, with the decisive participation of graduates from the Army School of Physical Education. The non-subliminal message transmitted by the official propaganda placed the World Cup as another great achievement of the military. The ruling class, in turn, sought to reproduce in the clubs the success gained internationally. Now, everyone wanted to access the formula of success.

What was this formula? It was a model grounded in discipline and in the hierarchical characteristics of the military ethos and was oriented to the production of athletic excess which led to the hypertrophy of the body and the detriment of the development of the soul.[39] This supported repressive practices dividing the world of sports between rulers and the ruled, describing the subordinate athletes as soldier-players. This militarised matrix housed the authoritarian utopia of Brazilian football.[40] However, this model faced the resistance of players to the exercise of power. It was present in the rebellion which erupted and manifested either as individual, or collective, in big or small teams, from one extreme to another in the country.

The rebellion

In the historical background of the *anos de chumbo* (the so-called 'years of lead'—the late 1960s and 1970s: the most repressive years of the military dictatorship), the rebellion of the young Botafogo player Afonso Celso Garcia Reis (or Afonsinho as he was usually called) acquired prominence and raised apprehensions in the ruling class. Incompatible with Mario Jorge Lobo Zagalo, Botafogo's coach, Afonsinho was loaned to Olaria, a small team of the suburbs of Rio de Janeiro, in the first half of 1970. Taking advantage of the break in the football season due to the World Cup tournament, Olaria went on a long tour to Asia, playing friendly matches in Hong Kong, South Korea and Indonesia. On returning to Brazil, however, Afonsinho left his team and went to Europe where he remained for about two months. Without his knowing, Afonsinho's prolonged absence aroused a wave of gossip and rumours in Rio de Janeiro concerning the whereabouts of this young football player and medical student. As Afonsinho would recall, it was said that, 'I had gone to China', or even 'I was stuck in Brazil because I was a subversive'.[41] However, following the World Cup in Mexico, the loan was cancelled. Afonsinho returned from Europe and was reintroduced to his club. When Botafogo's director of football, Xisto Toniato, saw him with a beard and long hair, he identified in the athlete's new look insidious signs that were seen as threatening in the world of football: 'This boy looks like Fidel Castro or even Che Guevara'.[42]

Based on the refusal of the player to obey the club's determination that he should shave and cut his hair, the club's management chose to apply the most feared punishment for a footballer: professional inactivity, preventing him from moving to another team by refusing to negotiate the discharge of his contract.

The case dramatically illustrates the arbitrariness of the *Lei do Passe* (Pass Law), how it could be used to restrict an athlete, leaving him cornered with apparently no other choice but to submit to the authoritarian rules of a club. However, instead of surrendering to the demands that were being made of him, Afonsinho openly questioned the rules with one simple enquiry: 'In what legal precept was Xisto Toniato using to forbid me to train with a beard?' Certain that the demands being made of him were purely arbitrary in nature, Afonsinho went to court to seek what he believed was his inalienable right to pursue his profession.[43] Who could resist this claim? Not even the military dictatorship felt able to, with the minister of education and culture, Colonel Jarbas Passarinho, publically stating that the legal mechanism of the *passe* 'enslaved and dehumanised' the football player.[44]

Thus, the struggle that many believed was lost in advance due to the forces historically in favour of the ruling class, allowed an unexpected outcome. It was no doubt decided that it would be best to avoid the risk of litigation and potentially setting a hostile precedent through losing the case. To prevent this, on Thursday, 4 March 1971, the Superior Tribunal de Justiça Desportiva (Superior Tribunal of Sports Justice) of the Confederação Brasileira de Futebol (Brazilian Football Confederation) decided unanimously to grant Afonsinho his *passe*, ignoring Álvaro Alonso, the lawyer representing Botafogo, who argued that the player was acting like a 'hippy', and that growing a beard was an act of disrespect towards the team.[45]

Once Afonsinho acquired the right to practice his profession, free from the legal dispute that had immobilised him for eight months, the player again chose to wear the jersey of the modest Olaria club, his masterful performances standing out in the Rio de Janeiro championships during the first half of 1971. Asked by sports journalists about the skills that he demonstrated on the field, Afonsinho offered an explanation that contained the deeper reasons for the conflict with Botafogo: 'The important thing is that we have freedom for everything: to move and to create. And, in football, especially for a player like me, the right to create is above everything'.[46] The critical mobility claimed by this rebel player contained three interrelated aspects: the development of creative intellectual activity; the elaboration of an artistic style of playing; and the democratisation of the team management. In these terms, the small team Olaria emerged as a refuge for Afonsinho to work on the cognitive, aesthetic and political elements of the practice of football, thus expressing his full potential. It was not by chance that the sports press considered him to be 'the best player in Rio' and it was considered 'almost certain' that he would be selected to represent Brazil in the *canarinho* team.[47] But his old nemesis, Zagalo, stated that he stood no chance: 'Afonsinho,' declared Brazil's coach, 'is not in my plans'.[48] But the question did not even arise: if the military regime believed that the national team represented the moral principles of national life, how could the presence of such a rebellious player who was stigmatised as 'damned', someone so clearly not the model of a soldier-footballer, be tolerated?[49]

Although excluded from the national team for reasons external to football, Afonsinho continued to play freely with Olaria—a small, somewhat impertinent club which faced the major teams as equals, vied for the Rio de Janeiro league, threatened the hegemony of Botafogo and eventually reached third place in the state's rankings. The success of this suburban team intrigued analysts and challenged them to find an explanation. The coach, Jair da Rosa Pinto, a former footballer who participated in the 1950 World Cup, provided the following reasons: 'good players, financial problems solved and no foreman who forces them to fulfil duties without rights'.[50] This is the paradox. Rather than acting as a stimulus for the freedom of movement of athletes both on and off the field and encouraging the view of football as an art form, winning a third World Cup for Brazil was interpreted by clubs' management in terms of an 'authoritarian utopia'. Consequently, clubs adopted regulations familiar in military barracks, with managers imposing financial punishments for acts classified as indiscipline, and sending warning letters to the athletes who did not follow tactical orders.[51] The measures also included the forced hospitalisation of injured players. The director of São Paulo Football Club, for example, decided that 'from now on the injured player will be a patient at the Morumbi clinic, forced to concentrate to speed his recovery'.[52] This was not an isolated initiative. In the rival Palmeiras team, the player Ademir da Guia expressed dissatisfaction with the information that 'he could be patient in a hospital for intensive treatment'.[53]

In Rio Grande do Sul, the situation was the same. There, the management of Grêmio—the club that President Médici supported—posted on the locker room door a draconian regulation prepared in order to 'supervise the overall activities of athletes'. The document contained the following points: a curfew on late entry at home; control of one's private life; rules on behaviour when in hotels and outside; control of players' levels of fatigue, alcohol intake and athletic condition; strict rules on the moral and social behaviour of each player; end of small subgroups within the squad; summary removal of prevaricators (those who do not comply determinations) in any circumstances.[54]

The authoritarian treatment by the club continued throughout the first half of the 1970s, incorporating new repressive practices. In these terms, invoking the urgent need to maintain team fitness during a break in the 1973 National Championship, Grêmio's director proposed that his players and members of their families should spend a period of relaxation on Tramandaí Beach—a resort 132 kilometres from Porto Alegre—with all the expenses covered by the club. Although it was claimed that the players 'spontaneously' agreed to the proposal, an 'image of coercion' remained.[55] The initiative certainly reflected a firm militarisation of the club—a process launched with the support of Grêmio's director of football, Renato Souza (who was also a chief of police)—by the field technician, Carlos Froner (an army captain), and by the coach, Mário Doernt (an army major).

Attempts, however, to circumvent the legislation relating to sport and suppress any political resistance from athletes was not successful. Grêmio's players 'rebelled' against the 'proposal' of a forced 'vacation'.[56] At the beginning of January only three players turned up for training. Gradually the other athletes joined the physical exercise routine on the beach, under the supervision of trainers.[57] In February, however, Grêmio did not qualify for the national competition. In the wake of this failure, the club's management fired the army and police officers who were supervising training, bringing to an end the period of 'almost military discipline'.[58] The political cost of the project had proved impossible. The conversion of players to soldiers did not materialise. And even worse, the symbolic construction of the worker-player, which is the other side of the character, would acquire a new meaning in the 1970s.

The Republic of Football

In mid-May 1978, Brazil's attention was focused on the World Cup tournament that was about to take place in Argentina. However, for the dictatorial regime, a disturbing event was unfolding that was gaining attention in the news. At 7.30am on Friday 12 May, 2,000 Scania-Vabis employees stood beside the machines, refusing to start them. The movement soon reached Ford, where about 9,000 metal workers also stopped work. With 8,000 Mercedes-Benz workers also downing tools, there was no way to ignore the historical dimensions of these strikes.[59] Exactly ten years after the last authentic working-class movements were witnessed in the São Paulo area, militant activities were recommencing. Now the stage was set to the immediate south of the city of São Paulo, in the ABCD Region, centred on the industrial municipalities of Santo André, São Bernardo, São Caetano and Diadema. Surprised by the outbreak of strikes in the motor vehicle industry, the authorities immediately phoned the radio and television stations, determined to ban news coverage of the stoppages.[60] But it was too late. About 40,000 employees linked their arms as the World Cup jamboree was about to commence in Argentina. On the eve of Brazil's debut, on Sunday 4 June, television stations devoted nine hours of programming to the tournament. But this was in vain. The strikes only spread, reaching factories in Osasco, mobilising workers in Santos, and challenging the repressive apparatus of the state which had started to arrest strikers.

There were problems both on and off the pitch. Indeed, everything seemed to conspire against the generals, including 'weak football' being played in Brazil's debut match, crystallising in a 1–1 draw with Sweden. This was only the beginning. In the match against Spain, there was another disappointing tie. The president's spokesman, Colonel Rubem Ludwig, went public in expressing the government's concerns with the campaign in Argentina, 'because football is sociologically a very important issue'.[61] Brasília was counting on the national team to 'improve the mood of the Nation' and stifle the symptoms of social discontent through a new sense of patriotism. 'Football', admitted *A Gazeta Esportiva*, was 'a powerful political instrument of social peace which the government operated with rigour and insight'.[62] However, the mechanism would only be effective if victorious. But the tournament did not go Brazil's way—nor had it in West Germany in 1974.

The strike wave that had started in the ABCD Region spread to various sectors of society, the struggle inspiring the whole working class. Amid the sports news that was still extensively dominated by the World Cup in Argentina, a small note in a small club indicated the historical nexus involving the factory and the field. After three months without being paid, players from the Comercial football club in Ribeirão Preto, a city in the interior of the state of São Paulo, took a stand: they went on strike.[63] The news showed the military's formula of handling players to have failed. Instead of football dissuading these workers from striking, it was the wider working class which persuade the athletes to mobilise. In effect, the years from the mid-1970s to the mid-1980s mark a historical period of increasing mobilisation of athletes to elevate the organisational capacity of unions, transforming them into combative, autonomous and representative organs. Between 1978 and 1980 alone, three gatherings of such athletes were held in Rio de Janeiro, Rio Grande do Sul and Piauí.[64]

Images that portrayed the professional athlete as a member of an atomised category, incapable of acceding to a critical consciousness, powerless to undertake an autonomous action had characterised the intrinsic condition of the football player. Such dominant representations were now starting to collapse.[65] This process began as the football rebels acquired a new political dimension to their actions. The dictatorship could no longer believe, with the same conviction, the idyllic picture of the alienated player that Brasília was circulating. Without doubt, the person most responsible for the unrest was José Reinaldo de Lima, a young striker with the Belo Horizonte team Atlético. On 6 March 1978, Reinaldo's political courage was clearly visible on the front page of *Movimento*, an alternative newspaper that was hostile to the military dictatorship.

At twenty-one years old, Reinaldo publically voiced the demands of the opposition to the regime, which included freedom of assembly, an amnesty for political prisoners and exiles and democratic presidential elections. Reinaldo defended collective action as the most appropriate way to allow players to have 'control of their own interests and destiny'. In an interview, Reinaldo stressed these demands and added a caustic comment about the World Cup in Argentina: 'We, players, are government canvassers. If we win the Cup, it will use our victory. I know this quite well'.[66] This phrase constituted the first public criticism by a footballer of the military regime, indicating the growing radicalisation of worker-players.

Against this background of increased radicalisation, gender-related issues in connection to the sport were coming to the fore. In the 1970s and 1980s, women's football was rapidly achieving prominence in Brazilian life, with the game being played on beaches, parks, wasteland and on whatever other space was available. By 1980, in the northeastern state of Pernambuco alone, there were over twenty thousand teams playing. In Recife, the state capital, women were particularly enthusiastic about the sport, and it was there that the first Women's Football Congress was held, with its main purpose being the establishment of a league and state championship.[67] Similar initiatives had taken place elsewhere in Brazil, sweeping aside the once covert position of women's football that struggled in the country's male-dominated sports environment. Women's football challenged the prohibition contained in decree-law 3.199 of 1941 and crossed the symbolic frontiers drawn by the patriarchy of football to impose itself and to create female and male roles within the sport. In this way the discussion about the many possibilities of being an athlete was enriched.[68] In effect, the Football Republic constituted the privileged scenario of a diverse game which attracted fans and created teams and organised leagues across Brazilian society. This process left the Conselho Nacional de Desportos (National Sports Council) with no other choice but to withdraw the prohibition which had proved incapable of stopping the dissemination of practices that seemed, in principle, against its own purposes and ideas.

Maria Feitosa of the Military Police's Sports Association stood out in the Women's Football League of São Paulo, a body that was founded in May 1982 with sixteen teams from the state capital and neighbouring municipalities. The twenty-one-year-old striker vehemently criticised the representation of her as a lesbian—a term riddled with prejudice directed at every woman who dared to enter the hitherto androcentric world of football.[69] Gradually, however, prejudices were at least partially overcome, as can be inferred from the resolution passed by the CND in early 1983 that officially recognised the practice of women's football.[70] In mid-1984, the magazine *Placar* had already recorded the existence of nearly 3,000 women's teams with a total of some 45,000 women players. Possibly the best of these teams at the time was Esporte Clube Radar, the champion of Rio de Janeiro's league and a two-time winner of the National Championship.[71] Created in 1981 on Copacabana, the team rapidly outgrew purely beach football. Soon, the majority of the team-members came from the poorest layers of society. Aged between fifteen and twenty-eight, the young women dedicated themselves to the sport, training three hours a day, Monday to Friday, on a rented pitch in Penha, a poor northern neighbourhood of Rio. It was not always an easy life, as the then eighteen-year-old Nancy recalled: 'One day, I was playing in secret. They [family members] saw me. I ran home and locked myself in the bathroom. In despair, I stumbled on some old bottles and

I cut my ass. I still have the scar, but that was the moment I decided to be a "*boleira*".[72] Discrimination, taunts and acts of physical violence were commonplace for women football players, victims of the male domination of society.[73] According to *Placar*, the young athlete Sally of the Rio de Janeiro Bangu team said when she kicked a ball about in the street 'she was beaten at home and believed that she faced a unique torment in the world'.[74]

Certainly, the Brazilian nation was represented by displays of the privileged male hegemonic world of football, stressing the supporting role of women both inside and outside of the sports arena.[75] Such images, however, involved a series of characteristics and values associated with the feminine universe. The veteran Baiano player Servílio de Jesus (1915–1984) was a case in point. He had arrived in São Paulo in 1937 to play with the Corinthians. Servílio's obituaries evoked his stylistic way of playing, which was distinguished by his ability to deceive his adversaries, appearing to go for the ball without actually touching it, putting 'his arms in a position which seemed to entrap an imaginary lady'.[76] Nicknamed 'the dancer', Servílio made the football field seem like a dance hall, crystallising a performance that was not recognised as a virile play.[77] But besides contemplate aspects related to the feminine universe, football as an art form included at its core practices of freedom.

Democracy at the Corinthians football club emerged in the context of the re-democratisation that Brazilian society was experiencing in the first half of the 1980s. At the time, the Corinthians president, Waldemar Pires, promoted the political liberalisation in the club, decentralising power, modernising the administration, and making management changes. This last initiative was reflected in the appointment to the football department of an outsider—Adílson Monteiro Alves, a young sociologist who was to bring the so-called rulers and ruled closer together. This project replaced the old hierarchical power structure that demanded obedience for a more democratic circle based on the ideal of isonomy,[78] that is, the equal participation of the athletes in decisions relating to the team.

Whether in reality players did have an impact on decision-making remains a contentious issue for historiography. Over time, two diametrically opposing interpretations emerged. On the one hand, democracy at Corinthians was portrayed as being essentially a mere slogan, though one that had induced chaos and mismanagement. On the other hand, the experience was idealised with no misconceptions or inconsistencies as the perfect example of citizenship within the sphere of sports. However, put in these terms, the debate did not allow for the dynamic and complex character of a movement which sought to reconcile in a contradictory way the economic values of a football business with the political principles of a self-governing team. This contradiction did not prevent, however, opening up and forging links with groups who shared similar ideals and whose main objective was to help bring about the downfall of the military dictatorship.[79]

Wladimir, a player of during the time of the 'Corinthians Democracy' and director of the Union of the Football Athletes of São Paulo, exchanged experiences and ideas with workers in São Bernardo and Diadema, participating in debates in the ABCD industrial areas which was the epicentre of the strike wave that was undermining the dictatorship. Casagrande, a young striker of the team and member of the Partido dos Trabalhadores, stood alongside the unemployed at demonstrations in Ibirapuera Park that were protesting in front of the state of São Paulo's legislative assembly against the severe economic crisis that society was then grappling with. Sócrates, in turn, joined the opposition to the military regime and was actively engaged with the Diretas Já (Direct Elections Now) campaign, the mass movement that emerged between November 1983 and April 1984 motivating millions of people to take to the streets demanding democracy. On the other side, the athletes of the Corinthians Democracy would meet after training sessions at Bar da Torre, in the Parque São Jorge. Wladimir, Casagrande and Sócrates appeared on stage with Rita Lee at her rock concert. In short, the Corinthians Democracy made inroads within São Paulo's bohemian set in search of an energy which kept football's counterculture alive.

By holding conversations within alternative spaces and rescuing the tradition of the autonomy of players, Corinthians's democratic project was effectively developing clear contours. The struggle against the hegemonic model deployed by clubs was characterised by a series of interrelated aspects: the authoritarianism in the social relations of work; the paternalistic management adopted by the ruling class; the athletic excess that favoured physical exercise to the detriment of thought; and the regime of control which led the player to ignore social, political and cultural life to satisfy the requirements of high performance. For players such as Sócrates, Wladimir and Casagrande, it was about undertaking the opposite path and urging the athletes to engage in crucial issues of their time, and they become citizens of the Republic of Football.

Conclusion

The contrast between the military's authoritarian utopia and the democracy movement's Republic of Football could not be greater. In the context of militarisation, the main objective of the holders of power constituted an expansion of sports practice, but at the same time controlling the meaning of game.[80] There were specific purposes for football depending on those involved, namely: to make soldiers popular through the Army Olympics; to pacify workers with the Worker Olympics; to civilise the Amerindians with the 'Games of Acculturation'; and as discussed throughout the chapter, to militarise professional athletes, both in the apparatus of clubs and in the national team.

In the context of democratisation, the new people joining the game offered multiple meanings, expanding the possibilities of who could be an athlete, establishing new bonds between factory and pitch and opening possibilities of sports contributing to a dynamic civil, autonomous and plural society.[81] The years 1978 to 1984 may not have been the most successful in terms of narrowly defined sporting achievement and methods, nor were these years the most favoured in terms of economics. Nevertheless, seen through the perspective of freedom, this is the most fascinating and inventive of periods, constituting revolutionary years for Brazilian football.

1. A match takes place at Witte Farm in São Paulo during the early part of the twentieth century. Source: Acervo Centro Pró-Memória Hans Nobiling (Esporte Clube Pinheiros).

2. Players in the traditional formation of the early teams of the twentieth century: the goalkeeper, two defenders, three midfielders and five strikers. Charles Miller, the man who introduced football to Brazil, is seated with the ball. Source: Collection of John Robert Mills/ SPAC.

3. Luiz Aranha, the president of the Brazilian Sports Confederation, with the Botafogo and Vasco da Gama players in the São Januário Stadium, Rio de Janeiro (circa 1930s). Source: Centro de Pesquisa e Documentação em História Contemporânea do Brasil/ CPDOC-FGV.

4. Players line up for a match between Rio de Janeiro (a combination of the best players of América FC and Fluminense FC) and the Italian side Pro Vercelli during the European club's tour of Brazil in 1914. Source: Acervo Fundação Biblioteca Nacional.

5. Players of Atlético, an amateur club from Rio Grande do Sul, pictured in 1960: The sashes worn by the players indicate victory in a tournament.
Source: Personal collection of Marta Cioccari.

6. The Atlético player Zoely with his wife.
Source: Personal collection of Marta Cioccari.

7. The São Paulo Chemical Workers Trade Union Football Club in the 1950s.
Source: Sindicato dos Trabalhadores Químicos e Plásticos de São Paulo.

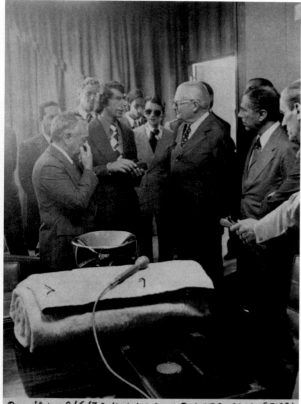

Brasília, 8/6/76-4. WILSON PIAZZA COM GEISEL E NEY BRAGA. Tele foto "Estado". Adão Nascimento.

8. The 1970 world champion Wilson Piazza (pictured with long hair) talks to the military dictator President Ernesto Geisel during the ceremony that approved the presidential decree officially recognising the footballing profession in Brazil, 25 May 1978. Source: Centro de Pesquisa e Documentação em História Contemporânea do Brasil/CPDOC-FGV.

9. The legendary player Garrincha in the América Fabril textile plant in Pau Grande, Magé, Rio de Janeiro in 1959. Garrincha was a textile worker in this plant before becoming a professional player. Source: Arquivo Público do Estado de SP—Fundo Última Hora.

10. Garrincha plays with one of his daughters in front of his house in Magé, Rio de Janeiro. Source: Arquivo Público do Estado de SP—Fundo Última Hora.

11. The Brazilian national team trains in the Maracanã in 1962.
Source: Arquivo Público do Estado de SP—Fundo Última Hora.

12. Didi, considered the best player of the 1958 World Cup at home with his wife in Sweden. Source: Arquivo Público do Estado de SP—Fundo Última Hora.

13. The Brazilian team celebrates Pelé's goal against Italy in the 1970 World Cup final in Mexico City. Source: Acervo Arquivo Nacional.

14. The professional contract of Leônidas da Silva, signed with São Paulo F.C. in 1944. Source: Acervo do São Paulo Futebol Clube.

15. The Maracanã in the 1950s. Source: Arquivo Público do Estado de SP—Fundo Última Hora.

16. Fans in the *geral* section of the Maracanã in March 1954 during a match between Brazil and Paraguay. Source: Arquivo Público do Estado de SP—Fundo Última Hora.

ARQUIVO PÚBLICO DO ESTADO DE SÃO PAULO - MEMÓRIA PÚBLICA

17. Police activity during the 2013 Confederations Cup in Rio de Janeiro. Source: Personal collection of Christopher Gaffney.

18. Popular demonstrations and police repression marked the 2013 Confederations Cup in Brazil. Source: Personal collection of Christopher Gaffney.

8

Public Power, the Nation and Stadium Policy in Brazil

The Construction and Reconstruction of the Maracanã Stadium for the World Cups of 1950 and 2014[1]

Bernardo Buarque de Hollanda

Introduction

This chapter discusses the construction of the Municipal Stadium of Rio de Janeiro, inaugurated in 1950, and puts forward a comparison with its contemporary situation on the eve of another international event. The comparison seeks to surpass the rigid dichotomy between past and present by confronting the meaning of its mid-twentieth-century construction in light of the stadium's partial reconstruction for the 2014 World Cup.

The stadium's remodelling—underway since 2000 when minor charges started to be made, but intensified and radically overhauled after the announcement in 2007 that Brazil would host the 2014 FIFA World Cup—has involved a series of structural changes. Taking into account the interval of over six decades, the historical underpinnings of two huge international sporting events that have the Maracanã Stadium at their epicentre will be analysed: the fourth and twentieth World Cup tournaments, held in 1950 and 2014 respectively.

The representation and discourse utilised in the late 1940s involved a plethora of social agents, such as the nation state, sporting entities, the media (radio and the press) and civil society more broadly. Nowadays, one must add to this list multinational sponsors, broadcasting networks (with a tremendous emphasis on television) and private transnational agencies which coordinate the complex organisation of major events.

Despite the changes in scale and magnitude, the image of the stadium as an icon of a modern nation was wielded as significant in the past just as it is now. The precaution concerning the anachronism demands clarification based on the criteria that each historical period employed to define nationality and the concept of modernity. The objective here is to present contrasting elements which may shed light on the public debate about the stadium and Brazilian society in both 1950 and 2014. This is possible because the spatial aspects of the stadium and the behaviour of the spectator in sporting arenas are vehicles for broader discussions throughout the country.

Thus, despite current capitalist transformations which have heralded a 'new football economy'[2] and the effects of the restriction of the public sphere in the so-called 'global age'—where the withering away of the nation state is in progress and in which the fan progressively becomes a citizen/consumer—[3] this sport continues to raise fundamental questions on the issue of the nation and its specificity in Brazil.

Recalling the controversies which surrounded the construction and remodelling of the stadium enables the drawing out of similarities and differences in the paradigms of modernisation the country has experienced, not only in the mid-twentieth century but also in the early twenty-first century. In the state's agenda for the 2014 event, one cannot but notice the introduction of two new features which undermine the existing criteria for inclusion/exclusion for the audience in the football arena.

The first is related to the arrival of television broadcasting of the games, entirely absent in 1950 (when people only had scarce newsreel reports) but which has since had a major impact on the fact that 'the crowd' as a category has become expendable inside the stadiums. The second new feature, closely connected to the first, regards the stadium having to meet the general guidelines and rigorous demands made by FIFA, as stipulated in FIFA's 'procedure rulebook' and in the provisions of Brazil's Ministry of Sports, ever since the coming into effect of the Estatuto do Torcedor in May 2003.

These two elements are by-products of the broader phenomena of gentrification, in this case the contemporary tendency to price non-elite citizens out of public sporting arenas. This is a direct result of a broader change in football's revenue sources, concurrent with the new international economic order. One can reach the conclusion that profits do not depend on the number of spectators who are actually physically present in a stadium, but rather on the consumption capacities of individual supporters and the versatility of sports merchandising before, during and after football spectacles.

That said, the basic set of norms and priorities of the 1950 World Cup repeat themselves in 2014. Measures ranging from road infrastructure and traffic management in the area surrounding the arena, to expectations regarding the behaviour of spectators inside the building, to the architectural elements of the stadium, can all serve as an index for determining the degree of development of the nation state.

With regards to the stadium building, although the demolition that was desired by some officials of the Confederação Brasileira de Futebol (CBF, Brazil's football governing body) never took place, there were a series of interventions including the introduction of high-tech equipment. Apart from the new audio and visual infrastructure, there has been an atomisation and segmentation of spectators, which suppresses their mass character from the era when—between the 1930s and 1960s—football mass culture was developing. Therefore, the result of the refurbishment will be a stadium that has retained only the shell-shaped outer structure of the original building.

Construction hallmarks

In 1947, the debate over the construction of a football stadium in Rio de Janeiro, then the capital city of Brazil, took place. At that time, football had already transcended its amateur boundaries. Brazil's first public stadium was built in São Paulo in the 1940s: the Pacaembu Municipal

Stadium[4]—now the Paulo Machado de Carvalho Stadium. With this landmark event, it was also decided to build a large-capacity public stadium in the nation's capital. That arena would be the Municipal Stadium of Rio de Janeiro (renamed the Journalist Mário Filho Stadium in 1966) or the Maracanã, the name of a nearby river, as it is usually called.

Until the creation of the Maracanã, Rio de Janeiro's largest stadiums were the medium-sized ones that were linked to the city's football teams. Considered grandiose achievements in their day, some of these stadiums were developed for the hosting of major international football competitions. This, for example, was the case of Laranjeiras Stadium, which belonged to Fluminense Football Club and was established in the early years of Brazilian football when the game was an amateur preserve of the upper classes. Located in a wealthy area of southern Rio on land owned by the Guinle family,[5] it was inaugurated in 1919 for the third South American Championship between the national teams of Argentina, Brazil, Chile and Uruguay, and could hold up to twenty thousand spectators.

Another noteworthy example was São Januário Stadium of the Club de Regatas Vasco da Gama. A milestone in the popularisation of football, the stadium was constructed in 1927 in the old royal borough of São Cristóvão, a district of northern Rio de Janeiro. With a capacity of forty thousand spectators, São Januário was the largest sporting arena in Latin America until the construction of Montevideo's Estádio Centenário which was built for the World Cup tournament hosted by Uruguay in 1930.

The need to accommodate the demand for larger sports arenas became more urgent in 1947 when FIFA announced that in 1950 Brazil would host the fourth World Cup. The choice came after a long interval without tournaments due to World War II. Both the federal and local authorities soon realised the urgency of building a stage that would meet the high standards that were expected.

The intention was to overcome the symbolic limitations inherent in a stadium that was not only associated with a particular football club, but also linked to a dictatorial regime as, under President Getúlio Vargas, São Januário had been used to stage political rallies and civic parades with overwhelmingly ideological content. The journalist Mário Filho, a great enthusiast of the 1950 tournament and a member of the organising committee, was handed the task of chaperoning FIFA's long-time president, Jules Rimet.[6]

PUBLIC POWER, NATION, STADIUM POLICY

Once the decision was made to build a new stadium in Rio, a great debate arose as to where it should be located. The controversy generated intense disagreement between the city's legislative representatives, with entirely different proposals being raised by two of the most well-known city council members representing the right-wing União Democrática Nacional (UDN)[7] in Rio's Municipal Assembly. On one side was Carlos Lacerda, an adversary of Mayor Ângelo Mendes de Morais, who supported construction on the very edge of the city, in the far-off western district of Jacarepaguá.[8] His key opponent was Ary Barroso, a celebrated sports radio broadcaster, who was in favour of a location somewhere in the city centre.

In a memoir written in the late 1970s, shortly before his death, Lacerda recounted the position he took thirty years earlier, at a time when he was just a novice in political life:

About Maracanã, which was built against my better judgement, there are good stories to tell. When I was a council member, they were intent on building the stadium in Maracanã and I suggested they do it by the Jacarepaguá Lagoon, at Barra da Tijuca. Firstly, because it was obvious that the city would grow in that direction; secondly, because ever since Napoleão Alencastro had been director of Central, there had been a project to build a 12-kilometer electrified railway, connecting Madureira and Leblon. You'd connect the city through its rear and, with the football world championship, it'd be very easy to convince the Federal Government to go ahead and build that railway.[9]

After heated exchanges, the city government went with the second option, which had also won over the council, and decided that the stadium would be constructed in a location considered uniformly distant to the different sections of the city—a point of spatial, economic and social convergence. It was located on a piece of land owned by the city which was then being used by the army. In the times of the Brazilian monarchy, the spot was famous due to the fact that it held the horse track of the Derby Club which attracted eminent political figures, the royal family and other members of the social elite.[10] The political reasoning behind the decision was based on the idea that the chosen location in northern Rio was strategic for the capital's image, due to its role as an intersecting point between southern Rio and the more distant suburbs.

From the south, one could arrive at the stadium by bus or car, while one could get there from more outlying parts of the city by the railway lines of Central do Brasil. This meant that the stadium would symbolically link the two extremes of the nation's capital, from the most affluent areas to some of the most impoverished, becoming what anthropologist José Sergio Leite Lopes called the 'heart of Brazil'.[11]

A public competition selected a group of architects and engineers with experience in the construction of sports arenas. The winning team was the same one that had, ten years earlier, been responsible for the expansion of Botafogo's General Severiano stadium,[12] when fragile wooden rafters were replaced with reinforced concrete—what would become a typical post-war structural material. A group of six architects—Rafael Galvão, Orlando da Silva, Pedro Bernardo Bastos, Antônio Dias Carneiro, Miguel Feldman and Waldir Ramos—prevailed over the five other competing plans that had made it to the final round of the competition. Amongst them was Oscar Niemayer who had some experience with the design of sports facilities, having designed Flamengo's nautical base by Lagoa Rodrigo de Freitas.[13]

While not yet having achieved the stature of being Brazil's leading architect—a mantra that would come with his involvement with the construction of Brasília—Niemayer had been part of Lúcio Costa's team which had built the strikingly modernist Ministry of Education and Health building between 1937 and 1943. He had already agreed to the request of the mayor of Belo Horizonte, Juscelino Kubitschek, to design the Pampulha Lake, in 1942. After a request from Minister Gustavo Capanema, Niemeyer drew a sketch of the National Olympic Stadium in 1941, in partnership with Emílio Baumgart. The project, however, would never take off. In the bid to build the Maracanã in 1947, he would take second place.

In his original plans, the ingenious structure planne[d] the Olympic stadium—with a capacity of 130,000— and an immense arch in the northern sector of the r[a] steel cables and inspired by Le Corbusier's 1931 pro[ject] the Soviets in Moscow. In addition to the athlet[ic] stadium, the area around the building was to hav[e] numerous sports courts, housing for athletes and school. The anthropologist and architect Lauro Cava[lcanti] reflect on the defeat of Niemayer's project:

What a pity it is that the jury's decision went in the direction of a different project, less beautiful and very unclear as to its insertion into the urban landscape and its coherence as a whole; Rio lost, therefore, a set of shapes and forms that would certainly join the select group of natural and man-made monuments that are the city's landmarks.[14]

The stadium was incorporated into a grandiose discourse, compared to the colossal effort of building the modern nation which had created it in a monumental and typically Brazilian form. Inaugurated on 16 June 1950, the stadium was built by 10,000 workers in one year and ten months between 1948 and 1950. The site's perimeter encompassed almost 190,000m² and made use of a massive 500,000 bags of cement. The project, carried out by six contractors, used some 10,000 tons of iron beams, 650,000m² of wood and 80,000m³ of concrete. According to contemporary newspaper reports, if stacked, the bags would reach twice the height of Rio's Sugar Loaf Mountain.[15]

In the political heart of Brazil, the Maracanã's task would be to serve as the most effective testament to the nation's claim of being a great power—and thus its grandiose title as 'the world's greatest stadium'. It was built for 150,000 spectators, but able to handle up to 200,000 people—equal to about 10 per cent of what was then the entire population of Rio. In order to reach these numbers, the architects had to scrap their original plan for an Olympic stadium and removed the athletics track from the blueprint. This would allow for standing spaces for hundreds more people, situated around and nearby the pitch, areas that would come to be known as the *geral*.

The term *geral* had been in use ever since the early years of football in Rio. The Estádio das Laranjeiras housed a section of its audience in similar areas: those who had seats and those congregating together in standing positions. Around the wooden fence that determined the boundaries of the pitch was a section also called *geral*. While this feature was not altogether original, the circular arrangement of the Brazilian stadium allowed for a freedom of movement unknown to the rectangular and segmented sporting arenas of Britain which had 'terraces' for standing spectators. The social homogeneity of British football terraces—also known as 'ends' or 'kops'—would eventually lead to the rise of hooliganism. In the Maracanã's case, however, the *geral* lacked organised groups of supporters due to the diversity of the social profile of those present in it.[16]

The international stature of the World Cup required great efforts regarding the hosting of foreign visitors. Football fulfilled a diplomatic role. Through it the state, in the midst of a re-democratisation process, would exhibit its national virtues to the world, and would thus promote educational campaigns to encourage good manners amongst the general public. The economic limitations of a young South American nation with regards to European countries that were still shaken by the trauma of totalitarianism—'the land of the future', according to a catchphrase widely credited to the Austrian writer Stefan Zweig, who had been a political refugee in Brazil—[17] were offset by the civility and good behaviour of Brazilian supporters. They were projected as reflecting the 'people' as a whole and told not to cause disturbances or throw objects into the pitch.

The election by *Jornal dos Sports* (Rio's main sports publication, headed by Mário Filho) of a representative of the supporters of Brazil's national team was also undertaken for similar reasons. This tradition had started with the 1938 World Cup in France, when both a male and a female ambassador were chosen from amongst supporters. The nomination of Jaime de Carvalho, the leader of Flamengo's supporters, as the official leader of Brazil's supporters was meant to create a figure of authority in the stands. He was in charge of leading events parallel to the football matches, with a festive and, at the same time, orderly character that the international tournament demanded.

Hallmarks of the name

Once built, the Maracanã soon transcended its purely sports-related functions and took on a public role. This process began with the roots of the terminology used for its various internal sections. An immediate connection can be drawn between the Municipal Stadium of Rio de Janeiro (Maracanã) and the names used for different sections of the audience of 'spectacle art forms', seen, according to tradition, to be solemn and tied exclusively to scholarly culture. In the capital city, the most evident prior example was the Theatro Municipal, inaugurated in 1909, in part as a by-product of the Pereira Passos Reforms (1902–6).[18] The new theatre was located in the square formed by what is currently Cinelândia, at the end of Avenida Central which led to Avenida Beira-Mar, another civilisational frontier of the nascent and expanding city. The theatre was surrounded by other grand public institutions such as the Biblioteca Nacional, the Câmara Municipal (the municipal assembly) and the Museu Nacional de Belas Artes.

According to most reports, the name 'Estádio Municipal do Rio de Janeiro' was inspired by that of the city's Theatro Municipal.[19] The same cannot be said of the names given to its internal sections, which have decidedly less distinguished origins. According to the historian Lilia Moritz Schwarcz, and based on the ideas of Peter Burke on the social history of language,[20] one can raise the hypothesis that the language of football and the names of the sections of the Maracanã's audience were inspired by popular sources of entertainment. At the turn of the nineteenth and twentieth centuries, one could include amongst these the cinematographic machine, a form of gambling called *jogo do bicho* and the circus. Circus audiences were the basis of the terminology used for the sections of sports audiences, since they were also split between *geral*, *arquibancada* (stands), *camarote* (boxes) and *cadeiras* (seats).[21]

Besides the name itself, architecture also brings the dimension of form, which points to revealing traces of the stadium's material insertion in the city and of the symbolic place it holds for the wider country. It is not as much a trait pertaining to the forms themselves as it is a presence—visible only from the air—of the stadium within the urban geography and topography. Circular, rectangular, polyhedral—how does one imagine the stadium? Where should it be placed in the city: in its centre or in the periphery? These are unexplored questions of a technical, iconic and political nature to which we can only allude to the authoritative words of philosopher Gaston Bachelard: 'matter is the content of form'.[22]

In Brazil's case, the role of the state in democratisation and in overcoming its condition as a peripheral nation has become central. Perhaps that is the reason why, historically, public power has been involved with stadium-building, a phenomenon seen less often in Europe or elsewhere in South America. Decades after the construction of the Maracanã, in the years of military dictatorship, several Brazilian stadiums adopted an elliptical shape extending this architectural model to many states in the federation, while 'national integration' was further promoted through a national football club championship from 1971. The only existing tournament of this nature up until that point had been the Taça de Prata, which did not include all regions of Brazil, especially in northern, northeastern and mid-western areas.

In 1970, by account of investments made by the military regime, of the fourteen largest stadiums in the world, six were in Brazil. The process started in 1965, when Magalhães Pinto Stadium, known as Mineirão, was inaugurated in Belo Horizonte, the capital of Minas Gerais. The Maracanã was the architectural inspiration for this and most of the other stadiums of mammoth proportions of the time. Therefore, the policy of the CBD, with the backing of high-ranking military officials, resulted in the construction of thirty sports arenas in just three years, from 1972 to 1975.[23]

The designation of names to the new sports complexes was another grand gesture of this period. Generally speaking, the names were given through the connection of two elements: the official name (usually a local politician) and a monumental sounding moniker suggested and/or appropriated by the football supporters and other stadium-goers. Thus, in Manaus, Vivaldo Lima Stadium (named after a federal deputy from Amazonas) became known as 'Vivaldão'—'Big Vivaldo'; in Aracaju, Lourival Batista Stadium (named for the then governor of the state of Sergipe) adopted 'Batistão'—'Big Batista'; in Fortaleza, Plácido Castelo Stadium (after a governor of the state of Ceará), through the same process would soon go by the name of 'Castelão'—'Big Castelo'.

The founding myth: anatomy of a 'democratic' stadium

Despite a discourse that emphasises the democratic character of the Maracanã as a space of widespread communion and unity, the ascending structure of the stadium mirrors a socioeconomic gradient. The spatial division in different levels is equivalent to social stratification. Whether seated or standing up, bunched together or spread apart, in a group or on one's own, the issue was always to allocate positions to the representatives of different economic and social strata and echelons, from the highest to the very lowest.

Without the Olympic structure planned initially, the stadium was conceived as two main levels divided into six hierarchical subsections. They are ranked in accordance to levels of comfort and the angle of view that the circular shape affords: *geral*, standard seating, stands, special seating and state—or honour—boxes for dignitaries and their guests.

Structural anthropologists have also shed light on the stadium's anatomy. With their capacity for distancing themselves from reality, even of complex societies to which they themselves belong, urban anthropologists were the first to analyse the social-spatial structure of the stadiums. Their descriptions have qualified the equality and underscored the inequalities concerning the categorisation of the audience. To quote one such author:

This segmentation in the audience follows mainly economic criteria: the sectors are organized in accordance to a price scale, the most expensive being the individual places: the seats. Other than criteria of an economic nature, professional (as in the case of subsections reserved for the press) and political conditions are determinant: honor boxes are places meant only for public authorities and their guests. With the best positioning and the most comfortable facilities, they are off limits for the rest of stadium goers and are not made available for seat purchase.

The worst places (with regards to comfort and field of view) are the cheapest and least well defined. The rafters and *Gerais* are occupied by masses; seats and boxes, on the other hand, are occupied by individuals. Another important element, taking Maracanã as an example: not only are the sectors located in distinct levels of the stadium (with the exception of the honor boxes, the press area and special seating which are, however, surrounded by steel bars), they have different colours. At the time this essay is being written, numbered and unnumbered seats were blue, special seating was yellow and the honor box was red. The possibility of there being an equivalence between the segmentation of the audience of football stadiums and the actual segmentation of the social sphere in Brazilian society would not be altogether improbable. On the contrary: it seems to actually be present in the sociological imagination of the supporter, when he associates the *Geral* with those who are 'penniless' and the honor boxes and special seating—whose tickets are subject to arbitrary distribution—with those who are 'protected', to quote two extreme examples.[24]

This perspective notwithstanding, official discourse as well as general opinion have raised the Maracanã to the status of a traditional place for social inclusion, due to its capacity to level out differences. It encompasses the most diverse segments of the population of Rio: in ethnic, social, cultural and geographical terms. In it are seen rich and poor, white and black, and residents of southern and northern Rio, all rubbing shoulders together. While subject to certain qualifications, the stadium could indeed be considered a mirror image of national integration, a microcosm of society, a synthesis of the then famed Brazilian 'racial democracy'; alternatively it could be seen as the ideal expression of rituals which suspend everyday life, in a similar way in which, in the 1970s, the anthropologist Roberto DaMatta interpreted carnival and popular culture.

In the case of the Maracanã, another significant element was the fact that its founding myth—the 1950 World Cup—was associated with the narrative of a defeat lived through as a collective demise. It was represented by Brazil's defeat by Uruguay on 16 July 1950, seemingly in disregard of the enormous construction and organisation efforts in which the host had displayed to the world. As highlighted in an essay written by another anthropologist, Arno Vogel, the 1950 World Cup can only be properly understood in light of the experience of the title match with Uruguay. The defeat was also responsible for introducing a 'Castilian-based' word, the *Maracanazo*, tragically experienced by the people—as in a burial rite—to be expiated only twenty years later when Brazil defeated the Uruguayans during the Mexico World Cup of 1970.[25]

'The Maracanã is all ours': the supporters' stadium

The Maracanã's spatial configurations had to coexist with a social dynamic, capable of giving new meaning to its structure. Owing to this, an unexpected consequence to its architects was the territorial takeover performed by organised groups of supporters, in tune with the logic of team rivalry.

If it is true that organised groups of supporters were already in existence since 1940, their reach was limited. The groups had a kind of community oriented dimension, without significant impact in terms of public performance. Until the construction of the Maracanã, bandanas were the main means of supporter identification and only in later decades were flags introduced and made progressively larger by fans. In the rafters, only one organised group of supporters was allowed so as to minimise conflict and threats to order.

Maintaining order in the stadiums, which were growing ever more enormous, was a constant worry for the authorities. Consequently, each club was to have an organised group of supporters who were to represent all their fans. Each organised group of supporters, in turn, was represented by a *chefe* (boss). The word *chefe* had the same ring of authority as in other areas of social life, such as the *chefe de polícia* (police boss), *chefe de família* (family boss), *chefe de repartição* (section boss) and *chefe da nação* (nation boss). In the 1940s, when organised and uniform-bearing groups of supporters came into play, the words 'organisation' and 'uniformity' were part of the educational project of 'moral adjustment' of the masses in stadiums.[26] Against the national and international context of totalitarian practices, a clear aim was to establish and maintain order in the stadiums. In São Paulo, according to media columnist Alberto Helena Júnior,[27] the model which has been adopted as an incentive by organised groups of supporters has curious origins. He argued that they were inspired by supporters of college sports in the United States and their colourful shirts and accessories. Apparently law students who were members of elite clubs in São Paulo travelled to the United States and brought home this new style of celebrating matches involving local teams such as São Paulo and Palmeiras. The pictorial record of these supporters can still be seen today thanks to the photographs of Hungarian Thomas Farkas, which document the supporters in action at Pacaembu Stadium in the 1940s.[28]

In Rio, the model was not an imported one, but instead was adapted from a cultural practice instituted in the 1930s: the samba-schools parade. Music of African origin had long been suppressed as part of the civilising project to eradicate so-called 'barbaric' influences on Portuguese popular traditions, but at this time it would come to be incorporated into national identity. In 1932, Mário Filho, the sports journalist after whom the Maracanã stadium was officially named in 1966 following his death, was responsible for the contest between samba-schools based on competitive criteria for awarding points: organisation, pace, harmony, costumes and rhythm.

Only a few years later from that samba-school institution, when football was also becoming professional, the same journalist took this competition format to the stadiums. The rafters also began having their own 'game', based on the same criteria used for samba-schools: liveliness, quality of the music, degree of organisation. The supporters in the exclusive boxes started wearing shirts with their team's colours instead of suits and ties or other such formal attire. There was mention of the rafters becoming carnival-like, with the introduction of the Concurso de Torcidas (Contest of Organised Supporter Groups), which were graded by sports journalists.

This festive model initiated in the 1940s would last until the end of the 1960s, when the principal of unity of supporter groups—one club, one supporters' association, one *chefe*—was challenged. Questions appear within the national context of the military dictatorship and in the international context of student rebellion. In the Maracanã, at the end of the 1960s, the *torcidas jovens* (young supporter associations) arose, made up of new generations of fans creating dissident groups inside established groups. In a new territorial claim, the young supporters placed themselves behind the goalposts and would jeer at the players, challenging the authority of the *chefe* of the traditional supporters and protesting freely against team management.

In the 1980s these very same young supporter associations would grow and become even more assertive, sometimes inciting in brawls inside the stadium. The number of these supporters grew, at times even skyrocketed. At first with just tens or hundreds of associates, soon there were thousands. Seduced by a wave of violence, the organised supporter groups were made up of various social segments. Most were poor young people from the periphery of the city and from the favelas. The new features introduced by these youthful supporters in the 1980s—a 'lost decade' of economic, social and political malaise—was the funk music that they heard on the radio and danced to in the hills of Rio, which was now present in the football stands. The image of organised groups of supporters became increasingly associated with urban violence, juvenile delinquency and drug use, conditions that were also on the rise more generally in the country's major cities.

The 1990s saw an ever more intense struggle between organised groups of supporters and the media and public authorities. In the Maracanã, at the initiative of the state government, the Grupo Especial de Policiamento em Estádio (Special Unit of Stadium Policing) or GEPE was created to contain the 'escalating violence' and to try and build community oriented links between police forces and supporters' groups. This initiative did not significantly alter the pattern of brawls, criminality and growing animosity around the stadium, which resulted from the increase in internal surveillance.[29]

In 1992, due to the precarious nature of the facilities at the Maracanã, a tragic incident occurred at the final of the Brazilian Championship, in a match between Flamengo and Botafogo. Before the start of the game and due to the overcrowding (there were over 150,000 fans inside the stadium) the railings from part of the rafters gave way as a result of fighting that broke out amongst the largest group of Flamengo supporters, the Raça Rubro-Negra (Red and Black Race). In the scuffle that made the railings collapse, dozens of fans plummeted down to the tier below. They landed on top of other fans, resulting in several deaths and hundreds of injuries. The game nevertheless carried on with a human curtain isolating the site of the accident from other spectators.

'Welcome to the new Maracanã': FIFA's stadium

Like earlier tragic events in European stadiums—in particular in 1985 at Heysel in Brussels and in 1989 at Hillsborough in Sheffield—the fatal incident at the Maracanã led to profound changes in the mind-set of public officials and sports entities. They reached the conclusion that there was a need to change the atmosphere and clean-up and moralise the stadiums through complete architectural restructuring. A new influx of renovated stadiums followed suit in the 1990s, with European stadiums set as the benchmark. The first time these design principles came into effect was in southern Brazil, with the construction of the Arena da Baixada—Atlético Paranaense's stadium in Curitiba.

As for Rio de Janeiro itself, changes took a long time to commence and came very slowly. In an effort to appease public opinion, one of the first measures the state government took was to close the rooms in the Maracanã belonging to the organised supporters' groups which they had used to store their flags and other kinds of sports materials. In 1994, two years after the tragedy, the twenty-three rooms that had been granted to supporters' groups were confiscated by the state. Officially intended for storage of those materials used by the supporters' groups, the rooms had in more recent times been misused with cases of brawls, break-ins and storage of guns and even hazardous substances in some of them.

Soon after, as a result of international recommendations, the *geral* sector of the stadium was closed. The more characteristically blue-collar section of the stadium, its elimination was also a consequence, among other reasons, of a criminal phenomenon called '*arrastão*'. This consisted of a mob which would run through a mass of supporters to steal their belongings while, through the creation of an opening in the crowd, preventing the police from intervening. The popularity of the *geral* resulted in it being reopened by the state secretary for sports and leisure,[30] in flagrant opposition to the desire of the managers of sport entities like the CBF.

In 2000, the Maracanã celebrated its fiftieth anniversary. With this special occasion in mind, FIFA decided to organise a World Championship of Football Clubs in Rio de Janeiro. A consequence of this decision was the almost immediate refurbishment of the stadium. The work was carried out hastily, it was only half-finished and would never be fully completed, with plans changing as often as local and federal political agendas did. The one major measure taken in this period was the decision to place numbered seats in the rafters and in the *geral* so supporters would no longer stand during games. In the rafters, besides the introduction of seats to cover the original cement structure, the sector was also divided into five subsections, each with different prices.

If in these circumstances it was impossible to eliminate organised supporter groups, authorities nevertheless reached the conclusion that they should at least curtail them. The splitting of the rafters into colour-coded compartments (white, green and yellow according to their position with respect to the pitch) was an effective way to limit the freedom of movement of those who were intent on engaging in fights at the stadium. In effect, the decision ended up having a perverse effect: while progressively under control inside the stadium, brawling migrated to its surrounding areas. With an expanded field of action, the territory where the fights took place became much more chaotic and out of control than before for the police.

The placement of seats in the Maracanã's inner ring changed the landscape of the rafters, but one must take into account the bargaining power of the organised groups, which gave them some leeway in the decisions that were made. They were able, for example, to negotiate with the stadium's administrators the introduction of seats without backrests in the green sector, reserved for the organised groups of supporters, which allowed for the congregation of the groups and the favoured visual aspect of 'rooting side by side'. Anyhow, if organised groups, in particular the *torcidas jovens*, were not entirely banned from stadiums as the authorities desired, the refurbishment of the stadium was still a subtle and effective strategy in the effort to isolate and stifle them.

Over the last few years, due to a reduction in capacity to one-third of its original configuration, and also as a result of a deliberate policy, the price of tickets to the Maracanã has increased fourfold. In this respect, a reaction from the organised supporters has been lacking, which was not the case in the late 1970s and 1980s when protests took place against price hikes at a time of runaway inflation. Even with the stadium's significant reconfiguration, with giant screens and boxes set aside for corporate sponsors, it may be a surprise that a new form of supporters' organisation has emerged entirely adapted to the new institutional framework. In the last four years, new groups of organised supporters have appeared in Rio de Janeiro and have, contrary to expectations, been rivalling the *torcidas jovens* in scale and visual terms, so far considered peerless and in control.

There are still very few studies on the social content of these groups. Based on first sight, these supporters appear to fit a white-collar profile, rooted in the middle class. They have brought innovations in terms of their principles—they are unconditional in their support; their behaviour—they speak out against violence; and their image—they do not promote their own symbols, only those of their club. Tuned in to the rhythms and musical styles of groups of supporters in Europe and Argentina—due to a more intensive use of the internet—the new groups have imported chants and visual routines. A notable example was displayed in the 2009 Brazilian Championship when a mosaic was produced by Fluminense's supporters, in the tradition of the Italian 'ultras', which demanded a much greater degree of coordination and preparation compared to the usual standards of improvisation in Brazilian supporters' groups.

The media quickly identified these new groups as the target for bonding with organised supporters, which had seemed out of the question with the *torcidas jovens*. For example, the songs brought by these new groups of supporters were broadcast by television during the airing of matches, as the lyrics did not make allusion to bad words and offenses to rivals. But to the degree that these new associations—which are much more submissive to the status quo—will stay faithful to their original principles remains to be seen; to what degree they will be able to become the new standard for organised supporters is another open question.

For the Maracanã after 2014, it seems more plausible that the organised groups of supporters, old and new, will gain new relevance as they adapt to the role that is expected of them in the next few years. Until then, signs of resistance have not been evident, nor has a traditionalist discourse opposed itself to 'modern football', as is seen more clearly—though not without ambiguity—in the case of the European 'ultras'.[31]

2014: farewell, Maracanã?

Throughout the last six decades, the Maracanã has had to face certain problems related to the workings of club-led football, owing to the fact that this form—with the rise of Rio de Janeiro state championship derbies—has come to assume a greater importance than the international version of the game. By the late sixties, the stadium was experiencing high turnouts with the so-called 'Fla-Flu' matches (those played between rivals Flamengo and Fluminense) that would attract 170,000 spectators.

Since the transfer of Brazil's capital from Rio de Janeiro to Brasília, the administration of the stadium was transferred from city to state level, being administered between 1960 and 1975 by ADEG (Sports Administration of the State of Guanabara) and since 1975 by SUDERJ (Sports Superintendence of the State of Rio de Janeiro). The relationship between public administration and the supporters of clubs requires a high degree of maintenance that has not been taken in consideration and some recurring issues must be addressed: 1) football as the people's form of leisure, characterised by catharsis, must be contained and kept in order by the police; 2) the monitoring of supporters—in particular of their organised groups—and the maintenance of orderly behaviour; and 3) the difficulties in offering plentiful and adequate means of transportation to spectators.

Naturally, these questions do not only concern the Maracanã, but it is important to highlight here the reconfiguration of the stadium for the 2014 World Cup. If the structural issues are of a similar nature as before—internal and external infrastructure—the new context of liberal-private encroachment into the world of football and the avowed weakening of the nation state in globalised times sets new challenges for the country.

Thus, a key condition of holding the World Cup in Brazil was the demolition of the existing Maracanã stadium, as was the case with Wembley Stadium in London, between 2003 and 2007, when the original structure was demolished and a new one was built in the same location. According to authorities such as Ricardo Teixeira, CBF's president from 1989 to 2012, the construction of a medium-sized stadium from the ground up in compliance with current FIFA demands was necessary. The reaction of uproar from the public and the subsequent awarding to the stadium of the status of a site of historical heritage, forbidden to be destructed, made the president of the Brazilian Football Confederation backtrack. After Brazil's confirmation as host of the World Cup, and with the possibility of demolition of the Maracanã's original structure ruled out, a large-scale transformation to its interior was undertaken, with plans to eliminate the gap between the two main levels of the stadium and becoming since then just one tier in order to meet international security standards.

If these changes are necessary, for they are supposedly made to benefit Brazil's national team, the image of the country as a whole and of the World Cup tournament, the effects of these great changes remain obscure for the regional and national club championships which will follow the international footballing festival, an event that only lasts for one month. A result is the progressively higher price for tickets and the change in the social profile of supporters. At the bottom line, it can be concluded that the tacit objective is the exclusion of the lower economic segments of the population, from which the members of the *torcidas jovens* hail, and who are seen as the main people responsible for acts of hooliganism and disorder in stadiums.

For the authorities, the sponsors and the football managers, the ideal type of supporter is that normally associated with other sports. In tennis, for example, spectators are more involved with applauding key plays rather than rooting for victory, which obviously does not fuel disputes and contentions. The current state of Brazilian football and of the 2014 World Cup therefore lies on the same plane as other contemporary transformations of the sporting world, with the conversion of the supporter into a potential consumer. Gentrification is a phenomenon observable in many public spaces in Latin America after the neo-liberal trends in the region in the 1990s.

Even so, in spite of the trend of stadiums becoming more and more elitist, one can say that football tends to preserve its status as the people's sport. To put it in broad strokes, with the dissemination of new standards of comfort and new security norms, the middle and upper classes will form the basic human landscape of the stadium, while the majority of the population will have to make do with watching matches on television.

9

A World Cup for Whom?

The Impact of the 2014 World Cup on Brazilian Football Stadiums and Cultures[1]

Christopher Gaffney

Introduction

In the run up to the 2014 World Cup in Brazil, there were twelve FIFA stadium projects underway, with a collective price tag of R$ 8,000,500,000, 97 per cent of which came from public sector financing.[2] This cost does not include the provision of thirty-two train-ing sites needed for each of the qualified World Cup teams. In the west-ern city of Cuiabá, in addition to the 42,000 seat World Cup stadium, three professional training facilities were planned, each with a spectator capacity greater than the average attendance at the city's pre-existing stadium. Cuiabá is not an anomaly as cities around Brazil are specula-tively building world-class facilities as they try to woo top teams. The

2014 World Cup has stimulated public investment in professional-grade sporting infrastructure at a cost, scope, pace and scale never before experienced in Brazil.

Infrastructure development for the world's biggest football tournament occurred at a propitious moment for the Brazilian economy. The massive public outlays for stadiums, airports, transportation, security and business subsidies are being born by a population that benefited, by and large, from the expansion of the Brazilian economy in the first decade of the twenty-first century. Yet the cost being paid by the Brazilian taxpayer cannot be limited to money spent on infrastructure but must be considered in relation to the use value of these projects once the World Cup has passed as well as the opportunity costs of mega-event financing. We know, for instance, that most Brazilian schools lack recreation areas and that investment in sporting facilities for public use is negligible. In Rio de Janeiro, which because of the 2016 Olympics is receiving more government investment than any other city, there are only nine public sport centres, the majority of these in very poor repair.[3] Rio de Janeiro has no municipally sponsored recreation leagues and active participation in sport is concentrated in the city's wealthiest neighbourhoods. The official discourse suggests that the World Cup will benefit society as a whole, bringing lasting benefits to cities and stimulating sporting culture. However, as of December 2013, there were no sporting or cultural projects associated with the World Cup, meaning that 100 per cent of public investment is being directed towards the development of professional-grade sporting infrastructure. All of the public World Cup stadiums have had their operations privatised through so-called public-private partnerships, with potentially devastating consequences for public space and Brazilian football culture.

This chapter will examine the development of stadium- and sport-related infrastructure projects associated with the 2014 World Cup. The analysis begins with a brief history of football in Brazil, noting that the radical changes to the Brazilian sporting landscape have been conditioned by shifts in the political economy of sport that have in turn shaped modes and cultures of spectatorship.

The construction of twelve new stadiums for the 2014 World Cup seems to be the culmination of a decade-long project aimed at changing the social and economic profile of Brazilian football. These changes appear inconsistent with the cultural milieu of Brazilian spectatorship and as such will not adequately serve the needs of cities and populations after the month long tournament.

The historical trajectory of Brazilian football

There is no question that association football, or *futebol*, is the most popular sport in Brazil. The sport emerged out of the cultural milieu of European expatriates in the late nineteenth century and was quickly adopted by Brazil's wealthy urbanites.[4] As the sons of expatriate and local elites kicked about, they eventually formalised their meetings and established clubs dedicated to football or brought organised football into already existing associations. The game gained in popularity as it was introduced to factories, played by dockhands and covered by the press. Stadiums emerged on the grounds of privately owned clubs and, by the 1910s, football was firmly entrenched as a spectator sport in rapidly growing Brazilian cities. Rio de Janeiro and São Paulo, as the political and economic centres of the country, saw the game spread among suburban and lower income populations, but the game also established itself in all of Brazil's coastal cities.[5] Football was a central part of Brazil's centennial celebrations in 1922, and with the advent of radio transmissions and improvements in transportation the game spread to Brazil's vast interior.[6]

As Brazil entered fully into industrial modernity in the 1920s and 1930s, its cities grew as workers flowed in from the countryside and new transportation lines stimulated migratory patterns from the impoverished northeast to the wealthy south. Because of its plasticity, football can be played on nearly any surface, with a huge variety of numbers, and under a wide range of physical constraints. This made the adaptation of football in both inner cities and worker's suburbs extremely easy. The spectacular success of football as a popular form of leisure was matched by its increasing commercial success.[7] Brazilian stadiums were getting larger, a specific press developed to cover the sport, and Brazilians were soon considered to be among the best players in the world. The centrality of football to Brazilian national identity was confirmed when the national team won a third place medal at the 1938 World Cup in France and tens of thousands gathered to welcome the team home on the docks of Rio de Janeiro.[8]

As a testament to this surging popularity, FIFA chose Brazil to host the 1950 World Cup. The tournament was well received in Brazil and attendances were high, though uneven. Notably, the Brazilian team played before crowds averaging 125,000. There were only two construction projects undertaken for this competition: the Independence Stadium (Estádio Sete de Setembro, also known as Estádio da Independência) in Belo Horizonte and Rio de Janeiro's Municipal Stadium (Estádio Municipal do Rio de Janeiro, later, Estádio Jornalista Mario Filho, but usually known simply as the Maracanã). The Brazilian team lost to Uruguay in the final game of the tournament in front of an estimated 200,000 fans. Known as the *Maracanazo*, or the failure in the Maracanã, this was a defining event in Brazilian history.[9] The effects of this game are still talked about as the 2014 World Cup approaches and because Brazil has never had major national traumas, the *Maracanazo* looms large in public consciousness.

In the post-war period and throughout the 1960s, 1970s, and 1980s, Brazilian football grew in size, stature and popularity. Politicians clearly understood the use of football and stadiums as political tools.[10] Stadiums such as Rio's Maracanã, São Paulo's Morumbi, Belo Horizonte's Minerão, and Fortaleza's Castelão had spectator capacities of over 100,000 and significant standing-only sections that offered cheap access for the working classes. These stadiums were well serviced by public transportation and the low cost of tickets facilitated the popularity of football. They were little more than containers for the performance of teams and their fans and reflected an architectural style that was consistent with the simplicity of the sport itself. It was within these spaces, however, that a complex football fan culture with rich traditions consolidated into something that was uniquely and identifiably Brazilian.

In 1970, Brazil won its third World Cup and by 1975, Brazil had more stadiums with capacities over 100,000 than any other nation. In general, we can assert that *futebol* and the places in which it was played followed a fairly consistent trajectory. Once consolidated as 'the people's game', new social formations such as *torcida organizada* (organised fan groups) entered the scene. This new element built upon the carnivalesque nature of Rio de Janeiro's public spaces and its traditions of public festival.[11] Rio's fans had long used costumes, music and decorations as means of creating spectacles, but the *torcidas organizadas* took this production to the next level. The tight relationship between the game on the field and the play in the stands made for a participatory and creative moment, a spatial and social conjuncture, the building blocks of culture and meaning. The openness of Brazilian stadiums allowed for a fluidity of movement and appropriation of space that made for a unique and participatory spectacle.

The very size and character of the Brazilian stadiums built in this 'popular' (if not 'populist') era reflected the zeitgeist. Between 1950 and 1980 Brazilian stadiums were large bowls of concrete and steel, commissioned by military leaders, regional strongmen and other political leaders. Used as political tools, the Brazilian geographer Gilmar Mascarenhas de Jesus has suggested that these public spaces had a hermeneutic effect. The spaces of the stadiums were so large that a single voice could never be heard, reducing an individual's sense of agency. It was only the union of five or ten or a hundred voices that could be heard from across the stadium, encouraging collective and coordinated action. State or federal governments financed the construction of the majority of stadiums built in this era and they remained under public administration into the twenty-first century.

The development of cable and satellite television services in the 1980s opened new revenue streams for the sport.[12] The growth of World Cup and Olympic television revenues brought record profits to FIFA (Fédération Internationale de Football Association) and the IOC (International Olympic Committee). In European domestic leagues and in the United States, improvements and expansion of broadcast services stimulated the sporting economy on a global scale. European teams gained increased purchasing power and accelerated the trend of buying Brazilian stars to play with them, much as had happened in the early decades of professionalisation. In the 1980s, this did not have an immediate impact on attendances or passion for football in the local context, but as this trend accelerated in the 1990s it led to a dilution of the talent pool and a weakening of the domestic game. The president of FIFA was a Brazilian, a condition that put Brazilian football in a powerful position internationally, but with a national football economy that was maintained in a state of dependency.[13]

The transition from dictatorship to democracy between the mid-1980s and the early 1990s occurred at the same time that the global economy was entering a period of accelerated integration. Improvements in communications (internet, cable, cell phones) and transportation technology (containers, expansion of air travel) opened pathways for flows of capital and cultural exchange in unprecedented volume. Brazil was physically unprepared for the demands of the 'global' economy.[14] At all levels, the Brazilian state had been unable to invest in basic urban infrastructures for more than a decade. The 1980s in all of Latin America is referred to as the 'lost decade' and Brazil was characterised by financial and political instability, low growth and emigration to Europe, Japan and the United States. During this period football retained much of its 'classic' characteristics but at the same time it became increasingly violent as the *torcidas organizadas* became mechanisms through which Brazil's marginalised youth could vent their frustration.

The growing social disturbances in football were partly a reflexive response to the deterioration of urban life in general. In the 1980s a series of collective and violent actions against trains in São Paulo and Rio de Janeiro demonstrated the level of frustration that the 'popular' classes experienced in their daily lives. The shoddy transportation lines that suburban dwellers depended upon to get to their jobs and the distant suburbs became the objects of their ire. The violent police repression that followed was consistent with the established relationships between the state and its working poor. These same people, '*o povo*', composed the majority of football fans, principally because ticket prices were reasonably affordable and the large urban stadiums had significant catchment areas for fans. In the biggest cities, intense local rivalries frequently resulted in running street battles. The rising perception of urban insecurity that had created new architectures of fear (gated condominiums, closed circuit television, private security) was exacerbated by the media's portrayal of all football fans as violent and aggressive.[15] While always limited to a minority of offenders and exacerbated by a police force that had retained characteristics from the military dictatorship, there were real problems of insecurity and violence in and around football stadiums.

When cable and satellite television arrived in Brazil in the 1990s, attendances at football matches began to decline. The perception of violent, uncomfortable stadiums kept many fans at home. And while there were real problems with violence, the institutional responses were often just as bad, assuming criminal intent on the part of ordinary fans. These factors combined with a crisis of institutional governance (for instance, the Brazilian league had thirty different formats in its first thirty years) and a lack of basic maintenance of aging stadiums further reduced attendances. This, in turn, increased the influence of the *torcidas organizadas* both within the clubs and on the streets surrounding stadiums on match day. In order to combat or control these well organised, rowdy and angry young men, the police further militarised stadium space, diminishing the appeal of live spectatorship even more. To make matters worse, the contracts signed between the Brazilian Football Confederation (Confederação Brasileira de Futebol, CBF) and the Globo media outlets ensured that many games would only start after the commercially important telenovelas at 10pm on a weekday. The lack of interest on the part of public authorities in providing transportation to and from stadiums made it difficult for all but the most dedicated fans to attend matches.

The institutional crisis of football was aggravated by the indifference and amateurism of football club directors.[16] The clubs remained opaque institutions governed by *cartolas*, or 'top hats', local or regional strongmen who negotiated club business behind closed doors, in many cases using their institutional authority to augment their own power, wealth and influence.[17] The clubs remained impassive and impenetrable to the demands of ordinary fans, and profited tremendously from the sale of players to European clubs. They also courted the favour of the *torcidas organizadas*, giving out political and economic favours in exchange for support on the terraces.

This incredible situation was aided and abetted by the institutional opacity of the CBF and FIFA, which actively pursued a policy of backroom negotiations, especially with the Globo television network. The Brazilian João Havelange was president of FIFA from 1974 to 1998 and his then son-in-law, Ricardo Teixeira, was head of the CBF from 1989 to 2012. This kind of familial relationship allowed for a never-ending series of scandals and sleights of hand in the management of contracts, the management of the Brazilian national team, and the governance of football at all levels. As Brazil won its fourth World Cup in 1994 and finished second in 1998, the controversies surrounding these institutional arrangements stimulated some government investigations, but the culture of indifference, private profit and impunity remained defining characteristics of Brazilian football. Despite all of this, Brazil continued to produce the best footballers in the world, winning their fifth World Cup in 2002.

Fin de siècle, again

The Brazilian public has never had a close relationship with the individuals and institutions responsible for the development, propagation and care of football.[18] As has already been noted, the game emerged from elite circles in the late nineteenth and early twentieth centuries, ensuring that well-established economic and political actors would maintain control of the game. Although many of the directors of Brazil's football clubs come from the world of business, there has never been significant professionalisation of club management and there are very few sport management courses in Brazilian universities. In the history of Brazilian football, there has never been an organisation that represented fans at a meaningful institutional level and it was not until 1999 that a federal level law was passed to regulate the football industry.

The *Lei Pelé* (Pelé's Law) was passed in 1999 under the government of President Fernando Henrique Cardoso.[19] The law was drafted under the influence of Pelé, who in 1997 was given the position of Extraordinary Minister of Sport in order to establish a more rigorous institutional framework to deal with the crisis of governance in Brazilian football. The details of the law are of interest in that they establish rules of conduct in a number of related fields but provide no regulatory mechanism. Thus, the fundamental elements of the *Lei Pelé* were difficult to enforce and business was allowed to carry on as usual.

The next major federal level intervention was the Parliamentary Inquisition Committee (CPI) CBF/Nike. The Committee's book-length report explained the contractual relationship between the Brazilian Football Confederation and Nike, one of its major sponsors. The inquisition resulted from the strange events that surrounded Brazil's 3–0 defeat to France in the 1998 World Cup final. The influence of Nike in the internal politics and decision making of the CBF was clearly demonstrated, yet no punitive or corrective action was taken. The public outrage soon dissipated and Ricardo Teixeira was able to maintain his position as president of the CBF. João Havelange left his position as president of FIFA in the months after Brazil's loss, but for reasons not associated with the CPI. For many Brazilians, the scandals associated with the 1998 World Cup were a turning point in their relationship with the national team as there was a general feeling that a sacred trust had been violated for the personal economic gain of the CBF directors. Curiously, the Minister of Sport in charge of delivering the World Cup,

Aldo Rebelo, was one of the co-authors of the CBF/Nike document during his time in the federal senate.

The crisis of Brazilian football did not improve with the *Lei Pelé*, nor did it with the CPI CBF/Nike. With the ascension of Luiz Inácio Lula da Silva to the presidency in 2003, it appeared that the Brazilian government was going to take the issue of fans' rights seriously for the first time. The first law passed by the Lula administration was the *Estatuto do Torcedor*, or Fan's Statute.[20] This statute elaborated on the expectations of fan behaviour as well as the rights that fans had to access to information, security and transparency in the management of sport. Upon signing the law, President Lula said, 'fans would never again be treated like a herd of animals'. The passing of the law unleashed a series of polemics within the CBF and the major football clubs that claimed they did not have the capacity to deal with the demands of the new law.[21] As ever, there was no group that represented fans' interests in the formulation of the statute.

The enforcement of the *Estatuto do Torcedor* has been uneven while its provisions have proven inadequate and controversial.[22] One of the intended effects of the law was to reduce violent incidents at football matches by making fan behaviour more transparent and predictable to authorities. Special punitive measures for football fans were introduced, yet no equivalent punishments were conditioned for the game's administrators or for the security forces that exaggerated in their heavy-handed attempts to enforce elements of the new statute. The *Estatuto do Torcedor* did bring some fundamental guarantees to football fans and it has had significant positive effects in some sectors such as ticketing, yet the institutional framework of football was not significantly altered and there continues to be no 'popular' representation in any of football's governing bodies.

The lack of transparent federal institutional frameworks is repeated at state and national levels, where participatory public or governmental oversight mechanisms do not hold accountable the private institutions responsible for the organisation of professional and amateur leagues. This lack of oversight has led to innumerable instances of corruption and influence peddling within Brazilian football.[22] There is wide acknowledgement that the amateur nature of football officials has contributed to a culture of corruption and impunity. Thus, the public has traditionally been unable to influence the workings of football, leaving the game in the hands of opaque and self-referential institutions.

At the turn of the twenty-first century, it was clear that Brazil was not prepared to host large-scale international sporting events. In most cases, public sporting facilities had suffered from a lack of investment and mismanagement while private facilities, such as the stadium of Atletico Paranaense in Curitiba, pursued North American style naming-rights agreements. Successive failures of Olympic bids underscored the gravity of problems in transportation, security and sporting infrastructure in Brazil's largest cities.

It is perhaps not accidental that the first stadium in Brazil to take a corporate name was in Curitiba, a city credited with adopting the tactics and techniques of city marketing.[23] The aggressive pursuit of mega-events by some of Brazil's urban administrations (Rio de Janeiro in particular) was closely tied to new forms of urban governance informed by the logics and ideological frames of neoliberalism. The selling of a city's image to international audiences in an attempt to attract highly mobile finance capital had 'successfully' transformed places like New York, Barcelona, Buenos Aires and Curitiba, and had become the Brazilian model for 'efficient urban planning'. Rio de Janeiro was one of the Brazilian cities that most eagerly pursued this model, hosting a series of spectacles that began in 2000 with the FIFA World Club Championship and will culminate with the 2016 Olympic Games.

In order to host the 2000 FIFA World Club Championship, the state government of Rio de Janeiro reduced the capacity of the Maracanã from 179,000 spectators to 129,000 and installed more than one hundred 'skyboxes' around the upper rim of the stadium. This was the first time that a Brazilian stadium had undergone significant reform in order to host a major international event. The reduction of capacity eliminated the proud claim that the stadium was *o maior do mundo* (the world's largest) and by creating air conditioned, sealed containers for VIPs while reducing traditional standing sections, the stadium's populist character was altered. Perhaps as a signal of things to come, construction of a FIFA Hall of Fame museum that was an appendage to the stadium began but was never completed.

Brazil gets its Games

As Brazil's most iconic and photogenic city, Rio de Janeiro led the country's twenty-first-century attempts to capture sport's mega-events as a way of selling the city and country as a place for business and tourism. Failed attempts to secure the 2004 and 2012 Olympic Games forced mega-event advocates to turn to smaller regional events. In 2003 the city won the right to host the 2007 Pan American Games.[24] This ushered in an era of sport-related infrastructure projects that has put Rio de Janeiro and Brazil at the epicentre of global mega-event production.

Soon after the conclusion of the wildly over-budget 2007 Pan American Games, FIFA awarded Brazil the 2014 World Cup. Strangely, Brazil was the only candidate as FIFA President Blatter had instituted (albeit briefly) a continental rotation for the tournament in 2000. Following Asia, Europe and Africa, 2014 was to be South America's turn and Brazil was the only country put forth by the regional football confederation CONMEBOL. While the FIFA technical report cited the need for a maximum of eight to ten host cities, eighteen Brazilian cities put forth candidature projects and in May 2009 the Brazilian government chose twelve of them. Once the cities were chosen, the wheels were set in motion to attend to the FIFA technical team's finding that 'none of the stadiums in Brazil would be suitable to stage 2014 FIFA World Cup™ matches in their current state'.[25]

The processes through which the 2014 host cities were selected and the methods employed to project and contract the myriad developments required in each city merits book-length treatment.[26] Current research demonstrates that an industrial complex has emerged around the production and consumption of mega-events.[27] The 2014 World Cup in Brazil has stimulated tens of billions of dollars of investment from all levels of the state and the private sector. This chapter's earlier sketch of the historical trajectory of Brazilian football and sporting culture has provided some of the background information necessary to make sense of the urban, institutional and social contexts in which the infrastructure projects for the 2014 World Cup are taking shape. While far from complete, this analysis has shown that the changes to Brazil's sporting landscape are conditioned by processes not visible on the surface. The following section examines data regarding football spectatorship, undertakes a brief analysis of select architectural projects and imagines the trajectory of Brazilian football in the post-World Cup era.

Realities and prospects

As was mentioned at the outset of this chapter, massive public expenditure on World Cup infrastructure is taking place as the Brazilian economy experiences consistent economic growth and an increase in purchasing power in all social segments. As the World Cup was announced to the Brazilian public in 2007, the government made guarantees that no public money would be spent. This was evidently a promise that should not have been made as there were no corporate partners supporting the 2014 bid and few potential host cities had prepared financial viability statements. As the World Cup has taken physical shape, public investment has been 98.5 per cent of the total expenditure.[28] Eager to justify the inevitable cost overruns, the minister of sport, Aldo Rebelo, quipped in November of 2011 that the government 'was not paying for the World Cup, but investing in Brazilian cities'.[29]

The extensive and monumental physical interventions undertaken for the 2014 FIFA World Cup stadiums are the most visible manifestation of a process referred to as *elitização*. This 'elitisation' implies a change in the social profile of stadium-going fans from lower and middle to upper-middle and upper class. With this, there is a perceived change in social comportment at football matches, moving from active to passive spectatorship. There are two distinct schools of thought regarding this process, but both agree on the character of the changes taking place.

The figures below show two interrelated phenomena. The first shows the average revenue streams for major Brazilian football clubs. The major sources of revenue are player sales and television contracts. The dominance of these sectors indicates that large media outlets have an important say in the programming and management of football and that the Brazilian teams continue to sell players abroad in order to remain financially viable. What this table does not show are the heavy debt burdens that most first division teams carry. For instance, the four biggest teams in Rio de Janeiro have a combined debt of R$ 1,045,400,000.[30] As the mega-events have caused more money to circulate through Brazilian sport (itself a reflection of the growing consumer economy) there has developed a need for more financial transparency and discipline. However, the semi-feudal conditions of the Brazilian football directorships have made a transition to efficient and professional management quite difficult.

A WORLD CUP FOR WHOM?

Returning to the economic structure of Brazilian football, of particular interest is the percentage of revenue derived from ticket sales: this figure stands at 11 per cent. This implies that clubs are not dependent on having paying fans in stadiums. For instance, if from one year to the next, Brazilian attendances were cut in half, there would only be a 5.5 per cent decrease in club revenues. This could easily be compensated for by the sale of extra players, a new sponsor or a more lucrative television contract. The general political and institutional conditions that were identified and explained earlier have both created and re-enforced the economic dynamics of clubs.

Fig. 1: Club revenue streams, 2010

Source of income	(%)
Ticket sales	11
Sponsors and advertising	12
Other receipts (merchandise sales)	12
Member dues and amateur sports	13
Television	24
Sale/transfer of players	28

Source: *Cadernos FGV Projetos*, 5, 13 (2010). ISSN 1984–4883.

Again, comparative data for the past ten years would reveal changing trends, but as yet data is not available. It can, however, be assumed that as the Brazilian economy has grown, the value of television contracts has increased. The expansion of Brazil's internal consumer market has likely increased the value of advertising and sponsorship contracts over time. Brazilian teams continue to sell their best young players to European and Middle Eastern markets, further weakening the domestic leagues.

As the second figure demonstrates, the decline in fan attendance at first division matches has been more than matched by an increase in the average ticket price. Figure 2 shows very clearly that while there are fewer fans in the stadiums per match, profits have soared. This means that average ticket prices have increased dramatically—by at least 70 per cent in five years. Ticket prices vary widely from city to city and from game to game. Research and observations in Rio de Janeiro have shown that a ticket priced between R$30 and R$40 is beyond the reach of most working-class fans.

While the average ticket price remains relatively low compared to leagues in Europe, Brazilians also earn much lower salaries and therefore pay a greater percentage of their income to attend matches. Brazilian football statistics are also skewed by the influence of what is known as the 'half-ticket', or half-price tickets for students, the elderly and state workers. Tickets are also sold in volume and at a discount to the *torcidas organizadas* who sell them on to other fans. To complicate the situation further, tickets given to the football federations, clubs and sponsors can account for up to 25 per cent of spectators at any given match. Hence, the data below cannot be considered absolutely accurate, but rather an indication of trends. If anything, the situation is even more alarming: as recently as 2005, standing tickets at Rio's Maracanã stadium were R$5. As Figure 3 shows, they had risen to R$30 by 2010. Following the reforms undertaken for the FIFA World Cup, ticket prices reached as much as R$60 for league matches, making them the most expensive in the world relative to minimum wage.[31]

Fig. 2: Average attendances and ticket prices at Brazilian Serie A football matches, 2007–2012

Year	Total Attendance	Average Attendance	Total gate receipts (R$)	Average ticket price (R$)
2007	6,582,976	17,461	80,040,848	12.20
2008	6,439,854	16,992	101,241,490	15.70
2009	6,766,471	17,807	125,764,391	18.60
2010	5,638,806	14,839	112,873,893	20.00
2011	5,660,987	14,976	117,665,714	20.80
2012	4,928,827	12,970	119,100,000	22.92
% Change	−15.2	−15.8	49	88

This graphic compares average ticket prices with the Brazilian federal minimum wage over the past sixty years. Since 2003, there has been a notable increase. If we were to continue this graph through 2014, the rise would be even more pronounced.

This new political economy of Brazilian football is being consolidated with the arrival of the World Cup. In 2012, Ricardo Trade of the 2014 Local Organising Committee said the following regarding the new stadiums under construction:

A WORLD CUP FOR WHOM?

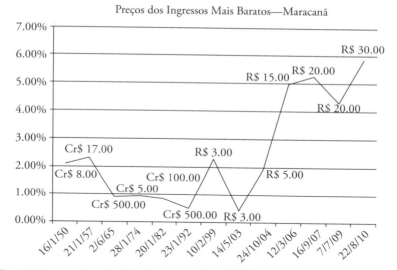

Preços dos Ingressos Mais Baratos—Maracanã

Fig. 3: Change in price for cheapest tickets for the Maracanã Stadium relative to minimum wage, 1950–2010. Graphic from Erick Omena de Melo, 2012

The stadiums sometimes attract people through their modern design, they become places for family outings and fans take stadium tours, they can visit the trophy room, see photos, arrive early for the game and consume club products.[32]

It is now clear that fewer people are able to attend matches because of the increased ticket prices that this 'consumptive football' has brought with it. The distancing of Brazil's lower and middle classes from their most popular form of leisure is bringing about significant changes to and challenges for 'traditional' Brazilian terrace cultures.

While it can be argued that the elevation of ticket prices is a 'natural' outcome of an expanding economy and inflationary processes, the same logic would suggest that greater purchasing power would cause attendances to remain constant or even increase. However, as has been argued, there has been what appears to be a deliberate attempt to reduce the presence of the working class in Brazilian stadiums with the goal of transforming 'traditional fans' into 'families of consumers'. This trend is entirely consistent with stadium and sport management practices in North America and Europe. As the new stadiums in Brazil are being paid for with public money, the government is actively subsidising the profits of private stadium operators and of professional sport teams. This intention was made clear as early as the FIFA Technical Evaluation of Stadiums in 2007:

The Brazilian model for the 2014 FIFA World Cup™ is to give priority to private finance in the construction and remodelling of the stadiums through long term concessions and eventually public private partnerships (PPPs).

This statement is misleading, in that the 'priority to private finance' should have been reflected in the appearance of private financing for the construction of stadiums. In fact, one of the pillars of the government's argument for hosting the World Cup was that it would be 100 per cent financed by private enterprise. Just the opposite has happened. A literal reading of the above sentence makes clear the government's real intent to privilege private interests through the public financing of projects that will then be handed to the private sector.

In addition to importing models of stadium development and sports management practices from abroad, the models for the stadiums under construction are heavily influenced by 'international best practice' in design. This partially results from the contracts signed between host cities and FIFA in which World Cup stadiums must conform to the guidelines established in the 'Technical Requirements for Stadia' manual. The 125-page manual treats ten primary areas ranging from pre-construction decisions to match-day security requirements. Stadium designers and event managers are thus slightly limited in their choices about which architectural elements to include and if they are to 'qualify' as a World Cup host, their stadium and game management plan must conform to FIFA's exigencies. Failure to comply with these exigencies within two years of the event could signal a breach of contract and the potential loss of the event.

There has developed an international stadium-building knowledge network that is comprised of multinational sports management firms such as Los Angeles-based IMG, and by multinational stadium design firms such as Populous, 360 Architecture and HKS Architects. Similar to other mega-events, with the production of the World Cup, a country enters into an international knowledge-sharing network. Teams of specialist technicians move around the globe, producing and reproducing sporting mega-events. The architecture, design, engineering and management contracts for World Cup stadiums are open to global bidding, though it is usually national-level civil construction firms that direct the projects. The 'internationalisation' of Brazilian football is bringing dramatic changes to stadium architecture, design and access, as well as consolidating a process of elitisation which will have enduring effects on Brazilian football culture.

Conclusion

The 2014 World Cup is a historical marker in Brazil. Much as in 1950, the country will use the tournament to project itself to an international audience through the construction of monumental stadiums. In the immediate post-World War II era, Brazil was anxious to demonstrate its engineering and architectural capacity, as well as the budding 'racial democracy' of the Brazilian people. The stadiums designed then reflected this ideal. Sixty-four years later, much in Brazil has changed and the new projects are a reflection of the goals and desires of Brazil's political and economic elite. As has been shown, there has been a change in the economics of Brazilian football in recent years which has resulted in the diminishing of crowds, an increase in ticket prices and the emergence of a commercially oriented model of fandom.[33]

These changes did not happen because of the World Cup, but they cannot be separated from it. The progressive territorialisation of Brazilian stadiums and urban space will reach its apogee between 13 June and 23 July 2014. Whereas previously fans were able to move relatively freely in the open terraces, they will now have individual seats, contained within demarcated sectors within which they can be more easily monitored and controlled. The new VIP (Very Important People) and VVIP (Very Very Important People) sections of the stadiums have exclusive access, differentiated services and come with a suite of privileges not available to the common fan. As the FIFA documents bear out, nearly every square metre of modern stadiums are controllable, regulated and conditioned. For instance, in the FIFA stadium requirements, VIP hospitality areas require $4.6m^2$ per person, while VVIPs are allotted $5.2m^2$ of space. This kind of hyper-rationalisation and differentiation of space extends to the stadium as a whole.

In truth, the boundaries of stadium space are highly flexible, as FIFA requires that a two-kilometre radius from the centre of the stadium be given over to their exclusive control for marketing purposes for the length of the tournament. Again, a large public subsidy can be identified for the generation of private profit. The militarisation of public space that accompanies global mega-events has been well documented, and in a society that has not yet fully made the institutional transition from military dictatorship to representative democracy, there are major concerns regarding the management of, and access to, public space during the 2014 World Cup. This is similar to processes observed in recent World Cups.[34]

It can be argued that the World Cup will bring something unique to Brazilians, namely the ability to see a World Cup match. While FIFA has made promises that 300,000 Category 4 tickets will be reserved for lower income Brazilians, the remainder of the tickets will remain well out of reach for most. The following figure indicates a progressive increase in the price of World Cup tickets. Those who wish to be close to the action for this 'once in a lifetime' opportunity will not only have to have an internet connection and a credit card to even attempt to make a booking, but will pay significantly more for tickets than South Africans or Germans did when World Cup tournaments were staged in their countries. The company MATCH won a third no-bid contract for selling 2014 World Cup tickets and tourist packages.[35] FIFA has consistently refused to release data regarding the number of tickets sold or reveal the processes through which individual ticket holders were selected in the various ticket lotteries.

Fig. 4: Ticket price comparisons for recent FIFA World Cups

	Category 1	Category 2	Category 3	Category 4
Germany 2006	$126	$75	$57	$45
South Africa 2010	$160	$120	$80	$20
Brazil 2014	$203	$192	$112	$25

The month-long World Cup will live in the memories of Brazilians, but what about the tournament's physical legacy once the event has passed? Though the once public stadiums have been privatised, relieving cities of the financial burden of maintenance, at least four cities (Cuiabá, Manaus, Natal and Brasília) have no permanent tenants and football cannot be counted on to generate sufficient revenue. The justification is that these new facilities are 'multi-use arenas' that can be used for shows, shopping and business. Given the trends in ticket prices, it can be assumed that Brazilian football clubs will continue to try to extract more money out of fewer fans by 'capturing' them within stadiums that have façades similar to shopping malls and office buildings. The commercial offerings of teams within the stadiums will likely increase as stadium demographics increasingly shift from the young working classes to the middle and upper-middle professional classes. The gradual and forceful displacement of traditional fans will be felt in the stadiums as a certain dulling of the experience as a formerly participatory environment turns to one of passive and comfortable consumption. Regardless of who goes to the new stadiums, the financial burden will fall upon the public in the form of increased taxes, higher ticket prices or the opportunity cost of investing public money in facilities that generate private profit.

The trends toward hyper-commercialisation can be observed in the architecture of the new stadiums and the documentation that has accompanied the selling of these projects to local, national and international audiences. Seen in the destruction of many of Brazil's traditional stadiums is the loss of architectural and cultural traditions. Of the twelve stadium projects underway, seven were existing stadiums demolished to be reconstructed in the same physical space, two are reforms of privately owned facilities, and three are being built from the ground up. While many of the projects are visually attractive, there is a sense that they are little more than stages upon which the ritual of football is to be carried out. There will be little to distinguish, for example, the new stadium in Cuiabá from stadiums in Portugal, Austria, Poland or South Africa. Similar to shopping malls, no new stadium allows for a visual connection or physical articulation with the urban environment. Financed with public money and controlled by private interests, World Cup stadiums will be worlds of consumption isolated from their urban and cultural contexts.

The accepted business wisdom of football suggests that this is the only way forward for Brazilian football. The private sector has undertaken no risk in developing the World Cup and the public sector has overachieved in its desire to put forth a 'positive image' of Brazil to the world. The wanton destruction of historic stadiums has been accompanied by a lack of transparency and accountability on the part of tournament organisers. Football's institutions have not recognised the very real threats to traditional football culture in Brazil. To the contrary, these very institutions have worked closely with private interests to change the form and function of Brazilian stadiums as well as the 'kind' of people that go there. These processes have the potential to permanently alter an essential element of Brazilian cultural identity. Ironically, it is the cultural weight of football as created and sustained by *o povo*, 'the people', that has made possible its saleability in the global marketplace.

NOTES

THE BEAUTIFUL GAME IN THE 'COUNTRY OF FOOTBALL'

1. Wisnik, J.M., *Veneno remédio: o futebol e o Brasil.* São Paulo: Companhia das Letras, 2008.
2. Hobsbawm, E., *The Age of Extremes: The Short Twentieth Century, 1914–1991.* London: Abacus, 1995, p. 198.
3. These studies originated in the Department of Social Anthropology at the Museu Nacional in Rio de Janeiro. Professor DaMatta was the leader of this group that broke the convention of football being a topic unworthy of study in Brazilian academia.
4. Examples of football-related research groups include LUDENS (Núcleo Interdisciplinar de Pesquisas sobre Futebol e Modalidades Lúdicas) in São Paulo; LESP (Laboratório de Estudos do Esporte) in Rio de Janeiro; and GEFUT (Grupo de Estudos sobre Futebol e Torcidas) in Belo Horizonte.
5. The works of the German sociologist Norbert Elias and of the French sociologist Pierre Bourdieu are among the most influential and inspiring. See Elias, N. and Dunning, E., *Quest of Excitement: Sport and Leisure in the Civilizing Process.* Oxford: Blackwell, 1985; and Bourdieu, P., *Questions de Sociologie.* Paris: Miniut, 1980.
6. See, among others, Souza, D.A. de, *O Brasil entra em campo: estado, trabalhadores e imprensa na construção da identidade nacional através do futebol (1930–1947).* São Paulo: Annablume, 2008; Negreiros, P.J.L. de C., 'Futebol nos anos 1930 e 1940: construindo a identidade nacional', *História: questões e debates*, 39 (2003); Silva, E.J. da, 'A seleção Brasileira nos jogos da Copa do Mundo entre 1930 e 1938', PhD Thesis, Department of History, Universidade Estadual Paulista, 2004; Franzini, F., *Corações na ponta da chuteira: capítulos iniciais da história do futebol Brasileiro (1919–1938.).* Rio de Janeiro: DP&A, 2003; Antunes, F.M.R.F., *Com brasileiro não há quem possa! Futebol e identidade nacional em José Lins do Rego, Mário Filho e Nélson Rodrigues.* São Paulo: Editora UNESP, 2004; Salvador, M.A.S., 'A memória da Copa de 1970: esquecimento e lembranças do futebol na construção da identidade nacional', PhD

thesis, Department of Physical Education, Universidade Gama Filho, Rio de Janeiro, 2005; and Hollanda, B.B. de, *O descobrimento do futebol: modernismo, regionalismo e paixão esportiva em José Lins do Rego*. Rio de Janeiro: Edições Biblioteca Nacional, 2004.

7. Gilberto Freyre's most significant study along these lines is *Casa-Grande e Senzala*. Rio de Janeiro, 1933, published in English as *The Masters and The Slaves: A Study in the Development of Brazilian Civilization*. For further social thought in relation to race in Brazilian football, see, for example, Freyre, G., *Sobrados & Mocambos: decadência do patriarcado rural e desenvolvimento do urbano*. Rio de Janeiro: Global Editora, 2003; Costa Pinto, L.A., *O negro no Rio de Janeiro: relações de raça numa sociedade em mudança*. Rio de Janeiro: UFRJ, 1998; Carneiro, E., 'Apresentação', in Rodrigues Filho, M., *O negro no futebol brasileiro*. Rio de Janeiro: Civilização Brasileira, 2nd edn, 1964; and Moraes, P. de, *Tradição e transformação no Brasil*. Rio de Janeiro: Civilização Brasileira, 1964.

8. Rodrigues Filho, M., *O negro no futebol brasileiro*. Rio de Janeiro: Edições Pongetti, 1947.

9. Gilberto Freyre's *The Masters and the Slaves* was first published in English in 1946 by Alfred A. Knopf in New York.

10. Anatol H. Rosenfeld, 'Das Fußballspiel in Brasilien', *Staden Jahrbuch*, 4 (1956). The article first appeared in Portuguese as 'O futebol no Brasil', *Argumento*, 1, 4 (1974) and it was later published in a collection of Rosenfeld's articles, edited by Modesto Carone, entitled *Negro, Macumba e Futebol*. São Paulo/Campinas: Perspectiva/EDUSP/Unicamp, 1993.

11. In this sense, the influential work of José Sergio Leite Lopes deserves special attention. See: Lopes, J.S.L., 'A vitória do futebol que incorporou a pelada. A invenção do jornalismo esportivo e a entrada dos negros no futebol brasileiro', *Revista USP*, 22 (1994); Lopes, J.S.L., 'Classe, etnicidade e cor na formação do futebol brasileiro', in Batalha, C. et al. (eds), *Culturas de Classe: identidade e diversidade na formação do operariado*. Campinas: Ed. Unicamp, 2004. Also see: Pereira, L.A. de M., *Footballmania: uma história social do futebol no Rio de Janeiro (1902–1938)*. Rio de Janeiro: Nova Fronteira, 2000. For a reading of the role of Mário Filho in the construction of the participation of black people in Brazilian football see: Soares, A.J.S., 'História e invenção das tradições no campo do futebol', *Estudos Históricos*, 23 (1999).

12. On football supporters, see the pioneering and important study by Luiz Henrique de Toledo, *Torcidas organizadas de futebol*. Campinas: Autores Associados, 1996. See also: Damo, A., 'Ah! Eu Sou Gaúcho! O nacional e o regional no futebol brasileiro', *Estudos Históricos*, 13, 23 (1999); Monteiro, R. de A., *Torcer, lutar, ao inimigo massacrar: raça rubro-negra!*, Rio de Janeiro: Ed. FGV, 2003; Teixeira, R. da C., *Os perigos da paixão: visitando jovens torcidas cariocas*. São Paulo: Annablume, 2004. See also Hollanda, B.B.B. de, *O clube como vontade e representação: o jornalismo esportivo e a formação das torcidas organizadas do Rio de Janeiro*. Rio de Janeiro: Ed. 7 Letras, 2010.

13. See Sarmento, C.E., *A regra do jogo: uma história institucional da CBF*. Rio de Janeiro: CPDOC/FGV, 2006.

14. See, for example, Gaffney, C.T. *Temples of the Earthbound Gods: Stadiums in the Cultural Landscapes of Rio de Janeiro and Buenos Aires*. Austin: University of Texas Press, 2008.

15. For a sample of this production, see the various articles published in the special issue on sports and workers of the journal *Cadernos AEL*, 6, 28 (2010), edited by Paulo Fontes and published by Unicamp.

16. Getúlio Vargas would again govern Brazil between 1951 and 1954, after being democratically elected as president through popular vote as the leader of the Partido Trabalhista Brasileiro (Brazilian Workers' Party).

1. THE EARLY DAYS OF FOOTBALL IN BRAZIL: BRITISH INFLUENCE AND FACTORY CLUBS IN SÃO PAULO

1. Mércio, Roberto, *A História dos Campeonatos Cariocas de Futebol*. Rio de Janeiro: Studio Alfa, 1985, p. 16.

2. Santos Neto, José Moraes dos, *Visão do jogo—primórdios do futebol no Brasil*. São Paulo: Cosac & Naify, 2002, pp. 18–19.

3. Ibid., pp. 22–3.

4. Várzea, Paulo, 'Começo e desenvolvimento do futebol em São Paulo', in Vários Autores, *60 Anos de Futebol no Brasil*. São Paulo: Federação Paulista de Futebol, 1955, p. 144.

5. Rodrigues Filho, Mário, *O negro no futebol brasileiro*. Rio de Janeiro: Mauad, 4th edn, 2003, p. 53.

6. Rodrigues Filho, Mário, *O negro no futebol brasileiro*. Rio de Janeiro: Civilização Brasileira, 2nd edn, 1964, p. 34.

7. On the development of football in Britain, see, for example, Sanders, Richard, *Beastly Fury: The Strange Birth of British Football*. London: Bantam Press, 2009; and also Allison, Lincoln, 'Association football and the urban ethos', in *Manchester and São Paulo: problems of rapid urban growth*. Stanford: Stanford University Press, 1978, pp. 203–28. On the spread of football elsewhere see, for example, David Goldblatt, *The Ball is Round: A Global History of Football*. London: Viking, 2006; Murray, Bill, *The World's Game: A History of Soccer*, Urbana: University of Illinois Press, 1996; Chapter 1 ('"The white man's burden": football and empire, 1860–1919') of Alegi, Peter, *African Soccerscapes: How a Continent Changed the World's Game*. Athens: Ohio University Press, 2010; and Tony Mason, *Passion of the People: Football in Latin America*. London: Verso, 1995.

8. For biographies of Charles Miller, see Lacey, Josh, *God is Brazilian: The Man Who Brought Football to Brazil*. Stroud: Tempus, 2005; and Mills, John R., *Charles Miller: o pai do futebol brasileiro*. São Paulo: Panda Books, 2005. See also Davis, Darién J., 'British football with a Brazilian beat: the early history of a national pastime (1894–1933)', in Marshall, Oliver, *English-Speaking Communities in Latin America*. London: Macmillan, pp. 261–84.

9. From the mid-nineteenth century, coffee farming had become the economic main-stay of the state of São Paulo. Coffee promoted wide commercial development, including the establishment of export houses in São Paulo, the city being favoured for its relatively benign climate and practical location between production areas and the port of Santos. British companies established themselves in the city, aiming to take advantage of the growing opportunities offered there.

10. Várzea, 'Começo e desenvolvimento', p. 154.

11. British technicians, engineers, administrators and workers started arriving in São Paulo in the mid-nineteenth century. Many of these men worked on the construction and maintenance of the São Paulo Railway, a line that linked São Paulo's coffee producing areas with Santos. In 1919, the São Paulo Railway Athletic Club, whose members were railway workers, was founded. In 1946, with the ending of the contract conceding services to the São Paulo Railway, the club adopted the name of Nacional Atlético Clube. This club is still active, competing in lower division professional tournaments and specialising in identifying new players for eventual sale to major teams. Other similar clubs formed by railway workers included the Associação Ferroviária de Esportes (Rail Sports Association) in Araraquara in the state of São Paulo, and the Paraná Clube in Curitiba.

12. Franzini, Fabio, 'A futura paixão nacional: chega o futebol', in Priore, Mary Del and Victor Andrade de Melo (eds), *História do Esporte no Brasil: do Império aos dias atuais*. São Paulo: Editora UNESP, 2009, p. 117.

13. Pereira, Leonardo Affonso de Miranda, *Footballmania: uma história social do futebol no Rio de Janeiro—1902–1938*. Rio de Janeiro: Nova Fronteira, 2000, p. 27.

14. Letter from the journalist Celso Araujo to the journalist Alcindo Guanabara, São Paulo, 16 August 1896, quoted in Neiva, Adriano, 'Escrevendo uma história', in Vários Autores, *60 Anos de futebol no Brasil*. São Paulo: Federação Paulista de Futebol, 1955, p. 33.

15. Ibid., p. 33.

16. Ibid., p. 57.

17. Silveira, Osvaldo da, 'Do Velódromo ao Morumbi', in Vários Autores, *60 Anos de Futebol no Brasil*. São Paulo: Federação Paulista de Futebol, 1955, p. 319.

18. According to Hilario Franco Júnior in, *A dança dos deuses: futebol, sociedade, cultura*. São Paulo: Companhia das Letras, 2007, pp. 34–5; and Franzini, 'A futura paixão nacional', p. 108.

19. Filho, *O negro no futebol brasileiro*, 2003, p. 29.

20. Antunes, Fatima Martin Rodrigues Ferreira, 'Futebol de fábrica em São Paulo', MSc thesis in sociology, Faculdade de Filosofia, Letras e Ciências Humanas/Universidade de São Paulo, 1992, pp. 196–211.

21. At this point, the described situation synthesises a part of the discussion developed in ibid.

22. The Ministerial Ordinance no. 254, on October 1 1941 (Ministry of Education and Health, National Council of Sports), instructed changes on the statuses of clubs and

sports associations. This document determined a common structure to the clubs, which was composed by a board of directors, a deliberative council and an audit committee. Each of these parts had a specific role in the administration of the club.

23. Rosenfeld, Anatol, 'O futebol no Brasil', *Revista Argumento*, 1, 4 (1973), pp. 61–85.

24. Caldas, Waldenyr, *O pontapé inicial. Memória do futebol brasileiro (1894–1933)*. São Paulo: IBRASA, 1990, p. 31.

25. Wahl, Alfred, 'Le footballheur français: de l'amateurisme au salariat (1890–1926)', *Le Mouvement Social*, 135 (1996), pp. 7–30.

26. Rosenfeld, 'O futebol no Brasil', p. 67.

27. Hardman, Francisco Foot, *Nem pátria, nem patrão. Vida operária e cultura anarquista no Brasil*. São Paulo: Brasiliense, 1983, p. 42.

28. Decca, Maria Auxiliadora Guzzo, *A vida fora das fábricas. Cotidiano operário em São Paulo (1920–1934)*. Rio de Janeiro: Paz e Terra, 1987, p. 121.

29. With the end of the Estado Novo, the Brazilian Communist Party (PCB) participated in the process of democratisation. It was at football clubs in workers' neighbourhoods and their social networks where the communists displayed their militancy. According to Paoli, Maria Célia and Adriano Luiz Duarte, 'São Paulo no plural: espaços públicos e redes de sociabilidade', in Porta, Paula (ed.), *História da Cidade de São Paulo: a cidade de São Paulo na primeira metade do século XX*, vol. III. São Paulo: Paz e Terra, 2005, pp. 67–92.

30. *Bicho* is the name given to the reward paid to professional players for a positive outcome in a match or championship. The expression originates from the *jogo do bicho*, an illegal betting on numbers, associated to animals.

31. Guedes, Simoni Lahud, 'Futebol brasileiro: instituição zero', MSc thesis in social anthropology, Museu Nacional/UFRJ, 1977, p. 146.

32. Wahl, 'Le footballheur français', p. 16.

33. Lopes, José Sergio Leite, 'La disparition de la "joie du peuple". Notes sur la mort d'un joueur de football', *Actes de la recherche en sciences sociales*, 79 (1989), pp. 21–36.

34. One of the most popular and well-known football players in Brazilian history, Garrincha was a key star of the national team during the World Cup tournaments of 1958 in Sweden and 1962 in Chile. Acclaimed as a 'naïve genius', he is probably the best representation of a 'romantic golden age' of Brazilian football. His tragic death in 1983 due to alcohol-related health problems paradoxically reinforced his reputation as a popular idol. In this regard see in this volume, José Sergio Leite Lopes, '"The people's joy" vanishes: considerations on the death of a soccer player'. For a biography of Garrincha, see Castro, Ruy, *Garrincha: The Triumph and Tragedy of Brazil's Forgotten Footballing Hero*. London: Yellow Jersey Press, 2004.

35. For a general business history of the 'Light', see McDowall, Duncan, *The Light: Brazilian Traction, Light and Power Company Limited, 1899–1945*. Toronto: University of Toronto Press, 1988.

36. *Boletim Histórico Eletropaulo*, 7 (1986), pp. 14–15.

37. According to the *Boletim Histórico Eletropaulo*, 5 (1986), p. 3, the initiative to light

the field came from Severino Rômulo Gragnani, president of the Sociedade Esportiva Linhas e Cabos. It was also decided to paint balls white for the subsequent matches. At the time, footballs were made of natural-coloured leather and, in the first night-time match there were problems with the visibility of the ball when it was not in the illuminated area. In 1924 the American journal *Electrical World* mentioned this issue.

38. The Light's associated companies were in the field of electric energy and included Companhia Ituana Força e Luz, Empresa Luz e Força de Jundiaí, Empresa Hidrelétrica da Serra da Bocaina S/A, Companhia Força e Luz de Jacareí e Guararema, Empresa de Eletricidade São Paulo e Rio S/A. Source: *Employment Bureau: Annual Report: 1945*, Allied Companies, Collection of the Fundação Energia e Saneamento de São Paulo. The Light gradually incorporated other local energy and telephone companies. With the construction of dams, reservoirs and thermoelectric and hydroelectric plants, the Light continued to expand its capacity of energy supply for São Paulo's rapidly growing industries, as well as to expand its public services such as urban transport and telephones. In the 1920s, the company had grown so much that the workers' press referred to it as 'the Canadian octopus' and criticised the quality of the services it provided, even to its own employees who invariably were brought to work in filthy vehicles. See Decca, *A vida fora das fábricas*, p. 113.

39. At the time of research for this chapter, the letters and reports cited here were held by the Divisão de Retenção e Recuperação de Documentos and the Departamento do Patrimônio Histórico da Eletropaulo—Eletricidade de São Paulo S/A. Subsequently, these documents were transferred to the Fundação Energia e Saneamento de São Paulo.

40. The União dos Trabalhadores da Light, founded on 29 November 1930, and affiliated to the Federação Operária de São Paulo (FOSP), brought together active and retired employees. The union had a medical clinic, which provided health services for its members, their children, spouses and parents. The organisation held its meetings at the headquarters of the workers' cooperative Classes Laboriosas. These meetings were mostly attended by employees of the Departments of Traffic (motormen and conductors), Workshops, Permanent Way and Lines & Cables. See *O Trabalhador da Light*, 3, 2 (1934); and 9 (1939).

41. Hardman, *Nem pátria*, p. 40.

42. In a study of the club of the Renault factory workers in France, Patrick Fridenson argues that workers, managers and executives had different interests in sports according to a classic process of distinction, regardless of region, country or time. Workers mainly dedicated themselves to mass sports, while foremen, technicians and white collar employees preferred individual and less common sports. Pierre Bourdieu suggested that different social classes have different interests on social profits and the distinction that the practice of a particular sport can provide. In addition, they also have different conceptions of the body and they make different use of it. See Fridenson, Patrick, 'Les ouvriers de l'automobile et le sport', *Actes de la Recherche en*

Sciences Sociales, 79 (1989), p. 51; and Bourdieu, Pierre, 'Como é possível ser esportivo?', *Questões de Sociologia*. Rio de Janeiro: Editora Marco Zero, 1983, p. 136–53.

43. Letter from Severino Gragnani to the president of the AAL&P, 23 September 1931.
44. Letter from Severino Gragnani to Odilon de Souza, 12 July 1937.
45. Decca, *A vida fora das fábricas*, p. 123.
46. The São Paulo Tramway, Light & Power Co. Ltd, *Employment Bureau: Annual Report: 1945*, Tramway Division, p. 6.
47. Apart from the lack of interest of the Canadian company to spread its name through the performance of its football clubs, the workers' teams of other major São Paulo companies experienced similar problems. The lack of a headquarters, the unpredictability of financial support, and the practice of a false amateurism also characterised factory clubs of the Indústrias Reunidas Francisco Matarazzo, Brazil's largest industrial conglomerate in the first half of the twentieth century. See Antunes, 'Futebol de fábrica em São Paulo', pp. 106–47.

2. *MALANDROS*, 'HONOURABLE WORKERS' AND THE PROFESSIONALISATION OF BRAZILIAN FOOTBALL, 1930–1950

1. Several versions of this rational for racial meaning and national identity have derived from the idea of a *raça brasileira*. See Gilberto Freyre preface in Mário Filho, *O negro no futebol brasileiro*. Rio de Janeiro: Pognetti, 1947; Frances Windance Twine, *Racism in a Racial Democracy: The Maintenance of White Supremacy in Brazil*. New Brunswick: Rutgers University Press, 1998; Brian Owensby, 'Towards a History of Brazil's "Cordial Racism", Race beyond Liberalism', *Comparative Studies of Society and History*, 47, 2 (2005), pp. 318–47; Anthony W. Marx, *Making Race and Nation*. Cambridge: Cambridge University Press, 1998.
2. Florestan Fernandes, *The Negro in Brazilian Society*. New York: Columbia University Press, 1969.
3. Edward Tells, *Race in another America, the Significance of Skin Color in Brazil*. Princeton: Princeton University Press, 2004.
4. Roberto DaMatta, *Universo do Futebol: esporte e sociedade brasileira*. Rio de Janeiro: Edições Pinakotheke, 1982.
5. Robert M. Levine, *Father of the Poor?: Vargas and his Era*. Cambridge: Cambridge University Press, 1998; and *The Vargas Regime, the Critical Year 1934–1938*. New York: Columbia University Press, 1969; and Thomas E. Skidmore, *Politics in Brazil, 1930–1964: An Experiment in Democracy*. New York: Oxford University Press, 1969.
6. Teresa Meade, *"Civilizing" Rio: reform and resistance in a Brazilian city, 1889–1930*. University Park: Pennsylvania State University Press, 1997.
7. Thomas E. Skidmore, *Black into White: Race and Nationality in Brazilian Thought*. Durham: Duke University Press, 1993.
8. Gregg P. Brocketti, 'Italian Immigrants, Brazilian Football, the Dilemma of National Identity', *Journal of Latin American Studies*, 40 (2008), pp. 275–302.

9. Gustavo Capanema, 'Letters to the President of the Republic Getúlio Vargas, from the Minister of Health and Education, Gustavo Capanema', 22 April 1936, Rio de Janeiro: Arquivo Gustavo Capanema, CPDOC-FGV, 2009.

10. Ibid.

11. Gregory E. Jackson, Jr, 'Building the New Brazilian Man: Football, Public Policy and Eugenics, 1894–1950', Doctoral Dissertation, Stony Brook University, 2013.

12. George Reid Andrews, *Blacks and Whites in São Paulo, 1888–1988*. Madison: University of Wisconsin Press, 1989.

13. Roger Bastide and Florestan Fernandes, *Relações raciais entre negros e brancos em São Paulo; ensaio sociológico sôbre as origens, as manifestações e os efeitos do preconceito de côr no município de São Paulo*. São Paulo: Editôra Anhembi, 1955.

14. This view that football facilitated social mobility among the poor is told in many versions and in many sources; see Roberto Assaf, *Bangú: bairro operário, estação do futebol e do samba*. Rio de Janeiro: Relume Dumará, 2001.

15. Mario de Moraes (ed.), *Futebol é Arte: série depoimentos, Zizinho, Domingos da Guia, Pelé*, Vols I and II. Rio de Janeiro: Editorial, FAPERJ, 2002.

16. 'Deportes Olimpicos', *La Prensa*, Buenos Aires, 28–31 May and 10–12 June 1924.

17. 'Uruguay's Victory', *Buenos Aires Herald*, 5, 30 May 1924.

18. Martin Curi, 'Arthur Friedenreich, 1892–1969: A Brazilian Biography', in *Football in Brazil*. New York: Routledge, 2013.

19. Ibid.

20. Twine, *Racism in a Racial Democracy*.

21. Carlos Eduardo Sarmento, *A regra do jogo: uma história institucional da CBF*. Rio de Janeiro: FGV-CPDOC, 2006; and Antonio Carlos Napoleão and Roberto Assaf, *Seleção Brasileira, 1914–2006*. Rio de Janeiro: Mauad, 2006.

22. 'O Vasco da Gama joga hoje no Hespanha', *Jornal dos Sports*, 9, 18 March 1931.

23. Ibid.

24. See Robert Levine's *Father of the Poor?: Vargas and his Era*. Cambridge: Cambridge University Press, 1998 for a detailed account of letters written to Getúlio Vargas himself by ordinary Brazilians who sought his personal intervention in public matters.

25. 'A Suspensão da Aragão', *Jornal dos Sports*, 1 December 1932.

26. 'Platinese'—pertaining to the River Plate (Argentina and Uruguay).

27. 'A Suspensão da Aragão'.

28. Carlos Eduardo Sarmento, *A regra do jogo: uma história institucional da CBF*. Rio de Janeiro: FGV-CPDOC, 2006.

29. Ibid.

30. 'Nunca vi um delegação assim!', *Jornal dos Sports*, 20 December 1932.

31. 'Uma Consagraçao do Aos Heróes do Triplice Triumpho', *Jornal dos Sports*, 20 December 1932.

32. José Sergio Leite Lopes, 'Class, Ethnicity, and Color in the Making of Brazilian Football', *Daedalus*, 129, 2 (2000), pp. 239–70.

33. Mário Filho, *Copa Rio Branco 1932*. Rio de Janeiro: Pognetti, 1943.

34. 'Querem arrancar nossos cracks', *Jornal dos Sports*, 20 December 1932.

35. 'Nunca vi um delegação assim!'.

36. Marcos Eduardo Neves, *Nunca Houve Um Homen Como Heleno*. Rio de Janeiro: Ediouro, 2006.

37. José Lins do Rego, Preface to *Copa Rio Branco 1932*.

38. Bernardo Buarque de Hollanda, *O clube como vontage e representação*. Rio de Janeiro: Viveiros de Castro Editora Ltd, 2009.

39. 'Pacto da Pacifcacai dos Esportes nacionaes', Rolo, 42, 6 June 1934.

40. Sílvio Romero and João Batista de Lacerda, intellectuals of the First Republic, had both advanced a vision of whitening the celebrated positive outcomes of miscegenation over the next several generations. See Skidmore, *Black into White*, p. 65.

41. Antonio Jorge Soares, 'Futebol brasiliero e sociadade: a interpretaçao culturalista de Gilberto Freyre', in Pablo Alabarces (ed.), *Fubologias Fútbol, identidad y violencia en América Latina*, Buenos Aires: CLASCO, 2003.

42. Jackson, 'Building the New Brazilian Man'.

43. 'Projeito de Decreitos de Leis sobre Educação Fisica', 24 December 1937, Rio de Janeiro: Arquivo Gustavo Capanema, CPDOC-FGV.

44. Gregg P. Brocketti, 'Italian Immigrants'.

45. Carlos Eduardo Sarmento, *A regra do jogo: uma história institucional da CBF*.

46. 'Flag Day, Estadio São Januário', Rolo, 44, Rio de Janeiro, 19 November 1941, G.C.1936. 010.22.

47. 'Grande Propaganda do Brasil na Italia', *Jornal dos Sports*, 13, 8 May 1934.

48. Filho, *O negro no futebol brasiliero*.

49. André Ribero, O *Diamante Eterno: biografia de Leônidas da Silva*. São Paulo: Gryphus, 1999, pp. 131.

50. In 1931 Leônidas was involved in a prolonged feud with Clube América that exposed ugly racial and class tensions when the player reneged on his 'commitment' to play for the amateur club during the era of false amateurism.

51. Ribero, O *Diamante Eterno*.

52. Ibid.

53. Ibid.

54. Referring to the player's salary, which was worth several times the average salary of professionals in non-sport related fields from the era.

55. Geraldo Romualdo da Silva, 'os Monstrous Sagrados', *Jornal dos Sports*, 10 April 1942.

3. FOOTBALL IN THE RIO GRANDE DO SUL COAL MINES

1. A slightly different version of this chapter was published in Portuguese in the journal *Cadernos AEL* in 2011. This text is a summarised version of a chapter of my doctoral dissertation from 2010. I would like to thank José Sergio Leite Lopes, Antônio

H. Oswaldo Cruz, Paulo Fontes and Bernardo Buarque de Hollanda for their comments on previous versions of this chapter. In the construction of the text I also benefited from the contributions of the work groups in the anthropology of sport during the VII and VIII Mercosul Anthropology Meeting (RAM) in Porto Alegre, Rio Grande do Sul, Brazil in 2007; and in Buenos Aires, Argentina in 2009. Translated by Dr Eoin O'Neill, whom I also would like to thank for his fine work.

2. In relation to this question, the principal results are in Cioccari, Marta, 'Do gosto da mina, do jogo e da revolta: um estudo antropológico sobre a construção da honra em uma comunidade de mineiros de carvão', Doctoral dissertation, Programa de Pós-Graduação em Antropologia Social (PPGAS), Museu Nacional, Universidade Federal do Rio de Janeiro, Rio de Janeiro, 2010; and 'Mina de jogadores: o futebol operário e a construção da pequena honra', *Cadernos Arquivo Edgard Leuenroth* (UNICAMP), 16 (2011), pp. 76–115.

3. I can cite, amongst the studies carried out in Brazil, Rodrigues Filho, Mário, *O negro no futebol brasileiro*. Rio de Janeiro: Civilização Brasileira, 1964; Guedes, Simoni L., 'Subúrbio: celeiro de craques', in DaMatta, R. et al. (eds), *Universo do futebol: esporte e sociedade brasileira*. Rio de Janeiro: Pinakotheque, 1982, pp. 59–74; Leite Lopes, José Sergio, *A tecelagem dos conflitos de classe na cidade das chaminés*. São Paulo/Brasília: Ed. Marco Zero/Ed. UnB, 1988; Leite Lopes, José Sergio and Maresca, Sylvain, 'A morte da "alegria do povo"', *Revista Brasileira de Ciências Sociais*, 20, 7 (1992), pp. 113–34; Antunes, Fatima, 'O futebol nas fábricas', *Revista USP*, Dossiê Futebol, 22 (1994), pp. 102–9; Caldas, Waldenyr, 'Aspectos sociopolíticos do futebol brasileiro', *Revista USP*, Dossiê Futebol, 22 (1994), pp. 40–9; Rosenfeld, Anatol, *Negro, macumba e futebol*. São Paulo: Perspectiva, 2007. In other contexts, the research in Nash, June, *Comemos a las minas y las minas nos comem a nosotros: dependencia y explotación en las minas de estaño bolivianos*. Buenos Aires: Antropofagia, 2008; Fridenson, Patrick, 'Les ouvriers de l'automobile et le sport', *Actes de la Recherche en Sciences Sociales*, 79, 1 (1989), pp. 50–62; Walvin, James, *The People's Game*. Edinburgh: Mainstream Publishing, 1994; Lindner, Rolf and Breuer, Heinrich, 'SV Sodingen: le dernier club de banlieue', *Actes de la recherche en sciences sociales*, 103, 1 (1994), pp. 52–4; Bromberger, Christian, *Football, la bagatelle la plus sérieuse du monde*. Paris: Bayard Éditions, 1998; Renahy, Nicolas, 'De l'appartenance ouvrière à la réprésentation territoriale', *Ethnologie française*, 31, 4 (2001), pp. 707–15; and Fontaine, Marion, 'Sport, sociabilité et culture politiques en territoire lensois, 1936–1955', *Les cahiers du Centre de Recherches Historiques*, 31 (2003), available at http://ccrh.revues.org/index308. html, last accessed 5 Nov. 2008, are of importance.

4. Bromberger, *Football*, pp. 29–58.

5. In the meaning adopted in Bailey, *Frederick G.* (ed.), *Gifts and Poison: The Politics of Reputation*, Oxford: Blackwell, 1971.

6. In the analysis of honour, I draw on the studies of honour carried out in Andalusia, especially Pitt-Rivers, Julian, *Anthropologie de l'honneur: la mésaventure de Sichem*. Paris: Le Sycomore, 1983; and 'Honra e posição social', in Peristiany, J.G. (ed.), *Honra*

e vergonha: valores das sociedades mediterrâneas. Lisboa: Fundação Calouste Gulbenkian, 1965, pp. 13–59; and research about the different modalities of honour (see Gautheron, Marie (ed.), *A honra: imagem de si ou dom de si—um ideal equívoco.* Porto Alegre: LP&M, 1992).

7. In this part of Brazil, there was a hierarchy between '*varzeano*' (which literally means meadow or grass field) football teams without official registration, and '*amador*' (amateur) football, members of the Federação Gaúcha de Futebol (Gaúcha Football Federation). There was not necessarily any difference in the quality of '*varzeano*' and '*amador*' teams, though the amateur players may have had similar physical preparation to professional players, while '*varzeano*' teams invested less in physical preparation.

8. Until November 1960 the municipality of São Jerônimo consisted of the central district of the town itself and the districts of Arroio dos Ratos, Butiá and Barão do Triunfo. It now has eight districts: the central one, as well as Charqueadas, Arroio dos Ratos, Butiá, Leão, Morrinhos, Barão do Triunfo and Quitéria.

9. Eraldo died in November 2007, a few months after the interview.

10. Interview with Butiá.

11. The reason for the nickname by which he is known in the region.

12. Interview with Eraldo.

13. These divisions remind us of the celebrated study by Elias & Scotson (*Os estabelecidos e os outsiders.* Rio de Janeiro: Zahar, 2000) about insiders and outsiders. In Minas do Leão, the 'insiders' are in the town centre, although at the time most were as poor as those living in Recreio.

14. Interview with Butiá.

15. This was the original name of the team.

16. A second division football club in Rio Grande do Sul, created in 1919.

17. The 'basic reforms' were structural changes proposed by President João Goulart in the areas of education, agrarian, politics and taxation.

18. According to Brizola's statement on 25 October 1963, made on the Mayrink Veiga radio chain and registered in 'O Comunismo no Brasil', *Inquérito Policial Militar*, 709 (1967) p. 393. Brizola used metaphors from the world of football for the functioning of the groups. The members of each *grupo dos onze* were intended to be the soldiers who would form the ranks of the Exercito Popular de Libertação (Popular Liberation Army) with branches in each of the most important Brazilian states. An extreme nationalist, Brizola was aware of the organisation of forces opposed to the Goulart administration and sought to prevent the military coup. In the movement's short life, 5,304 *grupos dos onze* were formed with a potential army of 58,344 people, but these projects were interrupted by the military coup of 31 March 1964.

19. In relation to the organisation of the *grupos dos onze* and the political context at the time, see Ferreira, Jorge, 'A estratégia do confronto: a frente de mobilização popular', *Revista Brasileira de História*, 24, 47 (2004), pp. 181–212.

20. One of the principal bodies used in repression during the military regime in Brazil (1964–1985).

21. See Salem, Tânia, 'Tensões entre gêneros na classe popular: uma discussão com o paradigma holista', *Mana*, 12, 2 (2006), pp. 419–49.
22. A documentary produced by the Sport-TV television channel in November 2007 and shown in 2008. The production was based on the research about the miner-players in Minas do Leão.
23. Procópio Farinha, who worked for Estrada de Ferro do Jacuí, led a strike mobilising railway workers and miners. A member of the Brazilian Communist Party (Partido Comunista Brasileiro), he was arrested by the military regime in 1964, along with the miner Gerino Lucas.
24. A reference to the celebrated Brazilian football player Manuel Francisco dos Santos, Mané Garrincha, who was notable for his talent and disconcerting dribbles in the 1958 and 1962 World Cups.
25. In relation to the trajectory of Garrincha, see Leite Lopes's article in this book and Leite Lopes & Maresca, 'A morte da "alegria do povo"'.

4. *FUTEBOL DE VÁRZEA* AND THE WORKING CLASS: AMATEUR FOOTBALL CLUBS IN SÃO PAULO, 1940s–1960s

1. A shorter version of this chapter was published as "The Cradle of Brazilian Soccer: working-class history and *futebol de várzea*', *Re:Vista: Harvard Review of Latin America*, 9, 3 (2012), pp. 22–24.
2. For a report of this match see http://futbolleiros.blogspot.nl/2011/11/grande-final-14-copa-kaiser-de-futebol.html, last accessed 15 Nov. 2013.
3. See, for instance, the recently released film documentaries *Futebol de Várzea*, directed by Marc Dordin (2011); *Várzea: A bola rolada na beira do coração*, directed by Akins Kintê (2012); *Contos da Várzea*, directed by Diego Vinas (2012); and *Várzea: essência do futebol*, directed by Rodrigo Viana (2012). There are many specialist blogs and websites on amateur football. In 2013, the Museu do Futebol in São Paulo initiated a series of cultural events highlighting the importance of the amateur game in the city. A new version of the municipal championship of amateur football, the Kaizer Cup, has been contested since 1995 and, in 2013, had more than 1,100 teams participating.
4. See http://esporte.uol.com.br/futebol/campeonatos/copa-kaiser/ultimas-noti-cias/2012/03/07/tecnico-da-selecao-mano-menezes-vai-montar-dream-team-de-joga-dores-de-varzea.htm, last accessed 12 Nov. 2013.
5. On this, see the chapter in this volume by Clément Astruc.
6. The 'centre-periphery model' and its class segregation features were analysed by Kowarick, Lucio et al., *Social Struggles and the City: The Case of São Paulo*. New York: Monthly Review Press, 1994. See also Caldeira, Teresa, *City of Walls: Crime, Segregation and Citizenship in São Paulo*. Berkeley: University of California Press, 2000.
7. See Colistete, Renato, *Labour Relations and Industrial Performance in Brazil: Greater São Paulo, 1945–1960*. New York: Palgrave, 2001, especially chapter 1.
8. See, among others, Fontes, Paulo, *Um Nordeste em São Paulo. Trabalhadores Migrantes*

em São Miguel Paulista (1945–1966). Rio de Janeiro: Editora da FGV, 2008; Negro, Antonio Luigi, *Linhas de Montagem: o Industrialismo Nacional-Desenvolvimentista e a Sindicalização dos Trabalhadores (1945–1978)*. São Paulo: FAPESP: Boitempo Editorial, 2004; and Neto, Murilo Leal Pereira, *A Reinvenção da Classe Trabalhadora (1953–1964)*. Campinas: Editora da Unicamp, 2011.

9. One of the most important and controversial political figures in Brazilian history, Getúlio Vargas served twice as president, first from 1930 to 1945, and again from 1951 until his suicide in 1954. He was brought to power as the leader of the so-called 'Revolution of 1930'. In 1934, Vargas was indirectly elected president by the members of a constituent assembly that also drafted a new constitution. Three years later, with the support of the military, he led a coup that installed the 'Estado Novo' (New State), a corporatist dictatorship that lasted until 1945. Vargas favored nationalism, industrialisation, centralisation, social welfare and labour rights. In 1943, he promulgated a national labour code, which continued to regulate labour relations for many years after his death. Very popular, Vargas was elected president democratically in 1950. He was supported by nationalistic forces and by the majority of the trade unions, but his second administration was fiercely opposed by conservatives and a great part of the media, leading to his suicide in 1954.

10. The political rivals Adhemar de Barros and Jânio Quadros were the two most prominent politicians in the state of São Paulo between the end of World War II and the military coup in 1964. Barros was the leader of the Partido Social Progressista (PSP), very strong in São Paulo. He was elected governor in 1947, mayor of São Paulo city in 1957 and governor again in 1962. Jânio Quadros had a meteoric political career. He was elected consecutively councilman (1947), member of the State parliament (1950), mayor of São Paulo (1953), governor (1954), member of the federal parliament (1958) and president of Brazil (1960). After seven months in office, Quadros resigned the presidency in a very obscure and controversial political move. His resignation opened a political crisis in Brazil that would end up in the military coup of 1964.

11. There is a huge and diverse literature on populism. Among others, see Weffort, Francisco, *O Populismo na Política Brasileira*. Rio de Janeiro: Paz e Terra, 1980; French, John, *The Brazilian Workers' ABC: Class Conflict and Alliances in Modern São Paulo*. Chapel Hill: University of North Carolina Press, 1992; Gomes, Angela de Castro, *A Invenção do Trabalhismo*. Rio de Janeiro: Instituto Universitário de Pesquisas do Rio de Janeiro; São Paulo: Vértice, 1988; and Ferreira, Jorge (ed.), *O Populismo e sua História: Debate e Crítica*. Rio de Janeiro: Civilização Brasileira, 2001. For an analysis of the political presence of Adhemar de Barros and Jânio Quadros in the city of São Paulo, see Duarte, Adriano and Fontes, Paulo, 'O populismo visto da periferia: adhemarismo e janismo nos bairros da Mooca e São Miguel Paulista (1947–1953)', *Cadernos AEL*, 11, 20/21 (2004), pp. 83–125.

12. See Mainwaring, Scott, *The Catholic Church and Politics in Brazil, 1916–1985*. Stanford: Stanford University Press, 1986; Iffy, Catherine, *Transformar a Metrópole:*

igreja Católica, territórios e mobilizações sociais em São Paulo 1970–2000. São Paulo: Editora da Unesp, 2011; and Sader, Eder, *Quando Novos Personagens Entraram em Cena: experiências, falas e lutas dos Trabalhadores da Grande São Paulo (1970–80)*. Rio de Janeiro: Paz e Terra, 1988.

13. See, for instance, the case of the 1957 generalised strike in São Paulo in Fontes, Paulo, 'The strike of 400,000 and the workers' organisation in São Paulo, Brazil, 1957', *Socialist History*, 17 (2000), pp. 17–35; and Fontes, Paulo and Macedo, Francisco Barbosa, 'Strikes and Pickets in Brazil: Working-Class Mobilization in the "Old" and "New" Unionism, the Strikes of 1957 and 1980', *International Labor and Working Class History*, 83 (2013), pp. 86–111. See also many interesting examples in Neto, *A Reinvenção da Classe Trabalhadora*; and Duarte, Adriano, 'Cultura Popular e Cultura Política no Após-guerra. Redemocratização, Populismo e Desenvolvimentismo no Bairro da Mooca, 1942–1973', PhD thesis, History Department, UNICAMP, Campinas, 2002.

14. See Cavalcanti, Claudio, 'As Lutas e os Sonhos. Um Estudo Sobre os Trabalhadores de São Paulo nos Anos 30', PhD thesis, Department of Sociology, Universidade de São Paulo, 1996, pp. 265–6.

15. See Antunes, Fatima, *Futebol de Fábrica em São Paulo*, MSc thesis, Department of Sociology, Universidade de São Paulo, 1992; and the chapter in this volume by the same author.

16. Weinstein, Barbara, *For Social Peace in Brazil: Industrialists and the Remaking of the Working Class in São Paulo, 1920–1964*. Chapel Hill, University of North Carolina Press, 1996, pp. 258–9.

17. *Gazeta Esportiva*, 6 April 1955.

18. Augusti, Waldir Aparecido, *Memórias de Ermelino Matarazzo. Um Bairro Paulistano, seu Povo, sua Gente*. São Paulo: Edição do autor, 2012, pp. 90–1.

19. See Jesus, Gilmar Mascarenhas, 'Várzeas, Operários e Futebol: uma outra geografia', *GEOgraphia*, 4, 8 (2002); and Santos Neto, José Moraes dos, *Visão de Jogo: primórdios do futebol no Brasil*. São Paulo: Cosac Naify, 2002.

20. Bosi, Ecléa, *Memória e Sociedade. Lembrança de Velhos*. São Paulo: Cia das Letras, 1994.

21. Freitas Marcondes, J.V., 'Aspectos do trabalho e do lazer em São Paulo', in Marcondes, J.V. and Pimentel, Osmar, *São Paulo: espírito, povo, instituições*. São Paulo: Livraria Pioneira Editora, 1968, p. 358.

22. For the relation between neighborhoods and football in Buenos Aires see Frydenberg, Julio, 'Os bairros e o futebol na cidade de Buenos Aires de 1930', *Cadernos AE*, 16, 28 (2010), pp. 175–208. The connections between working-class and urban politics through amateur football in Santiago, Chile were recently studied in the excellent book by Elsey, Brenda, *Citizen and Sportsmen. Fútbol and Politics in 20ᵗʰ Century Chile*. Austin: University of Texas Press, 2011.

23. *Notícias de Hoje*, 7 February 1954. On the canalisation and rectification of the Tietê and Tamanduateí rivers, see Seabra, Odete, *Meandros dos Rios nos Meandros do Poder*.

Tietê e Pinheiros: valorização dos rios e das várzeas na cidade de São Paulo, PhD thesis, Department of Geography, Universidade de São Paulo, 1987.

24. See Fontes, *Um Nordeste em São Paulo*, p. 149.

25. On the changes and geographical dislocations of working-class sociability see Duarte, 'Cultura Popular e Cultura Politica' for the case of the more central district of Mooca. On the lack of pitches and the main demands of peripheral clubs, see Hirata, Daniel, 'No meio do campo: o que está em jogo no futebol de várzea?', in Telles, Vera and Cabanes, Robert (eds), *Nas Tramas da Cidade. Trajetórias Urbanas e seus Territórios*. São Paulo: Humanitas, 2007. The survey about the current number of amateur football pitches in the city of São Paulo can be seen at 'Onde estão os campos de várzea de São Paulo' in http://esporte.uol.com.br/infograficos/2013/04/19/campos-de-varzea.htm, last accessed 24 June 2013.

26. Carrascoza, João Anzanello, et al., *A História do Tigre da Cantareira. Edição histórica ilustrada dos 75 anos do Lausanne Paulista F.C.* São Paulo: Edição do autor, 2002. p. 16.

27. Silva, Diana Mendes Machado, 'A Associação Atlética Anhanguera: imigração, associativismo e futebol de várzea na cidade de São Paulo (1928–1939)', Master thesis, Department of History, Universidade de São Paulo, 2013, pp. 51, 59; and Vicentini, Walter Scott, *O Segundo Chute*. São Paulo: Studio Art, 2005 p. 125.

28. Ibid., p. 76.

29. See Siqueira, Uassyr, *Clubes e Sociedades de Trabalhadores do Bom Retiro: organização, lutas e lazer em um bairro paulistano (1915–1924)*, Master thesis, Department of History, Universidade Estadual de Campinas, 2002, p. 70. For a pioneering analysis on the connections between popular leisure and local belonging in the case of São Paulo, see Magnani, José Guilherme, *Festa no Pedaço: cultura popular e lazer na cidade*. São Paulo: Editora Hucitec, 1998.

30. Interview with Maria Jensen, 20 April 2000, Archives of Universidade Cruzeiro do Sul.

31. Interview with Dino Sani, 3 June 2011, Project Futebol, Memória e Patrimônio, CPDOC/FGV and Museu do Futebol, São Paulo. See http://cpdoc.fgv.br/museu-dofutebol/dinosani#Transcricao, last accessed 28 June 2013.

32. Interview with Isidoro Del Vechio, 12 May 2000, conducted by Adriano Duarte. I thank Professor Duarte for allowing me to consult the interviews he has conducted for his research on neighbourhood organisations.

33. See Cavalcanti, 'As Lutas e os Sonhos', p. 268; Duarte, *Cultura popular e cultura política*, pp. 100–110; Siqueira, *Clubes e Sociedades*, pp. 97, 108; Witter, José Sebastião, 'Futebol: várzea e cidade de São Paulo', in *Estudo de Tombamento do Parque do Povo*. São Paulo: Condephaat, 1994; and Silva, 'A Associação Atlética Anhanguera', p. 70. For the match 'black people vs white people', see the documentary film *Preto Contra Branco* (2004) by Wagner Morales and the article by Schwarcz, Lilia, 'Pretos contra brancos ou dando e mudando nomes', in Cabral, João de Pina and Viegas, Susana de Matos (eds), *Nomes: Gênero, Etnicidade e Família*, Lisboa: Almedina, 2007.

NOTES

34. See Fontes, Paulo, *Um Nordeste em São Paulo*, p. 150.

35. Siqueira, *Clubes e Sociedades*, p. 101.

36. Silva, 'A Associação Atlética Anhanguera', pp. 118–22.

37. Duarte, *Cultura popular e cultura política*, p. 101; Seabra, Odete, 'Urbanização, bairro e vida de bairro', *Travessia*, 13, 38 (2000); and Jesus, 'Várzeas, Operários e Futebol', p. 6.

38. See Duarte, Adriano, 'Neighborhood Association, Social Movements, and Populism in Brazil, 1945–1953', *Hispanic Historical American Review*, 89 (2009).

39. Interviews with Waldomiro Macedo, 23 May 2000 and Nelson Bernardo, 7 August 2001 conducted by the author, Raimundo de Menezes Library. Interview with Isidoro Del Vechio 2 May 2000, conducted by Adriano Duarte.

40. See, as an example, Aesp, Deops sector (social and political police), Dossiers 30-C-1, fls.1.641 and the studies of Fontes, *Um Nordeste em São Paulo*; Fontes and Macedo, 'Strikes and Pickets in Brazil'; and Neto, *A Reinvenção da Classe Trabalhadora*.

41. Aesp, Deops sector (social and political police), Dossier 50-Z-591, fls.57.

42. Dias, Eduardo, *Um Imigrante e a Revolução. Memórias de um Militante Operário, 1934–1951*. São Paulo: Editora Brasiliense, 1983, pp. 60–1.

43. Interview with João Louzada, 6 November 1998, conducted by Adriano Duarte.

44. Vicentini, *O Segundo Chute*, p. 169.

45. Interview with Nelson Bernardo, 7 August 2001 conducted by the author, Raimundo de Menezes Library.

46. Vicentini, *O Segundo Chute*, p. 26.

5. THE 'PEOPLE'S JOY' VANISHES: CONSIDERATIONS ON THE DEATH OF GARRINCHA

1. Translated from Portuguese by Paulo Henriques Britto. Early versions of this chapter were published in French in *Actes de la Recherche en Sciences Sociales*, 79 (1989), with the collaboration of Sylvain Maresca; and in Portuguese at *Revista Brasileira de Ciências Sociais*, 20 (1992); as well as in English in *The Journal of Latin American Anthropology*, 4, 2/5, 1 (1999–2000), pp. 78–105.

2. Elza Soares supported Garrincha in the phase of decline of his football career and his deepest period of alcoholism. They lived together for fifteen years (1962–77), in which they had a son, they adopted a daughter and they lived abroad, in Rome.

3. In Brazil, it is quite common that fire engines carry victorious athletes in celebration parades after important sporting victories, such as a football World Cup title or winning a golden medal in an Olympic Games. Fire engines also sometimes transport the coffins of popular politicians, sports people and celebrities in general in farewell parades, as in the case of Garrincha.

4. On this new generation of players and their concern for the situation of footballers, see Ricardo Benzaquem de Araújo, 'Os Gênios da Pelota; um estudo do futebol como profissão', MA dissertation in social anthropology, Museu Nacional—UFRJ, Rio de Janeiro, 1980.

5. In fact, most of these people were entirely unrelated to the population of the region at the time when Garrincha lived there: since then, the inhabitants of the old workers' communities such as Pau Grande had been surrounded by a peripheral proletarian population located in new precarious neighbourhoods.

6. A heavy summer rainstorm fell soon after and washed away all the earth that covered the coffin. A few days later Nilton Santos read about this in the papers and returned to the Pau Grande cemetery to solve the problem.

7. I have drawn freely from Duby's (1984) analysis of the burial of Guillaume le Maréchal and the subsequent creation of the *chanson de geste* in his homage.

8. A *cronista* is a writer of *crônicas*, a literary form native to Brazil. The *crônica* is a short piece, typically published as a newspaper or magazine column that ranges freely from human-interest reporting to lyrical prose.

9. See Simoni Guedes's study of the lives of workers who had experience in neighbourhood soccer and professional sport in the Bangu workers' housing development: 'Subúrbio: celeiro de craques', in: DaMatta, R. et al., *Universo do Futebol*. Rio de Janeiro: Pinakotheque, 1982, pp. 59–74.

10. *Jornal do Brasil*, 21 January 1983.

11. Though a more detailed comparison with Pelé will be made later, for the moment it should be stressed that the styles of the two players were quite different. Garrincha used an 'ambush' strategy, out of the corners, while Pelé adopted a 'Light Brigade' approach, attacking down the centre of the field, facing his opponents always in full motion, using his impetus to outrun them, on the verge of falling.

12. Armando Nogueira, 'Mundo velho sem porteira', *Jornal do Brasil*, 23 January 1983.

13. One cannot be quite sure that he enjoyed himself as much as the audience. 'The look on Garrincha's face was serious, even stern. And the more people laughed, the sterner his expression, as if he could not understand what was going on, or understood it less than anyone else. This explains why he was never attacked. Any other player who tried to pull that sort of trick would never attempt it again: he would certainly be punched in the face. Many a player, after being made to fall by Garrincha, got up with a mind to fight, but was disarmed when he realised that Garrincha seemed awkward, humble, almost apologetic. The only thing to do was to keep on playing, and try once more, uselessly, to take the ball away from Garrincha, only to fall once again, legs flying, raising guffaws from the crowd', Mário Filho, *O negro no futebol brasileiro*. Rio de Janeiro, Civilização Brasileira, 1964, p. 384. Garrincha's deadpan seriousness suggests a comparison not with Chaplin but with Buster Keaton, 'the man who never smiles'—a comparison further encouraged by Garrincha's melancholy decline.

14. 'The Soviet player Boris Kuztnetsev went down in history, on 15 June 1958, as the first 'João' [John] in Garrincha's career. From then on, 'João' was the name of every opponent covering him. They were all interchangeable, whatever their team or nationality, and none of them were able to stop Garrincha', *Folha de S. Paulo*, 20 January 1984. In this case, the press was merely picking up and popularising a

term used by Garrincha himself, with which he expressed his indifference to football schemes and rivalries between players. The first 'João' in his career was actually Nilton Santos, whom he made fun of when he was being tested in Botafogo.

15. See DaMatta et al., *Universo do Futebol*, pp. 31–2. These studies coordinated by DaMatta analyse the social specificity of soccer which is, according to these authors, a dramatisation of Brazilian society, underscoring some of its aspects and downplaying others.

16. Here I am indebted to Guedes's (1993) analysis of the literature in 'O "povo brasileiro" no campo de futebol', *À Margem; Revista de Ciências Humanas* (1993).

17. On the social history of soccer in Brazil, see Mário Filho's *O negro no futebol brasileiro*, a book written in 1947, with a preface by Gilberto Freyre, and completed in 1964 to include the changes brought about by the 1950, 1954, 1958, and 1962 World Cups. See also Lever, Janet, *Soccer Madness*. Chicago & London: The University of Chicago Press, 1983; and Santos, Joel R. dos, *História Política do Futebol Brasileiro*. São Paulo: Brasiliense, 1981.

18. Many of the country's approximately 300 textile mills (as well as other kinds of factories) in the 1940s (when Garrincha was a boy) included housing for workers, and a large number of them were in rural districts or outlying suburbs. In Magé alone, in addition to América Fabril (with 1,200 workers at the time) there were three other textile mills.

19. See Willis, Paul, 'L'école des ouvriers', *Actes de la Recherche en Sciences Sociales*, 24 (1978), pp. 50–61; Leite Lopes, J. Sergio, *A tecelagem dos conflitos de classe na cidade das chaminés* [The weaving of class conflict in 'Chimneys' city']. São Paulo/Brasília: Marco Zero/Editora da UnB, 1988, ch.2; and Alvim, Rosilene & Leite Lopes, J. Sergio, 'Familles Ouvrières, Familles d'Ouvrières', *Actes de la Recherche en Sciences Sociales*, 84 (1990), pp. 78–84.

20. Companies often tampered with workers' birth certificates, with the help of local notaries. In other textile mills, certificates were forged so that boys under fourteen could be admitted, a violation of the law that was countenanced by parents. See Alvim, Rosilene, 'Constituição da Família e Trabalho Industrial', PhD thesis, Museu Nacional, Rio de Janeiro, 1985, ch.5.

21. Incidentally, the president of the Pau Grande Football Club was the head of Garrincha's department.

22. *Garrincha* is a Northeastern term (many working-class families in Pau Grande came from the Northeast, including Garrincha's) for a bird known in Rio by a different name. The term was so unfamiliar that in 1953 sportswriters tried to change the young player's moniker to 'Gualicho', the name of a horse that had just won Brazil's major race. But unlike his real name, which was modified by the factory, his nickname survived all newspapermen's attempts to tamper with it.

23. These supplementary activities are treated as paradoxical 'independent' work or 'accessory occupations' of workers living in company housing developments in Leite Lopes, J. Sergio & Machado da Silva, L.A., 'Introdução: estratégias de trabalho, for-

mas de dominação na produção e subordinação doméstica de trabalhadores urba-nos', in Leite Lopes, J. Sergio et al., *Mudança Social no Nordeste: a reprodução da subordinação*. Rio de Janeiro: Paz e Terra, 1979, pp. 16–17; and in Alvim & Leite Lopes, 'Familles Ouvrières, Familles d'Ouvrières'. Weber, Florence, *Le travail à côté; Étude d'ethnographie ouvrière*. Paris: Ed. EHESS/INRA, 1989 relied on the native category '*travail à côté*', used by French workers in her study of such activities in contemporary France.

24. Leite Lopes, *A tecelagem dos conflitos*, chs. 3 and 11.

25. *Garrincha, alegria do povo* begins with scenes of working-class children and youths playing informal soccer matches in the street, on vacant lots, on Copacabana Beach, as if Garrincha were the ultimate expression of the popular passion for playing soc-cer in any circumstances. A passage from Lever, *Soccer Madness*, p. 137 stresses this populist view, reducing the starting-point and the end of Garrincha's career to what she calls 'the slum', an umbrella term for any poor neighbourhood.

26. See Filho, *O negro no futebol brasileiro*, p. 390.

27. See Bourdieu, Pierre, 'Remarques provisoires sur la perception sociale du corps', *Actes de la Recherche en Sciences Sociales*, 14 (1977), pp. 51–4.

28. Garrincha signed his contracts before they were filled out, and was paid about half of what the other major players in the team were earning.

29. For information on Pelé's early life I have drawn on Filho, *O negro no futebol brasileiro*.

30. The now-famous epithet was the title of the first movie about Pelé, made by Carlos Hugo Christensen soon after Joaquim Pedro de Andrade directed his portrait of Garrincha.

31. See Hoggart, Richard, *The Uses of Literacy*. Harmondsworth, Penguin Books, 1969, ch.5.

32. In the late 1970s, one of Garrincha's illegitimate children came from Sweden to visit him.

33. See Guedes, 'Subúrbio: celeiro de craques'.

34. As convincing, pliable raw material, Garrincha was much more attractive than Pelé to this sort of intellectual and artistic consideration of the working classes. The two films on Pelé are not even mentioned in the catalogue of the Brazilian film retro-spective presented at the Centre Pompidou in 1987 (see Paranaguá, Paulo, *Le cin-ema brésilien*. Paris: Centre Georges Pompidou, 1987). *Garrincha, alegria do povo*, however, is praised as 'certainly one of the most intelligent Brazilian films about soc-cer ever made, for the multiple interpretations it suggests', as well as for the realis-tic innovativeness that makes it 'a new phenomenon in Brazilian cinema: the language of the streets is heard in the movie' (p. 170).

35. It would be necessary to place in a wider perspective the changes experienced by the working classes in the last thirty years in order to establish the social significance of these new forms of organised support to soccer teams. For some ethnographic data and explanations on the organised fans of Rio and São Paulo teams, see Lever, *Soccer Madness*, ch.5; and Toledo, Luís Henrique de, *Torcidas Organizadas de Futebol*. Campinas: Autores Associados/ANPOCS, 1996.

36. Between 1940 and the present, the 1950s were the decade in which real minimum wages were the highest.

6. FOOTBALL AS A PROFESSION: ORIGINS, SOCIAL MOBILITY AND THE WORLD OF WORK OF BRAZILIAN FOOTBALLERS, 1950s–1980s

1. This chapter has been written thanks to a research grant from the Réseau Français d'Etudes Brésiliennes (REFEB).
2. Morro do Alemão, a favela neighbourhood in northern Rio de Janeiro.
3. *Futebol*, first episode: 'O sonho', directed by Fontes, Arthur and João Moreira Salles. Rio de Janeiro: Vídeo Filmes, 1998. Translations in this chapter are mine.
4. Filho, Mário, *O negro no futebol brasileiro*. Rio de Janeiro: Mauad Ed./FAPERJ, 2003. The first edition of this book was published in 1947 by Pongetti Editores (Rio de Janeiro).
5. The Gold Law abolished slavery in Brazil in 1888 but the situation of black people during the next decades (especially until 1930) was particularly precarious because their social position did not enable them to benefit from the economical growth and the new opportunities it brought, Fernandes, Florestan, *O negro no mundo dos brancos*. São Paulo: Global Editora, 2nd edn, 2007, pp. 64–8.
6. Pereira, Leonardo Affonso de Miranda, *Footballmania. Uma história social do futebol no Rio de Janeiro, 1902–1938*. Rio de Janeiro: Editora Nova Fronteira, 2000.
7. Pereira, *Footballmania*, p. 325.
8. For a detailed reflection on the peculiarity of professional sportsmen's status, see Fleuriel, Sébastien and Manuel Schotté, *Sportifs en danger. La condition des travailleurs sportifs*. Bellecombes en Bauge: éditions du Croquant, 2008.
9. Bertrand, Julien, *La fabrique des footballeurs*. Paris: La Dispute, 2012, p. 11–12. This author highlighted how concepts such as passion and vocation are important for young people willing to turn professional.
10. In his study of Afonsinho's case, José Paulo Florenzano showed how *cartolas* often referred to amateur principles to defend their own interests, Florenzano, J.P., *Afonsinho e Edmundo: a rebeldia no futebol brasileiro*. São Paulo: Musa Editora, 1998, p. 46–7.
11. These oral sources, which are referred to throughout this chapter, were gathered between 2011 and 2012 by the Centro de Pesquisa em História Contemporânea do Brasil (CPDOC)—a research unit of the Fundação Getúlio Vargas—and the Museu do Futebol in São Paulo during a programme called 'Futebol, Memória e Patrimônio'. For further information, see the CPDOC's website (http://cpdoc.fgv.br/ museudofutebol).
12. Leite Lopes, J.S., 'Classe, etnicidade e cor na formação do futebol brasileiro', in Batalha, Cláudio, Fernando T.d. Silva and Alexandre Fortes (eds), *Culturas de classe: identidade e diversidade na formação do operariado*. Campinas: UNICAMP, 2004, p. 152–3. Few researches about footballers' history have focused on the immediate

post-1945 decades. Most of the analysis deals with the 1920s and 1930s or with the last decades of the twentieth century (from 1970). Since 1970, a wide process of modernisation of Brazilian football and new international dynamics drastically changed some features of the profession. For further information, see Florenzano, *Afonsinho e Edmundo*; Leite Lopes, J.S., 'Considerações em torno das transformações do profissionalismo no futebol a partir da observação da Copa de 1998', *Estudos Históricos*, 1, 23 (1999), pp. 170–90; Toledo, L.H., *Lógicas no futebol*. São Paulo: Hucitec, 2000; Damo, S.A., *Do dom à profissão: formação de futebolistas no Brasil e na França*. São Paulo: Hucitec, 2007; and Rodrigues, F.X.F., 'O fim do passe e a modernização conservadora no futebol brasileiro (2001–2006)', Doctoral thesis in sociology, Universidade Federal do Rio Grande do Sul, 2007.

13. The *seleção* is the Brazilian national team. See the decree no. 53.820 (1964), the law no. 6.269 (1975) and the law no. 6.354 (1976).

14. Araújo, Ricardo B., 'Os gênios da pelota, um estudo do futebol como profissão', Master's dissertation, Universidade Federal de Rio de Janeiro (UFRJ)/Museu Nacional, 1980. See Chapter One: 'Cálculo e prazer'. This research is based on the testimonies of eight football players who defined themselves as coming from the middle class.

15. The differences observed could be related to numerous factors. First, the individuals interviewed by researchers of CPDOC's and by the Museu do Futebol chose this occupation at an earlier time, when footballers' wages were probably lower. Secondly, their origins and opportunities of inclusion in the labour market were different. Then, the researchers' questions were not focused on that aspect of the players' life. Lastly, their testimony was recorded some decades after the end of their careers.

16. Astruc, Clément, 'Parcours de footballeurs. Récits, nature et diversité des trajectoires sociales et professionnelles des joueurs de l'élite du football brésilien des années 1950 aux années 1980', Master's dissertation, Ecole Normale Supérieure de Lyon, 2013, pp. 75–81.

17. See, for example, Amarildo's and Piazza's testimonies, Astruc, 'Parcours de footballeurs', pp. 60–4.

18. Chance and uncertainty are central in the working environment of footballers. For example, their selection in a competitive team is often related to a stroke of luck, Astruc, 'Parcours de footballeurs', p. 64. Other decisive aspects of their careers such as injuries or their collective team's performance hardly depend on them.

19. Ado's testimony. Part of the testimonies are on CPDOC's website.

20. Caldas, Waldenyr, *O pontapé inicial: memória do futebol brasileiro (1894–1933)*. São Paulo: Instituição Brasileira de Difusão Cultural, 1990, pp. 51–2.

21. Approximately one-third of the interviewees said that at least one of his parents had a hostile reaction or showed reluctance when he started to dedicate himself to football or announced his choice of occupation. I am unable to provide more precise data because classifying parents' reaction was barely possible sometimes. First, their attitude towards their son's orientation could change over time. Secondly, some wit-

nesses did not give an opinion. Then, as all the individuals interviewed finally became professional, the study excluded potential cases of youth wanting to do this job but who were prevented to do so by their parents. Finally, even some players whose family backed them mentioned footballers' bad reputation.

22. The *malandro* is a likeable urban figure in Brazilian society linked to non-conformist and mixed-race circles. He lives by his wits, can be something of a con-artist and is dismissive of established social conventions, Schwarcz, Lilia Moritz, *Nem preto nem branco, muito pelo contrário*. São Paulo: Claro Enigma, 2012, pp. 59–60.

23. Carlos Alberto Torres's testimony.

24. Joel Camargo's testimony.

25. Pepe's testimony.

26. According to Waldir Peres's and Lima's testimonies, footballers had the reputation of going out excessively, drinking and frequenting prostitutes.

27. Marinho Peres's testimony. In this extract, Marinho referred to Brazil's third victory in the 1970 World Cup tournament.

28. The striker Dadá embodies this social figure. He related that his mother committed suicide when he was very young and that he had been cared for in a public children's home, created under the Getúlio Vargas government in 1941, called the Serviço de Assistência aos Menores. Describing his youth, he mentioned juvenile crime and precariousness, linking his start in football to an immediate necessity: 'And I did not start for fun, no, I started, as I told you, for a plate of food', Dadá's testimony.

29. Fifteen out of forty-three players mentioned a previous working experience while some witnesses were not asked about it. More than two out of three players became professional between seventeen and nineteen years old.

30. Jair da Costa's testimony. He was hired to work for Cobrasma and to play in the company team.

31. This analysis is based on the footballers' accounts. Some did not mention their parents' job and others employed evasive language, or indicated for which company their father or mother worked but did not specify what their position was. Twelve of the sportsmen said that their mother worked outside the home, while one performed work at home. As a consequence, I provide indications about this population rather than offer an exhaustive sociological profile.

32. Two played for the Brazilian national team and the others had a more modest career. One of them continued working as a tailor following his career in football.

33. By comparison, Wahl and Lanfranchi established that in France since the 1970s a reproduction phenomenon could be observed among football players. In 1991, 5 per cent of professional footballers were the sons of professional players, Wahl, Alfred and Pierre Lanfranchi, *Les footballeurs professionnels: des années trente à nos jours*. Paris: Hachette, 1995, pp. 210–11 and 237–9.

34. See Araújo, 'Os gênios da pelota', ch.2: 'Arte e ofício'; and Damo, *Do dom à profissão*, ch.6: 'O espectro do dom'.

35. See Astruc, 'Parcours de footballeurs', ch.2.

36. Novais, Fernando and João Manuel Cardoso de Mello, 'Capitalismo tardio e socia-bilidade moderna', in Novais, Fernando and Lilia Moritz Schwarcz (eds), *História da vida privada no Brasil. Contrastes e intimidade contemporânea*, vol.IV. São Paulo: Companhia das Letras, 1998, pp. 560–4 and 618–20. The growth of the Brazilian economy accelerated between the 1950s and the late 1970s, but significant changes occurred after 1964. The military dictatorship involved a change in economic policy that had major social consequences including a lower minimum wage. Due to the growth in their numbers, jobs that had previously been considered semi-skilled were depreciated. Generally speaking, the dynamism of the Brazilian economy between 1964 and the late 1970s led to the creation of new opportunities of employment; nonetheless, this spectacular growth did not generate a proportional income increase for the majority of workers but deepened socioeconomic inequalities.

37. Novais and Cardoso de Mello, 'Capitalismo tardio', pp. 585–6.

38. Valdomiro's testimony.

39. Ibid.

40. Alfredo Mostarda's testimony. This professional training was free.

41. José Baldocchi's testimony.

42. Fernandes, *O negro no mundo dos brancos*.

43. Novais and Cardoso de Mello, 'Capitalismo tardio', pp. 583–4 and 598–9.

44. I based my conclusions of the racial breakdown of the interviewees by examining photographs, which can only provide a general indication of the proportion who were black or of mixed race. Racial categories and the person who attributes them—for example, the researcher—have varied over time in the history of Brazilian statistics. More generally speaking, what determines the affiliation to one group or another in Brazil is skin colour and facial features more than the origins. But this attribution is dynamic and also integrates social considerations: one could get 'whiter' due to his/her social status (if he/she gets rich or has superior education for instance), Schwarcz, *Nem preto nem branco*, pp. 97–106.

45. Carlos Maranhão, 'A profissão dos pobres', *Placar*, 300 (1975), pp. 3–8.

46. Investment in real estate is often mentioned in the players' accounts. They are a good indicator of social ascension because these investments often benefited an entire family, especially the parents, while *fugir do aluguel* (avoid renting) was a preoccupation of all the salaried employees, especially those on low wages, Novais and Cardoso de Mello, 'Capitalismo tardio', p. 601. These properties were also part of an economical strategy directed at the constitution of a private income. For this aspect, see in particular Carlos Alberto's testimony.

47. These investments—real estate, shares, and bills of exchange—were brought up as the good way of spending the money rapidly earned thanks to football by professional players at the end of the 1970s, Araújo, 'Os gênios da pelota', pp. 7–11.

48. 'Profissão: jogador', *Placar*, 80 (1971), pp. 6–11.

49. Leite Lopes, 'Classe, etnicidade', pp. 152–6.

50. The notion of domination has been central to much social science research; many

authors have conceptualised it (Marx, Marcuse, Foucault, Bourdieu, for instance) and it has been used to study various kinds of relationships (between classes, sexes, colonisers and colonised people). Here, in the context of the relationship between employer and employee, 'dominated' should be understood in the common sense of the word and indicates people who do not fully dispose of themselves, who often cannot make sovereign decisions regarding their own careers.

51. Mirandinha's testimony.

52. In relation to this profession at the beginning of the twenty-first century, Damo wrote: 'There are few social spaces nowadays that transform, without ethical restrictions, people into objects as does football', Damo, *Do dom à profissão*, p. 68.

53. César Lemos's testimony.

54. Paraná's testimony.

55. Preamble to the decree no. 53.820 from 24 March 1964.

56. The retain-and-transfer system was created in England in the early 1890s. For further information, see Taylor, Matthew, *The Leaguers: The Making of Professional Football in England, 1900–1939.* Liverpool: Liverpool University Press, 2005, pp. 98–101.

57. Araújo, 'Os gênios da pelota', p. 75.

58. See for instance the statements of Flamengo's president in *Passe livre*, a documentary directed by Oswaldo Caldeira (Filmes da Matriz and Oswaldo Caldeira Prod. Cinematográficas, 1974); and the words of the *cartola* Felisberto Pinto Filho in *Placar*, 94, 31 (1971), p. 37.

59. Decree no. 53.820, from 24 March 1964 and law no. 6.354, from 2 September 1976.

60. The Pelé Law abolished the *passe*. For further information about this text and the changes it generated in Brazilian footballers' world of work, see Rodrigues, 'O fim do passe'.

61. Araújo, 'Os gênios da pelota', p. 75. See also the comparison made by Florenzano between industrial workers and football players, his conclusion being that: '[…] through the *passe* mechanism the club appropriated the players' bodies and in this way guaranteed their domination', Florenzano, *Afonsinho e Edmundo*, p. 102.

62. 'O passe no banco dos réus' [The *passe* in the dock], *Placar*, 93 (1971), pp. 18–19.

63. See for, example, 'Lei do passe. Lei de cão' [The law of *passe*. A law for dogs], *Placar*, 63 (1971), pp. 16–17. The comparison between football players and slaves was not specific of Brazil. For instance, this connection has also been made in France, Wahl and Lanfranchi, *Les footballeurs professionnels*, p. 147.

64. Indio's testimony.

65. The *cartolas* were described by some players and journalists as being dishonest and abusive managers, Araújo, 'Os gênios da pelota', pp. 70–4; 'O lamentável mundo dos cartolas' [The deplorable world of the managers], *Placar*, 20 (1970), pp. 15–17.

66. In his analysis, Leite Lopes uses the notion of habitus. For further information, see his chapter in this volume.

67. *Diário de Noticias*, 10 Aug. 1973, p. 19; and *Placar*, 181 (1973), pp. 3–4.

68. *Diário de Noticias*, 10 Aug. 1973, p. 19 and 11 Aug. 1973, p. 19.

69. *Placar*, 182 (1973), pp. 10–11.

70. *Jornal do Brasil*, 16 Feb. 1974, p. 23.

71. *Diário de Noticias*, 23 Oct. 1975, p. 15.

72. *Diário de Noticias*, 24 Oct. 1975, p. 15 and 24 Dec. 1975, p. 16.

73. José Guilherme Baldocchi's testimony.

74. *Placar*, 352, (1976), p. 10.

75. According to a paragraph published in *Placar*, 775 (1985), p. 54.

76. Florenzano, *Afonsinho e Edmundo*, pp. 85–105.

77. Similar cases existed in the 1970s, Florenzano, *Afonsinho e Edmundo*, pp. 106–7.

78. Baldocchi's testimony; Florenzano, *Afonsinho e Edmundo*, pp. 118–19.

79. According to Florenzano, Afonsinho is a figure of players' resistance against the modernisation of Brazilian football, notably characterised by a growing will to discipline footballers' life, including their private life, ibid.

80. The National Federation of Professional Athletes (Federação Nacional dos Atletas Profissionais de Futebol; FENAPAF) was created in 1990.

81. *Placar*, 63 (1971), p. 17.

82. *Placar*, 90 (1971), p. 10.

83. See Gérson's testimony and Pelé's interview in *Placar*, 90 (1971), p. 10. It is to be noted that the military government increased the regulation of the profession of footballer: a law of 1975 (no. 6.269) created a fund—the Fundo de Assistência ao Altleta Profissional—intended to help sportsmen succeed in their occupational reconversion; then, a law of 1976 (no. 6.354) was passed to determine the working conditions of professional athletes.

84. *Placar*, 29 (1970), p. 33.

85. *Placar*, 459 (1979), p. 7.

86. *Placar*, 584 (1981), p. 21.

87. *Placar*, 719 (1984), p. 22.

88. *Placar*, 387 (1977), pp. 19–20 and 501 (1979), p. 9. The Foundation of Guarantee of the Professional Athlete (FUGAP) has existed since 1963 but was not a trade union. I found mentions of two former trade unions—the Sindicato dos Jogadores Profissionais da Guanabara and the Sindicato de Empregados de Confederações Desportivas—but the organisation created in 1979 seems to be the first independent and significant trade union of football players in the state.

89. *Placar*, 684 (1983), p. 50.

90. *Placar*, 724 (1984), p. 46 and 926 (1988), p. 51.

91. Waldir Peres's testimony.

92. Astruc, 'Parcours de footballeurs', ch.3.

93. Araújo, 'Os gênios da pelota', in particular p. 81.

NOTES

7. DICTATORSHIP, RE-DEMOCRATISATION AND BRAZILIAN FOOTBALL IN THE 1970s AND 1980s

1. 'Costa: governo procurou apoio político e foi traído', *O Estado de S. Paulo*, 28 December 1968.
2. Gramsci, A., *Cadernos do cárcere*, vol. III, *Maquiavel. Notas sobre o Estado e a Política*. Rio de Janeiro: Civilização Brasileira, 2000, p. 73.
3. 'Os craques vão às urnas', *Placar*, 601 (1981).
4. Rosanvallon, P., *L'age de l'autogestion*. Paris: Seuil, 1976.
5. 'Paraná abre Olimpíada', *O Estado de S. Paulo*, 4 April 1970.
6. Thomaz, O.R., *Ecos do Atlântico Sul*. Rio de Janeiro: URFJ/FAPESP, 2002.
7. 'Cariocas e mineiros abrem Olimpíada', and 'Começam os jogos militares', *O Estado de S. Paulo*, 3 June 1971.
8. Almeida, A.T.S. de, *O regime militar em festa*. Rio de Janeiro: Apicuri/FAPERJ, 2013, p. 187.
9. 'Médici instala jogos militares', *O Estado de S. Paulo*, 26 April 1972.
10. 'Exército fecha sua Olimpíada', *O Estado de S. Paulo*, 8 April 1973.
11. 'Ô Olimpíadas do Exército', *O Estado de S. Paulo*, 23 April 1974.
12. 'Até índios festejam a independência', *O Estado de S. Paulo*, 3 September 1969.
13. 'A missão', caderno *Ilustríssima*, *Folha de S. Paulo*, 11 November 2012.
14. '90 índios juram fidelidade ao País', *O Estado de S. Paulo*, 5 February 1970.
15. 'A missão', caderno *Ilustríssima*, *Folha de S. Paulo*, 11 November 2012; Gorender, J., *Combate nas trevas*. São Paulo: Ática, 1998, p. 258.
16. 'A Funai quer logo o índio aculturado', *O Estado de S. Paulo*, 1 May 1971.
17. The expression *Brasil Grande* was used in political advertisements during the 1964 military dictatorship. It proclaimed the regime's economic and geopolitical aspirations to turn Brazil in a global superpower.
18. 'O mito do genocídio índio', João de Almada, *O Estado de S. Paulo*, 1 October 1972.
19. 'Acusada a Guarda Indígena', *O Estado de S. Paulo*, 7 June 1971.
20. Vianna, F. de L.B., *Boleiros do cerrado: índios xavantes e o futebol*. São Paulo: Annablume/FAPESP/ISA, 2008.
21. 'Quando o Xavantes não está bem a solução é colocar em campo mais de 11', *Placar*, 75 (1971).
22. 'Jogos Desportivos Operários: recreação na pausa do trabalho', *O Estado de S. Paulo*, 3 April 1969.
23. 'Prefeito Paulo Maluf comanda revolução no esporte. Um clube em cada canto da cidade!', *A Gazeta Esportiva*, 20 April 1969.
24. 'Trabalhador, sua Olimpíada está chegando', *A Gazeta Esportiva*, 22 October 1969.
25. 'BH centraliza comemoração do trabalho', *O Estado de S. Paulo*, 30 April 1972.
26. 'Sesi abre sua 25º Olimpíada Operária', *O Estado de S. Paulo*, 2 May 1972.
27. 'O 1º de Maio no Pacaembu vazio', *Folha de S. Paulo*, 2 May 1979.
28. 'Médici telefonou à Seleção', *O Estado de S. Paulo*, 5 June 1970.

29. 'Brasil vence mas fica sem Rivelino', *O Estado de S. Paulo*, 9 June 1970.

30. 'Vamos gritar gooool', *O Estado de S. Paulo*, 10 June 1970.

31. Gorender, *Combate nas trevas*, p. 184.

32. Villa, M.A., *Vida e morte no sertão. História da seca no Nordeste nos séculos XIX e XX.* São Paulo: Editora Ática, 2000, p. 198.

33. 'Saque faz 20 feridos no Ceará', *O Estado de S. Paulo*, 3 June 1970.

34. 'Nordeste é problema nacional', *O Estado de S. Paulo*, 7 June 1970.

35. 'É o Brasil de há 20 anos quem recorda', *O Estado de S. Paulo*, 17 June 1970.

36. 'O manifesto', *O Estado de S. Paulo*, 13 June 1970.

37. '4 a 1, palpite do presidente', *O Estado de S. Paulo*, 20 June 1970.

38. Fico, C., 'A pluralidade das censuras e das propagandas da ditadura', in Daniel Aarão Reis et al., *O golpe e a ditadura militar: quarenta anos depois (1964–2004)*. Bauru, SP: EDUSC, 2004.

39. Gorender, J., *Prefácio*, in Carlos Fico, *Como eles agiam. Os subterrâneos da Ditadura Militar: espionagem e polícia política*. Rio de Janeiro: Record, 2001; Foucault, M., *História da sexualidade*, vol. II, *O uso dos prazeres*. Rio de Janeiro: Edições Graal, 1984.

40. Damo, A.S., *Do dom à profissão: a formação de futebolistas no Brasil e na França*. São Paulo: Hucitec/ANPOCS, 2007, p. 39; Fico, 'A pluralidade', p. 273.

41. 'Lá vai Afonsinho…', entrevista publicada na revista *Bondinho*, 1972.

42. 'Afonsinho (ou: o crime de ser barbudo)', *O Estado de S. Paulo*, 17 August 1970.

43. 'Afonsinho leva a lei do passe ao tribunal', *O Estado de S. Paulo*, 10 February 1971.

44. 'CBD julga hoje a lei que todos condenam', *O Estado de S. Paulo*, 11 February 1971.

45. 'Afonsinho ganha o Passe no STJD', *O Estado de S. Paulo*, 5 March 1971.

46. 'Olaria, uma esperança', *O Estado de S. Paulo*, 24 April 1971.

47. 'Afonsinho pode ser convocado', *O Estado de S. Paulo*, 21 May 1971.

48. 'Zagalo diz tudo sobre dispensa de Afonsinho', *Folha de S. Paulo*, 19 June 1971.

49. 'Os renegados', *Placar*, 36 (1970).

50. 'Um alegre time de subúrbio', *O Estado de S. Paulo*, 9 June 1971.

51. 'Bonetti traz paz ao Parque', *O Estado de S. Paulo*, 5 May 1971.

52. 'São Paulo multa Gérson, Jurandir e Tenente', *O Estado de S. Paulo*, 3 February 1971.

53. 'Ademir não aceita internamento', *O Estado de S. Paulo*, 19 February 1971.

54. 'O Grêmio estabelece linha dura', *O Estado de S. Paulo*, 30 September 1971.

55. 'Grêmio ignora ameaça e mantém férias especiais', *O Estado de S. Paulo*, 30 December 1973.

56. 'Grêmio quer treinar nas férias, mas os jogadores rejeitam', *O Estado de S. Paulo*, 22 November 1973.

57. 'Férias ou concentração?', *Placar*, 200 (1974).

58. 'Hoje, Froner dirige o Grêmio pela última vez', *O Estado de S. Paulo*, 9 February 1974.

59. Sader, E., *Quando novos personagens entraram em cena: experiências, falas e lutas dos trabalhadores da Grande São Paulo (1970–1980)*. Rio de Janeiro: Paz e Terra, 1988.

60. 'Rádio e TV sob censura', *O Estado de S. Paulo*, 17 May 1978.

61. 'Seleção preocupa até o presidente Geisel', *O Estado de S. Paulo*, 9 June 1978.

62. 'Reformular é o imperativo do momento', *A Gazeta Esportiva*, 10 July 1974.

63. 'O time do Comercial entra em greve', *O Estado de S. Paulo*, 12 July 1978.

64. 'Ainda somos o País do Futebol?', *Folhetim, Folha de S. Paulo*, 15 February 1981.

65. Sader, *Quando novos personagens entraram em cena*, p. 32.

66. 'Futebol é religião, é ópio no Brasil', *Movimento*, 154 (1978).

67. 'No Recife, luta do futebol feminino', *O Estado de S. Paulo*, 14 September 1980.

68. 'Radar contra o preconceito', *O Globo*, 30 September 2007.

69. 'Mulheres só esperam o sinal verde da FIFA', *Folha de S. Paulo*, 22 August 1982.

70. 'Mulheres, novo problema', *Folha de S. Paulo*, 29 March 1983.

71. '3.000 times. 45.000 mulheres em campo', revista *Placar*, 13 July 1984.

72. 'As meninas do Radar driblam o preconceito', *Folha de S. Paulo*, 13 March 1984. The term *boleiro* is used to describe a football player who comes from a lower social class. This term is also used to indicate the transition of the elitist football played in the first decades of the twentieth century by sportsman (wealthy young people from Rio de Janeiro and São Paulo) to the popular soccer, seen as a profession for poor, blacks and workers, Pereira, L.A. de M., *Footballmania: uma história social do futebol no Rio de Janeiro, 1902–1938*. Rio de Janeiro: Nova Fronteira, 2000.

73. Bourdieu, P., *A dominação masculina*. Rio de Janeiro: Bertrand Brasil, 2003.

74. 'O charme vai a campo', revista *Placar*, 13 July 1984.

75. Souza, M.A. de, 'A "Nação em Chuteiras": raça e masculinidade no futebol brasileiro', Dissertação de Mestrado, Antropologia Social, Universidade de Brasília, 1996.

76. 'Morre Servílio, o bailarino', *Folha de S. Paulo*, 11 April 1984.

77. Oriard, M., 'Muhammad Ali: the Hero in the age of mass media', in Elliott J. Gorn (ed.), *Muhammad Ali: The People's Champ*. Urbana and Chicago: University of Illinois Press, 1997, p. 10.

78. Vernant, J.P., *As origens do pensamento grego*. São Paulo: DIFEL, 5th edn, 1986.

79. Sader, *Quando novos personagens entraram em cena*.

80. Guedes, S.L. and Gastaldo, E., *Nações em campo: Copa do Mundo e identidade nacional*. Niterói, RJ: Intertexto, 2006, p. 9.

81. Coutinho, C.N., *Cultura e sociedade no Brasil: ensaios sobre ideias e formas*. Rio de Janeiro: DP&A, 2000, p. 36.

8. PUBLIC POWER, THE NATION AND STADIUM POLICY IN BRAZIL: THE CONSTRUCTION AND RECONSTRUCTION OF THE MARACANÃ STADIUM FOR THE WORLD CUPS OF 1950 AND 2014

1. Translation from the Portuguese by Victor Strazzeri. Text revision by Tara McGuinnes and André Linn.

2. Cruz, A.H.O, 'A nova economia do futebol: uma análise do processo de moderniza-

ção de alguns estádios brasileiros', Doctoral thesis, Museu Nacional—UFRJ, Rio de Janeiro, 2005.

3. Key works which have guided the general understanding of the nation state are those of Eric Hobsbawn and of Benedict Anderson. Hobsbawm, E., *Nações e nacionalismo desde 1780*. Rio de Janeiro: Paz e Terra, 1990. Balakrishnan, G. (ed.), *Um mapa da questão nacional*. Rio de Janeiro: Contraponto, 2000.

4. Negreiros, Plínio Labriola, 'A nação entra em campo: futebol nos anos 30 e 40', Doctoral thesis, PUC-SP, São Paulo, 1998.

5. The Guinles were one of the wealthiest Brazilian families in the early twentieth century. The family was the owner of the Companhia Docas de Santos, in the state of São Paulo's main port. In Rio de Janeiro, the Guinles owned numerous buildings, such as the Copacabana Palace Hotel, which remain to this day important landmarks.

6. Moura, G. de A., *O Rio corre para o Maracanã*. Rio de Janeiro: Editora FGV, 1998.

7. The UDN was a right-wing political party created in Brazil in 1945 after the end of the dictatorial period of the Getúlio Vargas government (1930–1945). During Vargas's second term (1951–54) this party was his biggest opponent.

8. Correa, M., *O sertão carioca*. Rio de Janeiro: Imprensa Nacional, 1936.

9. Lacerda, C., *Depoimento*. Rio de Janeiro: Nova Fronteira, 1978, p. 299.

10. With the recent lowering of the pitch of the Maracanã, archeological evidence of the golden age of horse racing in this location was found.

11. Lopes, J.S.L., 'Le Maracanã: coeur du Brésil', *Sociétés & representations*, 7 (1998).

12. Porto, C.H.R., 'Os espaços da paixão: estádios de futebol no Rio de Janeiro (1900–1960)', Final paper in the bachelor's programme for social history of culture, PUC-Rio, Rio de Janeiro, 2006.

13. Hollanda, B.B.B. de, *O descobrimento do futebol: modernismo, regionalismo e paixão esportiva em José Lins do Rego*. Rio de Janeiro: Edições Biblioteca Nacional, 2004.

14. Cavalcanti, L., *Quando o Brasil era moderno: guia de arquitetura 1928–1960*. Rio de Janeiro: Aeroplano, 2001, p. 259.

15. *Jornal Do Brasil*, 16 June 1950.

16. On the architectural varieties of stadiums around the world, see Gaffney, C.T., *Temples of the Earthbound Gods: Stadiums in the Cultural Landscapes of Rio de Janeiro and Buenos Aires*. Texas: University of Texas Press, 2008.

17. For a piercing portrayal of the writer, see Garcia, Jr, A., 'Stefan Zweig, prophète de la nation brésilienne', *Cahiers d'études hongroises*, 14 (2009).

18. Reforma Pereira Passos was the name given to an ensemble of urban and architectural reforms made in downtown Rio de Janeiro, then the capital of Brazil. This big campaign of modernisation and sanitisation was conducted by the city hall of Rio and the reform was popularised with the name of the mayor, Francisco Pereira Passos (1836–1913).

19. Lucchesi, M., *Teatro alquímico: diário de leituras*. Rio de Janeiro: Artium Editora, 1999.

NOTES

20. Burke, P. and Roy, P. (eds), *História social da linguagem*. São Paulo: UNESP, 1997.

21. Schwarcz, L.M. and COSTA, A.M. da, *1890–1914: no tempo das certezas*. São Paulo: Companhia das Letras, 2000, p. 72.

22. Bachelard, G., *A poética do espaço*. São Paulo: Martins Fontes, 1989.

23. Franco, Jr, H., *A dança dos deuses: futebol, sociedade, cultura*. São Paulo: Companhia das Letras, 2007.

24. Baeta Neves, L.F., 'Na zona do agrião: sobre algumas mensagens ideológicas do futebol', in DaMatta, R. (ed.), *Universo do futebol: esporte e sociedade brasileira*. Rio de Janeiro: Edições Pinakotheque, 1982, p. 54.

25. Vogel, A., 'O momento feliz: reflexões sobre o futebol e o *ethos* nacional', in DaMatta, R. (ed.). *Universo do futebol: esporte e sociedade brasileira*. Rio de Janeiro: Edições Pinakotheque, 1982; Perdigão, P., *Anatomia de uma derrota: 16 de Julho de 1950—Brasil X Uruguai*. Porto Alegre: L&PM, 2000.

26. The expression was coined by Luiz Henrique Toledo. Toledo, L.H. de, *Lógicas no futebol*. São Paulo: Huicitec/Fapesp, 2000.

27. Apud Silva, E.M. da, 'A violência no futebol e a imprensa esportiva', in Costa, M.R. da (ed.), *Futebol, o espetáculo do século*. São Paulo: Musa Editora, 1999.

28. To consult these images, see Farkas, T., *Pacaembu*. São Paulo: DBA Artes Gráficas, 2008.

29. Bodin, D., *Le hooliganisme: vérites et mensonges*. Paris: ESF Éditeur, 1999.

30. On the character of the '*geraldino*'—the supporter that stays in the cheapest and most uncomfortable place of the Maracanã stadium—see the classic film by Joaquim Pedro de Andrade, *Garrincha, alegria do povo* (1962); and, more recently, Anna Azevedo's award-winning short film, *Geral* (2010).

31. The 'ultras' can generally be defined as groups of organised fans emerging in Italy during the 1970s. The movement spread across continental Europe. Nowadays, covered by television images, they influence South America. The ultras are largely young men and teenagers. They introduced in stadiums the contemporary 'culture' of fandom: collective songs, choreographies, mosaics, devices and flags. They are critical of the 'football business' and, when necessary, the use physical force against their rivals. Houcarde, N., 'La place des supporters dans le monde du football', in *Pouvoirs—Revue. Française d'Études Constitutionelles et Politiques*, 101 (2001).

9. A WORLD CUP FOR WHOM? THE IMPACT OF THE 2014 WORLD CUP ON BRAZILIAN FOOTBALL STADIUMS AND CULTURES

1. An abridged version of this article was published as 'From Culture to Spectacle, the new logics of Brazilian football', *Territorio*, 64, 1 (2013), pp. 34–9.

2. Gaffney, Christopher, 'Copa Do Mundo No Brasil: Futebol, Esporte E Negocios', presented at the Simpósio Internacaional: *Os impactos dos megaeventos esportivos nas metropóles no Brasil*, Rio de Janeiro, Brazil, 12 October 2013. Available at: http://prezi.com/rgxik-2eyej9/?utm_campaign=share&utm_medium=copy.

3. 'Na Cidade-Sede Dos Jogos Olímpicos, 45% Das Escolas Públicas Não Têm Sequer Uma Quadra de Esportes', *O Globo Online*, 10 October 2009. Available at: http://oglobo.globo.com/rio/rio2016/mat/2009/10/10/na-cidade-sede-dos-jogos-olimpicos-45-das-escolas-publicas-nao-tem-sequer-uma-quadra-de-esportes-768006155.asp.

4. Melo, Victor Andrade de, *Cidadesportiva: Primórdios Do Esporte No Rio de Janeiro*. Relume Dumará, 2000.

5. 'Várzeas, Operários E Futebol: Uma Outra Geografia', *Geografia*, 4, 8 (2002), pp. 115–29.

6. Caldas, Waldenyr, *O Pontapé Inicial: memória do futebol brasileiro (1894–1933)*. São Paulo: Ibrasa, 1990.

7. Mascarenhas de Jesus, Gilmar, 'Construindo a Cidade Moderna: A Introdução Dos Esportes Na Vida Urbana Do Rio de Janeiro', *Estudos Históricos*, 23, 1 (2000), pp. 17–37.

8. Rodrigues Filho, Mário, *O negro no futebol brasileiro*. Rio de Janeiro: Civilização, 1964.

9. Gaffney, Christopher, *Temples of the Earthbound Gods: Stadiums in the Cultural Landscapes of Rio de Janeiro and Buenos Aires*. Texas: University of Texas Press, 1st edn, 2008.

10. Helal, Ronaldo, Antonio Jorge Soares and Hugo Louisolo, *A Invenção Do País Do Futebol: mídia, raça, e idolatria*. Rio de Janeiro: Mauaad, 2001.

11. Murad, Maurício, *Dos Pés À Cabeça: elementos básicos de sociologia do futebol*. Irradiação Cultural, 1996; DaMatta, Roberto, *A Bola Corre Mais Que Os Homens: duas copas, treze crônicas e três ensaios sobre futebol*. Rocco, 2006.

12. Aidar, Antônio Carlos Kfouri, Marvio Pereira Leoncini and João José de Oliveira, *A Nova Gestão Do Futebol*. FGV Editora, 2000.

13. Yallop, David A., *Como Eles Roubaram O Jogo: segredos dos subterrâneos da FIFA*. Rio de Janeiro: Record, 1998.

14. Harvey, David, *Spaces of Capital: Towards a Critical Geography*. Routledge, 2001.

15. Caldeira, Teresa P.R., *City of Walls: Crime, Segregation, and Citizenship in São Paulo*. Berkeley: University of California Press, 2000; Alabarces, Pablo, *Futbologías: fútbol, identidad y violencia en América Latina*. Buenos Aires: CLACSO, 2003.

16. Helal, Soares, and Louisolo, *A Invenção Do País Do Futebol*.

17. Bellos, Alex, *Futebol: The Brazilian Way of Life*. London: Bloomsbury, 2003.

18. Alvito, Marcos, and Christopher Gaffney, Juca Entrevista ANT, 4 December 2010.

19. *Lei Pelé*.

20. *Estatuto Do Torcedor*.

21. Magalhães, Luis António and Marinilda Carvalho, 'Estatuto Do Torcedor, Vitória Da Sociedade', *Observatório Da Imprensa*, 5 (2003). Available at: http://www.observatoriodaimprensa.com.br/banners/banners_int.htm.

22. Kfouri, Juca, 'Lula, O Cartola', *Blog Do Juca Kfouri*, 1 (2010). Available at: http://blogdojuca.uol.com.br/2010/01/lula-o-cartola/.

NOTES

23. Sanchez, Fernanda, *A Reinvenção Das Cidades Para Um Mercado Global*. Chapeco, Santa Catarina: ARGOS, 2010.

24. Mascarenhas de Jesus, Gilmar, Glauco Bienenstein and Fernanda Sánchez, *O jogo continua: megaeventos esportivos e cidades*. Rio de Janeiro: EdUERJ, 2011.

25. FIFA, 'FIFA Inspection Report', 30 October 2007. Available at: http://www.fifa. com/mm/document/affederation/mission/62/24/78/inspectionreport_e_24841.pdf.

26. Savarese, Maurício, 'The World Cup and Politics—a Love Story', *From Brazil—Folha de S.Paulo*, 29 November 2013. Available at: http://frombrazil.blogfolha.uol. com.br/2013/11/29/the-world-cup-and-politics-a-love-story/.

27. Boykoff, Jules, *Celebration Capitalism and the Olympic Games*. Abingdon: Routledge, 2014.

28. Articulação Nacional das Comitês Populares da Copa, *Megaeventos E Violações de Direitos Humanos No Brasil*. Rio de Janeiro, 2012. Available at: http://comitepopulario.files.wordpress.com/2012/06/dossie_megaeventos_violacoesdedireitos2012. pdf.

29. Associação dos Corrospondentes Internacionais. Aldo Rebelo, 16 November 2011.

30. Ferreira, Fernando, 'Clubes Brasileiros Acumulam R$ 1,8 Bi de Prejuízo Nos Últimos 6 Anos', Pluri Consultoria, 10 (2013). Available at: http://www.pluriconsultoria. com.br/uploads/relatorios/pluri%20ESPECIAL%20-%20 Prejuizosacumuladosclubes.pdf.

31. Oliveira, Rafael, 'Ingressos Para Futebol No Brasil São Os Mais Caros Do Mundo, Aponta Pesquisa', *Extra Online*, 24 March 2013. Available at: http://extra.globo. com/esporte/ingressos-para-futebol-no-brasil-sao-os-mais-caros-do-mundo-aponta-pesquisa-7927470.html.

32. Fialho, Gabriel, 'Diretor Do COL Avalia Que Seleção Brasileira Pode Aumentar Sustentabilidade de Arenas', 16 May 2012. Available at: http://www.copa2014.gov. br/pt-br/noticia/ diretor-do-col-avalia-que-selecao-brasileira-pode-aumentar-sustentabilidade-de-arenas.

33. Durão, Vera Saavedra, 'Maracanã Ganha Cara Nova Para Copa 2014', *Valor Econômico*, 31 March 2010. http://www.valor.com.br/seminarios/investinrio/suplemento/suplemento16.shtml.

34. Alegi, Peter, '"A Nation To Be Reckoned With": the politics of World Cup stadium construction in Cape Town and Durban, South Africa', *African Studies*, 67, 3 (2008), pp. 397–422; Maennig, Wolfgang and Stan du Plessis. 'World Cup 2010: South African economic perspectives and policy challenges informed by the experience of Germany 2006', *Contemporary Economic Policy*, 25, 4 (2007), pp. 578–90; Pithouse, Richard, *Business as Usual? Housing Rights and 'slum eradication' in Durban, South Africa*. Genebra, Suiça: The Centre on Housing Rights and Evictions (COHRE), September 2008. Available at: http://www.cohre.org/news/documents/south-africa-business-as-usual-housing-rights-and-slum-eradication-in-durban; Rodrigues, Cris, 'South Africa's World Cup Is a Disgrace', *The Guardian*, 5 June 2010. Available

at: http://www.guardian.co.uk/commentisfree/2010/may/06/south-africa-world-cup-spending-disgrace.

35. Jennings, Andrew, 'No Tendering for World Cup Tickets', *Transparency in Sport*, 13 November 2011. Available at: http://www.transparencyinsport.org/No_tendering_for_World_Cup_tix_contract/no_tender_for_world_cup_tickets.html.

Bibliography

Aidar, Antônio Carlos Kfouri, Marvio Pereira Leoncini and João José de Oliveira, *A Nova Gestão Do Futebol*. FGV Editora, 2000.

Alabarces, Pablo, *Futbologías: fútbol, identidad y violencia en América Latina.* Buenos Aires: CLACSO, 2003.

Alegi, Peter, '"A Nation To Be Reckoned With": The Politics of World Cup Stadium Construction in Cape Town and Durban, South Africa', *African Studies*, 67, 3 (2008), pp. 397–422.

Almeida, A.T.S. de, *O regime militar em festa*. Rio de Janeiro: Apicuri/FAPERJ, 2013.

Alvim, Rosilene, 'Constituição da Família e Trabalho Industrial', PhD thesis, Museu Nacional, Rio de Janeiro, 1985.

Alvim, Rosilene and J. Sergio Leite Lopes, 'Les jardins secrets de l'usine; logiques paysanne et ouvrière dans la gestion de la main d'oeuvre industrielle au Brésil', *Cahiers d'Economie et Sociologie Rurales*, 21, 4 (1991), pp. 71–98.

———— 'Familles Ouvrières, Familles d'Ouvrières', *Actes de la Recherche en Sciences Sociales*, 84 (1990), pp. 78–84.

Alvito, Marcos and Christopher Gaffney, Juca Entrevista ANT, 4 December 2010.

Andrews, George Reid, *Blacks and Whites in São Paulo 1888–1988*. Madison: University of Wisconsin Press, 1989.

Antonio Carlos Napoleão, Roberto Assaf, *Seleção Brasileira, 1914–2006*. Rio de Janeiro: Mauad, 2006.

Antunes, Fatima Martin Rodrigues Ferreira, 'Futebol de fábrica em São Paulo', MSc thesis in sociology, Faculdade de Filosofia, Letras e Ciências Humanas/ Universidade de São Paulo, 1992.

———— 'O futebol nas fábricas', *Revista USP*, Dossiê Futebol, 22 (1994), pp. 102–9.

BIBLIOGRAPHY

Arbena, Joseph, 'Sport and Nationalism in Latin America 1880–1970: The Paradox of Promoting and Performing European Sports', *The History of European Ideas*, 16, 4 (1993), pp. 837–44.

———— *Sport and Society in Latin America: Diffusion, Dependency and the Rise of Mass Culture*. New York and London: Greenwood Press, 1988.

Articulação Nacional das Comitês Populares da Copa, *Megaeventos E Violações de Direitos Humanos No Brasil*. Rio de Janeiro, 2012. Available at: http://comitepopulario.files.wordpress.com/2012/06/dossie_megaeventos_violacoesdedireitos2012.pdf.

Assaf, Roberto, *Bangu Operário, Estação Do Futebol E Samba*. Rio de Janeiro: Relume Dumara, 2001.

Associação dos Correspondentes Internacionais. Aldo Rebelo, 16 November 2011.

Astruc, Clément, 'Parcours de footballeurs. Récits, nature et diversité des trajectoires sociales et professionnelles des joueurs de l'élite du football brésilien des années 1950 aux années 1980', Master's dissertation, École Normale Supérieure de Lyon, 2013.

Augusti, Waldir Aparecido, *Memórias de Ermelino Matarazzo. Um Bairro Paulistano, seu Povo, sua Gente*. São Paulo: Edição do autor, 2012.

Bachelard, Gaston, *A poética do espaço*. São Paulo: Martins Fontes, 1989.

Baeta Neves, Luiz Felipe, 'Na zona do agrião: sobre algumas mensagens ideológicas do futebol', in DaMatta, Roberto (ed.), *Universo do futebol: esporte e sociedade brasileira*. Rio de Janeiro: Edições Pinakotheque, 1982.

Bailey, Frederick G. (ed.), *Gifts and Poison: the Politics of Reputation*, Oxford: Blackwell, 1971.

Balakrishnan, Gopal (ed.), *Um mapa da questão nacional*. Rio de Janeiro: Contraponto, 2000.

Bastide, Roger and Florestan Fernandes. *Relações Raciais Entre Negros E Brancos Em São Paulo; ensaio sociológico sôbre as origens, as manifestações e os efeitos do preconceito de côr no município de São Paulo*. São Paulo: Editôra Anhembi, 1955.

Bellos, Alex, *Futebol: The Brazilian Way of Life*. London: Bloomsbury, 2003.

———— *Futebol: Soccer the Brazilian Way*. New York: Bloomsbury, 2002.

Benzaquem de Araújo, Ricardo, 'Os Gênios da Pelota; Um Estudo do Futebol como Profissão', MA dissertation in social anthropology, Museu Nacional—UFRJ, Rio de Janeiro, 1980.

Bertrand, Julien, *La fabrique des footballeurs*. Paris: La Dispute, 2012.

Bodin, Dominique, *Le hooliganisme: vérites et mensonges*. Paris: ESF Éditeur, 1999.

Boletim Histórico Eletropaulo, 5 (1986), p. 3.

Boletim Histórico Eletropaulo, 7 (1986), pp. 14–15.

Bosi, Ecléa, *Memória e Sociedade. Lembrança de Velhos*. São Paulo: Cia das Letras, 1994.

BIBLIOGRAPHY

Bourdieu, Pierre, *A dominação masculina*. Rio de Janeiro: Bertrand Brasil, 2003.

——— *Distinction: A Social Critique of the Judgement of Taste*, trans. Richard Nice. Cambridge, Massachusetts: Harvard University Press, 11th edn, 2002.

——— *Questões de Sociologia*. Rio de Janeiro: Editora Marco Zero, 1983.

——— 'Sport and Social Class', *Social Science Information*, 17, 6 (1978), pp. 819–40.

——— 'Remarques provisoires sur la perception sociale du corps', *Actes de la Recherche en Sciences Sociales*, 14 (1977), pp. 51–4.

Boykoff, Jules, *Celebration Capitalism and the Olympic Games*. Abingdon: Routledge, 2014.

Brocketti, Gregg P., 'Italian Immigrants, Brazilian Football, the Dilemma of National Identity', *Journal of Latin American Studies*, 40 (2008), pp. 275–302.

Bromberger, Christian, *Football, la bagatelle la plus sérieuse du monde*. Paris: Bayard Éditions, 1998.

Burke, Peter and Roy Porter (eds), *História social da linguagem*. São Paulo: UNESP, 1997.

Butler, Kim, *Freedoms Given Freedoms Won: Afro-Brazilians in Post-Abolition São Paulo and Salvador*. New Jersey: Rutgers University Press, 1998.

Caldas, Waldenyr, 'Aspectos sociopolíticos do futebol brasileiro', *Revista USP*, Dossiê Futebol, 22 (1994), pp. 40–9.

——— *O pontapé inicial. Memória do futebol brasileiro (1894–1933)*. São Paulo: IBRASA, 1990.

Caldeira, Teresa P.R., *City of Walls: Crime, Segregation, and Citizenship in São Paulo*. Berkeley: University of California Press, 2000.

Carrascoza, João Anzanello et al., *A História do Tigre da Cantareira. Edição histórica ilustrada dos 75 anos do Lausanne Paulista F.C.* São Paulo: Edição do autor, 2002.

Castro, Ruy, *Garrincha: The Triumph and Tragedy of Brazil's Forgotten Footballing Hero*. London: Yellow Jersey Press, 2004.

Caulfield, Sueann, *In Defense of Honor: Sexual Morality, Modernity and Nation in Early Twentieth Century Brazil*. Durham: Duke University Press, 2000.

Cavalcanti, Claudio, 'As Lutas e os Sonhos. Um Estudo Sobre os Trabalhadores de São Paulo nos Anos 30', PhD thesis, Department of Sociology, Universidade de São Paulo, 1996.

Cavalcanti, Lauro, *Quando o Brasil era moderno: guia de arquitetura 1928–1960*. Rio de Janeiro: Aeroplano, 2001.

Cioccari, Marta, 'Mina de jogadores: o futebol operário e a construção da pequena honra', *Cadernos Arquivo Edgard Leuenroth* (UNICAMP), 16 (2011), pp. 76–115.

——— 'Do gosto da mina, do jogo e da revolta: um estudo antropológico sobre a construção da honra em uma comunidade de mineiros de carvão',

BIBLIOGRAPHY

Doctoral dissertation, Programa de Pós-Graduação em Antropologia Social (PPGAS), Museu Nacional, Universidade Federal do Rio de Janeiro, Rio de Janeiro, 2010.

Clastres, P., *Arqueologia da violência*. São Paulo: Cosac Naify, 2011.

Colistete, Renato, *Labour Relations and Industrial Performance in Brazil: Greater São Paulo, 1945–1960*. New York: Palgrave, 2001.

Correa, Magalhães, *O sertão carioca*. Rio de Janeiro: Imprensa Nacional, 1936.

Coutinho, C.N., *Cultura e sociedade no Brasil: ensaios sobre ideias e formas*. Rio de Janeiro: DP&A, 2000.

Coutinho, Filipe, 'Receita Federal Multa a CBF Em R$ 3 Milhões Por Sonegação de Imposto de Renda', *Folha de São Paulo*, 29 August 2010. Available at: http://www1.folha.uol.com.br/esporte/790573-receita-federal-multa-a-cbf-em-r-3-milhoes-por-sonegacao-de-imposto-de-renda.shtml.

Cruz, Antônio Holzmeister Oswaldo, 'A nova economia do futebol: uma análise do processo de modernização de alguns estádios brasileiros', Doctoral thesis, Museu Nacional—UFRJ, Rio de Janeiro, 2005.

Curi, Martin, 'Arthur Friedenreich, 1892–1969: a Brazilian biography', in *Football in Brazil*, New York: Routledge, 2013.

DaMatta, Roberto, *A Bola Corre Mais Que Os Homens: duas copas, treze crônicas e três ensaios sobre futebol*. Rocco, 2006.

——— Roberto, *Carnavais, malandros e heróis: para uma sociologia do dilema brasileiro*. Rio de Janeiro: Zahar, 1983.

——— Roberto, *Universo Do Futebol: esporte e sociedade Brasiliera*. Rio de Janeiro: Edições Pinakotheke, 1982.

——— Roberto et al. (eds), *Universo do futebol: esporte e sociedade brasileira*. Rio de Janeiro: Pinakotheque, 1982.

——— Flores, Luís Felipe B.N., Guedes, Simone & Vogel, Arno, *Universo do Futebol*. Rio de Janeiro: Pinakotheque, 1982.

Damo, A.S., *Do dom à profissão: a formação de futebolistas no Brasil e na França*. São Paulo: Hucitec/ANPOCS, 2007.

Dávila, Jerry, *Diploma of Whiteness: race and social policy in Brazil, 1917–1945*. Durham: Duke University Press, 2003.

Davis, Darién J., 'British Football with a Brazilian Beat: The Early History of a National Pastime (1894–1933)', in Marshall, Oliver, *English-Speaking Communities in Latin America*. London: Macmillan, pp. 261–84.

Decca, Maria Auxiliadora Guzzo, *A vida fora das fábricas. Cotidiano operário em São Paulo (1920–1934)*. Rio de Janeiro: Paz e Terra, 1987.

Degler, Carl N., *Neither Black nor White: Slaves and Race Relations in Brazil and the United States*. New York: Macmillan, 1971.

de Moraes, Mario, *Futebol é Arte: serie depoimentos, Zizinho, Domingos da Guia Pelé*, vols I–II. Rio de Janeiro: Editorial, 2002.

Dias, Eduardo, *Um Imigrante e a Revolução. Memórias de um Militante Operário, 1934–1951*. São Paulo: Editora Brasiliense, 1983.

BIBLIOGRAPHY

Duarte, Adriano, 'Neighborhood Association, Social Movements, and Populism in Brazil, 1945–1953', *Hispanic Historical American Review*, 89 (2009).

———— 'Cultura Popular e Cultura Politica no Após-guerra. Redemocratização, Populismo e Desenvolvimentismo no Bairro da Mooca, 1942–1973', PhD thesis, History Department, UNICAMP, Campinas, 2002.

Duarte, Adriano and Fontes, Paulo, 'O populismo visto da periferia: adhemarismo e janismo nos bairros da Mooca e São Miguel Paulista (1947–1953)', *Cadermos AEL*, 11, 20/21 (2004), pp. 83–125.

Duby, George, *Guillaume le Marechal*. Paris: Fayard, 1984.

Durão, Vera Saavedra, 'Maracanã Ganha Cara Nova Para Copa 2014', *Valor Econômico*, 31 March 2010. http://www.valor.com.br/seminarios/investinrio/suplemento/suplemento16.shtml.

Elias, Norbert and Scotson, John, *Os estabelecidos e os outsiders*. Rio de Janeiro: Zahar, 2000.

Elsey, Brenda, *Citizens and Sportsmen: Fútbol and Politics in Twentieth-Century Chile*. Austin: University of Texas Press, 2011.

Estatuto Do Torcedor. L10671, 2003. https://www.planalto.gov.br/ccivil_03/leis/2003/l10.671.htm.

Farkas, T., *Pacaembu*. São Paulo: DBA Artes Gráficas, 2008.

Fernandes, Florestan, *O negro no mundo dos brancos*. São Paulo: Global Editora, 2nd end, 2007.

———— *The Negro in Brazilian Society*. New York: Columbia University Press, 1969.

Ferreira, Fernando, 'Clubes Brasileiros Acumulam R$ 1,8 Bi de Prejuízo Nos Últimos 6 Anos', Pluri Consultoria, 10 (2013). Available at: http://www.pluriconsultoria.com.br/uploads/relatorios/pluri%20ESPECIAL%20-%20Prejuizosacumuladosclubes.pdf.

Ferreira, Jorge, 'A estratégia do confronto: a frente de mobilização popular', *Revista Brasileira de História*, 24, 47 (2004), pp. 181–212.

———— (ed.), *O Populismo e sua História: debate e crítica*. Rio de Janeiro: Civilização Brasileira, 2001.

Fialho, Gabriel, 'Diretor Do COL Avalia Que Seleção Brasileira Pode Aumentar Sustentabilidade de Arenas', 16 May 2012. Available at: http://www.copa2014.gov.br/pt-br/noticia/diretor-do-col-avalia-que-selecao-brasileira-pode-aumentar-sustentabilidade-de-arenas.

Fico, C., 'A pluralidade das censuras e das propagandas da ditadura', in Daniel Aarão Reis et al., *O golpe e a ditadura militar: quarenta anos depois (1964–2004)*. Bauru, SP: EDUSC, 2004.

FIFA, 'FIFA Inspection Report', 30 October 2007. Available at: http://www.fifa.com/mm/document/affederation/mission/62/24/78/inspectionreport_e_24841.pdf.

Filho, Mário, *O negro no futebol brasileiro*. Rio de Janeiro: Mauad, 4th edn, 2003.

BIBLIOGRAPHY

———— *O negro no futebol brasileiro*. Rio de Janeiro: Civilização Brasileira, 2nd edn, 1964.

———— *Viagem em tôrno de Pelé*. Rio de Janeiro: Editora do Autor, 1963.

Fischer, Brodwyn, *A Poverty of Rights: citizenship and inequality in twentieth-century Rio De Janeiro*. Stanford: Stanford University Press, 2008.

Fleuriel, Sébastien and Manuel Schotté, *Sportifs en danger. La condition des travailleurs sportifs*. Bellecombes en Bauge: éditions du Croquant, 2008.

Florenzano, J.P., *A Democracia Corinthiana: práticas de liberdade no futebol brasileiro*. São Paulo: Fapesp/Educ, 2009.

———— *Afonsinho e Edmundo: a rebeldia no futebol brasileiro*. São Paulo: Musa Editora, 1998.

Fontaine, Marion, 'Sport, sociabilité et culture politiques en territoire lensois, 1936–1955', *Les cahiers du Centre de Recherches Historiques*, 31 (2003), available at http://ccrh.revues.org/index308.html, last accessed 5 Nov. 2008.

Fontes, Paulo, *Um Nordeste em São Paulo. Trabalhadores Migrantes em São Miguel Paulista (1945–1966)*. Rio de Janeiro: Editora da FGV, 2008.

———— 'The Strike of 400,000 and the Workers' Organisation in São Paulo, Brazil, 1957', *Socialist History*, 17 (2000), pp. 17–35.

Fontes, Paulo and Macedo, Francisco Barbosa, 'Strikes and Pickets in Brazil: working-class mobilization in the "old" and "new" unionism, the strikes of 1957 and 1980', *International Labor and Working Class History*, 83 (2013), pp. 86–111.

Foucault, M., *História da sexualidade*, vol. II, *O uso dos prazeres*. Rio de Janeiro: Edições Graal, 1984.

Franco Júnior, Hilário, *A dança dos deuses: futebol, sociedade, cultura*. São Paulo: Companhia das Letras, 2007.

Franzini, Fabio, 'A futura paixão nacional: chega o futebol', in Priore, Mary Del and Victor Andrade de Melo (eds), *História do Esporte no Brasil: do Império aos dias atuais*. São Paulo: Editora UNESP, 2009.

French, John, *The Brazilian Workers' ABC: Class Conflict and Alliances in Modern São Paulo*. Chapel Hill: University of North Carolina Press, 1992.

Fridenson, Patrick, 'Les ouvriers de l'automobile et le sport', *Actes de la Recherche en Sciences Sociales*, 79, 1 (1989), pp. 50–62.

Frydenberg, Julio, 'Os bairros e o futebol na cidade de Buenos Aires de 1930', *Cadernos AE*, 16, 28 (2010).

Gaffney, Christopher, 'Copa Do Mundo No Brasil: Futebol, Esporte E Negocios', presented at the Simpósio Internacaional: *Os impactos dos megaeventos esportivos nas metropóles no Brasil*, Rio de Janeiro, Brazil, 12 October 2013. Available at: http://prezi.com/rgxik-2eyej9/?utm_campaign=share&utm_medium=copy.

———— *Temples of the Earthbound Gods: Stadiums in the Cultural Landscapes of Rio de Janeiro and Buenos Aires*. Texas: University of Texas Press, 1st edn, 2008.

BIBLIOGRAPHY

Garcia, Jr, Afrânio, 'Stefan Zweig, prophète de la nation brésilienne', *Cahiers d'Études Hongroises*, 14 (2009).

Gautheron, Marie (ed.), *A honra: imagem de si ou dom de si—um ideal equívoco*. Porto Alegre: LP&M, 1992.

Gomes, Angela de Castro, *A Invenção do Trabalhismo*. Rio de Janeiro: Instituto Universitário de Pesquisas do Rio de Janeiro; São Paulo: Vértice, 1988.

Gorender, J., *Prefácio*, in Carlos Fico, *Como eles agiam. Os subterrâneos da Ditadura Militar: espionagem e polícia política*. Rio de Janeiro: Record, 2001.

——*Combate nas trevas*. São Paulo: Ática, 1998.

Gramsci, A., *Cadernos do cárcere*, vol. III, *Maquiavel. Notas sobre o Estado e a Política*. Rio de Janeiro: Civilização Brasileira, 2000.

—— *Cadernos do cárcere*, Vol.I, *Introdução ao estudo da filosofia. A filosofia de Benedetto Croce*. Rio de Janeiro: Civilização Brasileira, 1999.

Guedes, Simone, 'O "povo brasileiro" no campo de futebol', *À Margem; Revista de Ciências Humanas* (1993).

—— 'Subúrbio, celeiro de craques', in DaMatta, Roberto, Flores, Luís Felipe B.N., Guedes, Simone & Vogel, Arno, *Universo do Futebol*. Rio de Janeiro: Pinakotheque, 1982.

Guedes, Simoni Lahud, and Gastaldo, E., *Nações em campo: Copa do Mundo e identidade nacional*. Niterói, RJ: Intertexto, 2006.

—— 'Subúrbio: celeiro de craques', in DaMatta, R. et al. (eds), *Universo do futebol: esporte e sociedade brasileira*. Rio de Janeiro: Pinakotheque, 1982, pp. 59–74.

—— 'Futebol brasileiro: instituição zero', MSc thesis in social anthropology, Museu Nacional/UFRJ, 1977.

Guttmann, Allen, *Games and Empire: Modern Sports and Cultural Imperialism*. New York: Columbia University Press, 1994.

—— *The Olympics: A History of the Modern Games*. Urbana: University of Illinois Press, 1992.

—— *From Ritual to Record: The Nature of Modern Sports*. New York: Columbia University Press, 1978.

Hardman, Francisco Foot, *Nem pátria, nem patrão. Vida operária e cultura anarquista no Brasil*. São Paulo: Brasiliense, 1983.

Harvey, David, *Spaces of Capital: Towards a Critical Geography*. Abingdon: Routledge, 2001.

Helal, Ronaldo, 'A Construção De Narrativas De Idolatria No Futebol', in Antonio Jorge Soares, Ronaldo Helal, Hugo Rodolfo Lovisolo (eds), *A Invençãao Do País Do Futebol: midia raça e idolatria*. Rio de Janeiro: PUC, 2003.

—— 'As Idealizaçoes De Sucesso No Imaginario Brasileiro: un estudo de caso', in Antonio Jorge Soares, Ronaldo Helal, Hugo Rodolfo Lovisolo (eds), *A Invençãao Do País Do Futebol: mídia, raça e idolatria*. Rio de Janeiro: PUC, 2003.

────── *Passes E Impasses: futebol e cultura de massa no Brasil*. Petrópolis: Vozes, 1997.

────── *O Que É Sociologia Do Esporte*. São Paulo: Brasiliense, 1990.

Helal, Ronaldo, Antonio Jorge Soares and Hugo Louisolo, *A Invenção Do País Do Futebol: mídia, raça, e idolotria*. Rio de Janeiro: Mauaad, 2001.

Hellerman, Steven L. and Andrei S. Markovits, *Offside: Soccer and American Exceptionalism*. Princeton: Princeton University Press, 2001.

Hirata, Daniel, 'No meio do campo: o que está em jogo no futebol de várzea?', in Telles, Vera and Cabanes, Robert (eds), *Nas Tramas da Cidade. Trajetórias Urbanas e seus Territórios*. São Paulo: Humanitas, 2007.

Hobsbawm, Eric, *Nações e nacionalismo desde 1780*. Rio de Janeiro: Paz e Terra, 1990.

Hoggart, Richard, *The Uses of Literacy*. Harmondsworth, Penguin Books, 1969.

Hollanda, Bernardo Borges Buarque de, *O Clube Como Vontage E Representação: o jornalismo esportivo e a formação das rorcidas orginizadas de Rio De Janeiro*. Rio de Janeiro: Viveiros de Castro Editora Ltd, 2009.

────── *O descobrimento do futebol: modernismo, regionalismo e paixão esportiva em José Lins do Rego*. Rio de Janeiro: Edições Biblioteca Nacional, 2004.

Houcarde, Nicolas, 'La place des supporters dans le monde du football', *Pouvoirs—Revue Française d'Études Constitutionelles et Politiques*, 101 (2001).

Iffy, Catherine, *Transformar a Metrópole: igreja Católica, territórios e mobilizações sociais em São Paulo 1970–2000*. São Paulo: Editora da Unesp, 2011.

Jackson, Jr, Gregory E., 'Building the New Brazilian Man: Football, Public Policy and Eugenics, 1894–1950', Doctoral Dissertation, Stony Brook University, 2013.

Jennings, Andrew, 'No Tendering for World Cup Tickets', *Transparency in Sport*, 13 November 2011. Available at: http://www.transparencyinsport.org/No_tendering_for_World_Cup_tix_contract/no_tender_for_world_cup_tickets.html.

Jesus, Gilmar Mascarenhas, 'Várzeas, Operários e Futebol: Uma outra Geografia,' *GEOgraphia*, 4, 8 (2002).

Kfouri, Juca, 'Sobre a CBF E O Clube Dos 13', *Blog Do Juca Kfouri*, March 2010. Available at: http://blogdojuca.uol.com.br/2010/03/sobre-a-cbf-e-o-clube-dos-13–3/.

────── 'Lula, O Cartola', *Blog Do Juca Kfouri*, January 2010. Available at: http://blogdojuca.uol.com.br/2010/01/lula-o-cartola/.

Kowarick, Lucio et al., *Social Struggles and the City: the case of São Paulo*. New York: Monthly Review Press, 1994.

Lacerda, Carlos, *Depoimento*. Rio de Janeiro: Nova Fronteira, 1978.

Lacey, Josh, *God is Brazilian: The Man Who Brought Football to Brazil*. Stroud: Tempus, 2005.

Larson, Brooke, *Trials of Nation Making: liberalism, race and ethnicity in the Andes, 1810–1910*. Cambridge: Cambridge University Press, 2004.

BIBLIOGRAPHY

Lei Pelé L9615, 1998. Available at: http://www.planalto.gov.br/ccivil_03/leis/l9615consol.htm.

Leite Lopes, José Sergio, A tecelagem dos conflitos de classe na cidade das chaminés [The Weaving of Class Conflict in 'Chimneys' City']. São Paulo/Brasília: Marco Zero/Editora da UnB, 1988.

——— 'A Vitória do Futebol Que Incorporou a Pelada: a invenção do jornalismo esportivo e a entrada dos negros brasileiro', Revista USP, 1 (1994).

——— 'Success in "Multiracial" Brazilian Football', in Gary Armstrong, Nicole Toulis, Richard Giulianotti (eds), *Entering the Field: New Perspectives on World Football*. New York: Berg Publishing, 1997.

——— 'Le Maracanã: coeur du Brésil', Sociétés & représentations, 7 (1998).

——— 'Considerações em torno das transformações do profissionalismo no futebol a partir da observação da Copa de 1998', *Estudos Históricos*, 1, 23 (1999).

——— 'La disparition de la "joie du peuple". Notes sur la mort d'un joueur de football', Actes de la recherche en sciences sociales, 79 (1989), pp. 21–36.

——— 'Class, Ethnicity, and Color in the Making of Brazilian Football', *Daedalus*, 129, 2 (2000), pp. 239–70.

——— 'Classe, etnicidade e cor na formação do futebol brasileiro', in Batalha, Cláudio, Fernando T.d. Silva and Alexandre Fortes (eds), *Culturas de classe: identidade e diversidade na formação do operariado*. Campinas: UNICAMP, 2004.

Leite Lopes, J. Sergio & Machado da Silva, L.A., 'Introdução: estratégias de trabalho, formas de dominação na produção e subordinação doméstica de trabalhadores urbanos', in Leite Lopes, J. Sergio et al., *Mudança Social no Nordeste: a reprodução da subordinação*. Rio de Janeiro: Paz e Terra, 1979, pp. 9–40.

——— *O 'vapor do diabo': o trabalho dos operários do açúcar* [The 'Devil's Steam': The Labour of Sugar Workers], Rio de Janeiro: Paz e Terra, 1976.

Leite Lopes, José Sergio and Maresca, Sylvain, 'A morte da "alegria do povo"', *Revista Brasileira de Ciências Sociais*, 20, 7 (1992), pp. 113–34.

Lesser, Jeffery, *Negotiating National Identity: Immigrants, Minorities and the Struggle for Ethnicity in Brazil*. Durham: Duke University Press, 1999.

Lever, Janet, *Soccer Madness: Brazil's Passion for the World's Most Popular Sport*. Illinois: Waveland Publishing, 1995.

——— *Soccer Madness*. Chicago & London: The University of Chicago Press, 1983.

Levine, Robert M., *Father of the Poor?: Vargas and his Era*. Cambridge: Cambridge University Press, 1998.

——— 'Sport as Dramaturgy for Society: A Concluding Chapter', in Joseph L. Arbena (ed.), *Sport and Society in Latin America: Diffusion, Dependency and the Rise of Mass Culture*. New York: Greenwood Publishing, 1988.

BIBLIOGRAPHY

———— 'The Case of Brazilian Futebol', *Luso Brazilian Review*, 17, 2 (1980).

———— *The Vargas Regime: The Critical Year, 1934–1938*. New York: Columbia University Press, 1969.

Lindner, Rolf and Breuer, Heinrich, 'SV Sodingen: le dernier club de banlieue', *Actes de la recherche en sciences sociales*, 103, 1 (1994), pp. 52–4.

Lucchesi, Marco, *Teatro alquímico: diário de leituras*. Rio de Janeiro: Artium Editora, 1999.

Lyra Filho, João, *Taça do Mundo, 1954*. Rio de Janeiro: Irmãos Pongetti, 1954.

Maennig, Wolfgang and Stan du Plessis. 'World Cup 2010: South African economic perspectives and policy challenges informed by the experience of Germany 2006', *Contemporary Economic Policy*, 25, 4 (2007), pp. 578–90.

Magalhães, Luis António and Marinilda Carvalho, 'Estatuto Do Torcedor, Vitória Da Sociedade', *Observatório Da Imprensa*, 5 (2003). Available at: http://www.observatoriodaimprensa.com.br/banners/banners_int.htm.

Magnani, José Guilherme, *Festa no Pedaço: cultura popular e lazer na cidade*. São Paulo: Editora Hucitec, 1998.

Mainwaring, Scott, *The Catholic Church and Politics in Brazil, 1916–1985*. Stanford: Stanford University Press, 1986.

Marcondes, J.V. and Pimentel, Osmar, *São Paulo: Espírito, Povo, Instituições*. São Paulo: Livraria Pioneira Editora, 1968.

Mascarenhas de Jesus, Gilmar, 'Várzeas, Operários E Futebol: Uma Outra Geografia', *Geografia*, 4, 8 (2002), pp. 115–29.

———— 'Construindo a Cidade Moderna: A Introdução Dos Esportes Na Vida Urbana Do Rio de Janeiro', *Estudos Históricos*, 23, 1 (2000), pp. 17–37.

Mascarenhas de Jesus, Gilmar, Glauco Bienenstein and Fernanda Sánchez, *O jogo continua: megaeventos esportivos e cidades*. Rio de Janeiro: EdUERJ, 2011.

Mascarenhas, Gilmar and Christopher Gaffney, 'The Soccer Stadium as a Disciplinary Space', *Revista Esporte & Sociedade*, 1 (2005/2006). Available at: www.esportesociedade.com.

Mason, Tony., *Passion of the People? Football in South America*. New York: Verso, 1995.

McCann, Bryan, *Hello Hello Brazil: Popular Music and the Making of Modern Brazil*. Durham: Duke University Press, 2004.

McCarthy, Thomas, *Race, Empire, and the Idea of Human Development*. Cambridge: Cambridge University Press, 2009.

McDowall, Duncan, *The Light: Brazilian Traction, Light and Power Company Limited, 1899–1945*. Toronto: University of Toronto Press, 1988.

Meade, Teresa, *"Civilizing" Rio: Reform and Resistance in a Brazilian City, 1889–1930*. University Park: Pennsylvania State University Press, 1997.

Melo, Victor Andrade de, *Cidadesportiva: Primórdios Do Esporte No Rio de Janeiro*. Relume Dumará, 2000.

BIBLIOGRAPHY

Mércio, Roberto, *A História dos Campeonatos Cariocas de Futebol*. Rio de Janeiro, Studio Alfa, 1985.

Mills, John, *Charles Miller: o pai do futebol brasileiro*. São Paulo: Panda Books, 2005.

Moura, Gisella de Araújo, *O Rio corre para o Maracanã*. Rio de Janeiro: Editora FGV, 1998.

Murad, Maurício, *Dos Pés À Cabeça: elementos básicos de sociologia do futebol*. Irradiação Cultural, 1996.

Nascimento, Abidias do, *Brazil Mixture or Massacre? Essay in the Genocide of a Black People*. Dover, Massachusetts: Majority Press, 1989.

'Na Cidade-Sede Dos Jogos Olímpicos, 45% Das Escolas Públicas Não Têm Sequer Uma Quadra de Esportes', *O Globo Online*, 10 October 2009. Available at: http://oglobo.globo.com/rio/rio2016/mat/2009/10/10/na-cidade-sede-dos-jogos-olimpicos-45-das-escolas-publicas-nao-tem-sequer-uma-quadra-de-esportes-768006155.asp.

Nash, June, *Comemos a las minas y las minas nos comem a nosotros: dependencia y explotación en las minas de estaño bolivianos*. Buenos Aires: Antropofagia, 2008.

Needell, Jeffery, *A Tropical Belle Epoque: Elite Culture and Society in Turn of the Century Rio de Janeiro*. Cambridge: Cambridge University Press, 1987.

Negreiros, Plínio Labriola, *A nação entra em campo: futebol nos anos 30 e 40*. São Paulo: Tese de Doutorado/PUC-SP, 1998.

Negro, Antonio Luigi, *Linhas de Montagem: o industrialismo nacional-desenvolvimentista e a sindicalização dos trabalhadores (1945–1978)*. São Paulo: FAPESP: Boitempo Editorial, 2004.

Neiva, Adriano, 'Escrevendo uma história', in Vários Autores, *60 Anos de Futebol no Brasil*. São Paulo: Federação Paulista de Futebol, 1955.

Neto, Murilo Leal Pereira, *A Reinvenção da Classe Trabalhadora (1953–1964)*. Campinas: Editora da Unicamp, 2011.

Neves, Marcos Eduardo, *Nunca Houve Um Homen Como Heleno*. Rio de Janeiro: Ediouro, 2006.

Novais, Fernando and João Manuel Cardoso de Mello, 'Capitalismo tardio e sociabilidade moderna', in Novais, Fernando and Lilia Moritz Schwarcz (eds), *História da vida privada no Brasil. Contrastes e intimidade contemporânea*, vol. IV. São Paulo: Companhia das Letras, 1998.

'O Comunismo no Brasil', *Inquérito Policial Militar*, 4, 709. Rio de Janeiro: Biblioteca do Exército, 1967.

Oliveira, Rafael, 'Ingressos Para Futebol No Brasil São Os Mais Caros Do Mundo, Aponta Pesquisa', *Extra Online*, 24 March 2013. Available at: http://extra.globo.com/esporte/ingressos-para-futebol-no-brasil-sao-os-mais-caros-do-mundo-aponta-pesquisa-7927470.html.

Oriard, M., 'Muhammad Ali: The Hero in the Age of Mass Media', in Elliott

BIBLIOGRAPHY

J. Gorn (ed.), *Muhammad Ali: The People's Champ*. Urbana and Chicago: University of Illinois Press, 1997.

Owensby, Brian, 'Towards a History of Brazil's "Cordial Racism": Race Beyond Liberalism', *Comparative Studies of Society and History*, 47, 2 (2005), pp. 318–47.

Paoli, Maria Célia and Adriano Luiz Duarte, 'São Paulo no plural: espaços públicos e redes de sociabilidade', in Porta, Paula (ed.), *História da Cidade de São Paulo: a cidade de São Paulo na primeira metade do século XX*, vol. III. São Paulo: Paz e Terra, 2005, pp. 67–92.

Paranaguá, Paulo, *Le cinema brésilien*. Paris: Centre Georges Pompidou, 1987.

Patterson, Orlando, *Slavery and Social Death: A Comparative Study*. Cambridge: Harvard University Press, 1988.

Pearson, Roger, *Eugenics and Race*. Los Angeles: Noontide Press, 1966.

Perdigão, Paulo, *Anatomia de uma derrota: 16 de Julho de 1950—Brasil x Uruguai*. Porto Alegre: L&PM, 2000.

Pereira, Leonardo Alfonso de Miranda, *Footballmania: uma história social do futebol no Rio De Janeiro, 1902–1938*. Rio de Janeiro: Editora Nova Fronteira, 2000.

Perelman, Marc, *L'ère des stades: genèse et structure d'un espace historique*. Paris: Infolio, 2010.

Pithouse, Richard, *Business as Usual? Housing Rights and 'Slum Eradication' in Durban, South Africa*. Genebra, Suiça: The Centre on Housing Rights and Evictions (COHRE), September 2008. Available at: http://www.cohre.org/news/documents/south-africa-business-as-usual-housing-rights-and-slum-eradication-in-durban.

Pitt-Rivers, Julian, *Anthropologie de l'honneur: la mésaventure de Sichem*. Paris: Le Sycomore, 1983.

———— 'Honra e posição social', in Peristiany, J.G. (ed.), *Honra e vergonha: valores das sociedades mediterrâneas*. Lisboa: Fundação Calouste Gulbenkian, 1965, pp. 13–59.

Porto, Carlos Henrique Ribeiro, 'Os espaços da paixão: estádios de futebol no Rio de Janeiro (1900–1960)', Monografia de Graduação em História Social da Cultura, PUC—Rio, Rio de Janeiro, 2006.

Rebelo, Aldo and Silvio Torres, *CBF Nike*. Rio de Janeiro: Casa Amarela, 2001.

Rego, José Lins do, 'Preface', in Rodrigues Filho, Mário, *Copa Rio Branco 1932*. Rio de Janeiro: Pognetti, 1943.

Renahy, Nicolas, 'De l'appartenance ouvrière à la réprésentation territoriale', *Ethnologie française*, 31, 4 (2001), pp. 707–15.

Ribeiro, Péris, *Didi: O Gênio Da Folha-Seca*. Rio de Janeiro: Gryphus, 2009.

Ribero, André, *O Diamante Eterno: biografia de Leônidas Da Silva*. São Paulo: Gryphus, 1999.

Rodrigues, Cris, 'South Africa's World Cup Is a Disgrace', *The Guardian*, 5 June

BIBLIOGRAPHY

2010. Available at: http://www.guardian.co.uk/commentisfree/2010/may/06/south-africa-world-cup-spending-disgrace.

Rodrigues, F.X.F., *O fim do passe e a modernização conservadora no futebol brasileiro (2001–2006)*, Doctoral thesis in sociology, Universidade Federal do Rio Grande do Sul, 2007.

Rosanvallon, P., *L'age de l'autogestion*. Paris: Seuil, 1976.

Rosenfeld, Anatol, *Negro, macumba e futebol*. São Paulo: Perspectiva, 2007.

———— 'O futebol no Brasil', *Revista Argumento*, 1, 4 (1973), pp. 61–85.

Sader, Eder, *Quando Novos Personagens Entraram em Cena: experiências, falas e lutas dos trabalhadores da Grande São Paulo (1970–80)*. Rio de Janeiro: Paz e Terra, 1988.

Salem, Tânia, 'Tensões entre gêneros na classe popular: uma discussão com o paradigma holista', *Mana*, 12, 2 (2006), pp. 419–49.

Sanchez, Fernanda, *A Reinvenção Das Cidades Para Um Mercado Global*. Chapeco, Santa Catarina: ARGOS, 2010.

Santos, J.R. dos, *História política do futebol brasileiro*. São Paulo: Brasiliense, 1981.

Santos, Joel R. dos, *História Política do Futebol Brasileiro*. São Paulo: Brasiliense, 1981.

Santos Neto, José Moraes dos, *Visão do jogo—primórdios do futebol no Brasil*. São Paulo: Cosac & Naify, 2002.

Sarmento, Carlos Eduardo, *A Regra Do Jogo: uma história institucional da CBF*. Rio de Janeiro: FGV-CPDOC, 2006.

Savarese, Maurício, 'The World Cup and Politics—a Love Story', *From Brazil—Folha de S.Paulo*, 29 November 2013. Available at: http://frombrazil.blogfolha.uol.com.br/2013/11/29/the-world-cup-and-politics-a-love-story/.

Schwarcz, Lilia Moritz, *Nem preto nem branco, muito pelo contrário*. São Paulo: Claro Enigma, 2012.

———— 'Pretos contra brancos ou dando e mudando nomes', in Cabral, João de Pina and Viegas, Susana de Matos (eds), *Nomes: gênero, etnicidade e família*. Lisboa: Almedina, 2007.

Schwarcz, Lilia Moritz and Costa, Ângela, *Moreira da. 1890–1914: no tempo das certezas*. São Paulo: Companhia das Letras, 2000.

Seabra, Odete, 'Urbanização, bairro e vida de bairro', *Travessia*, 13, 38 (2000).

———— 'Meandros dos Rios nos Meandros do Poder. Tietê e Pinheiros: valorização dos rios e das várzeas na Ccdade de São Paulo', PhD thesis, Department of Geography, Universidade de São Paulo, 1987.

Silva, Diana Mendes Machado, 'A Associação Atlética Anhanguera: imigração, associativismo e futebol de várzea na cidade de São Paulo (1928–1939)', Master thesis, Department of History, Universidade de São Paulo, 2013.

Silva, Elisabeth Murilho da, 'A violência no futebol e a imprensa esportiva', in

BIBLIOGRAPHY

Costa, M.R. da (ed.), *Futebol, o espetáculo do século*. São Paulo: Musa Editora, 1999.

Silveira, Osvaldo da, 'Do Velódromo ao Morumbi', in Vários Autores, *60 Anos de Futebol no Brasil*. São Paulo: Federação Paulista de Futebol, 1955.

Siqueira, Uassyr, 'Clubes e Sociedades de Trabalhadores do Bom Retiro: organização, lutas e lazer em um bairro Paulistano (1915–1924)', Master thesis, Department of History, Universidade Estadual de Campinas, 2002.

Skidmore, Thomas E., *Black Into White: Race and Nationality in Brazilian Thought*. Durham: Duke University Press, 1993.

———— *Politics in Brazil, 1930–1964: An Experiment in Democracy*. New York: Oxford University Press, 1969.

Soares, Antonio Jorge, 'Futebol Brasiliero E Sociadade: a interpretaçao culturalista de Gilberto Freyre', in Pablo Alabarces (ed.), *Fubologias: fútbol, identidad y violencia en América Latina*. Buenos Aires: CLASCO, 2003.

———— 'O Racismo No Futebol Do Rio De Janeiro Nos Anos 20: uma história de identidade', in Antonio Jorge Soares, Ronaldo Helal, Hugo Rodolfo Lovisolo (eds), *A Invençãao Do País Do Futebol: Mídia, Raça E Idolatria*. Rio de Janeiro: PUC, 2003.

Souza, M.A. de, 'A "Nação em Chuteiras": raça e masculinidade no futebol brasileiro', Dissertação de Mestrado, Antropologia Social, Universidade de Brasília, 1996.

Stepan, Nancy Leys, *"The Hour of Eugenics": Race, Gender and Nation in Latin America*. Ithaca: Cornell University Press, 1991.

———— *Beginnings of Brazilian Science*. New York: Science History Publications, 1978.

Taylor, Matthew, *The Leaguers. The Making of Professional Football in England, 1900–1939*. Liverpool: Liverpool University Press, 2005.

Tells, Edward, *Race in Another America, the Significance of Skin Color in Brazil*. Princeton: Princeton University Press, 2004.

———— *Torcidas Organizadas de Futebol*. Campinas: Autores Associados/ANPOCS, 1996.

The São Paulo Tramway, Light & Power Co. Ltd, *Employment Bureau: Annual Report: 1945*, Tramway Division.

Thomaz, O.R., *Ecos do Atlântico Sul*. Rio de Janeiro: URFJ/FAPESP, 2002.

Toledo, Luiz Henrique de, *Lógicas no futebol*. São Paulo: Huicitec/FAPESP, 2000.

Twine, Frances Windance, *Racism in a Racial Democracy: The Maintenance of White Supremacy in Brazil*. New Brunswick: Rutgers University Press, 1998.

O Trabalhador da Light, 3, 2 (1934).

O Trabalhador da Light, 9 (1939).

'Une Mine De Footballeurs', *Relais*, Charbonnages de France, 1991, p. 207.

BIBLIOGRAPHY

Várzea, Paulo, 'Começo e Desenvolvimento do Futebol em São Paulo', in Vários Autores, *60 Anos de Futebol no Brasil*. São Paulo: Federação Paulista de Futebol, 1955.

Vernant, J.P., *As origens do pensamento grego*. São Paulo: DIFEL, 5th edn, 1986.

Vianna, F. de L.B., *Boleiros do cerrado: índios xavantes e o futebol*. São Paulo: Annablume/FAPESP/ISA, 2008.

Vianna, Hermano, *The Mystery of Samba: Popular Music and National Identity in Brazil*, trans. John Chasteen. Chapel Hill: University of North Carolina Press, 1999.

Vicentini, Walter Scott, *O Segundo Chute*. São Paulo: Studio Art, 2005.

Villa, M.A., *Vida e morte no sertão. História da seca no Nordeste nos séculos XIX e XX*. São Paulo: Editora Ática, 2000.

Vogel, Arno, 'O momento feliz: reflexões sobre o futebol e o *ethos* nacional', in DaMatta, Roberto (ed.), *Universo do futebol: esporte e sociedade brasileira*. Rio de Janeiro: Edições Pinakotheque, 1982.

Wade, Peter, *Race, Nature and Culture: An Anthropological Perspective*. London: Pluto Press, 2002.

——— *Race and Ethnicity in Latin America*. London: Pluto Press, 1998.

Wahl, Alfred, 'Le footballheur français: de l'amateurisme au salariat (1890–1926)', *Le Mouvement Social*, 135 (1996), pp. 7–30.

Wahl, Alfred and Pierre Lanfranchi, *Les footballeurs professionnels: des années trente à nos jours*. Paris: Hachette, 1995.

Walvin, James, *The People's Game*. Edinburgh: Mainstream Publishing, 1994.

Weber, Florence, *Le travail à côté; Étude d'ethnographie ouvrière*. Paris: Ed. EHESS/INRA, 1989.

Weffort, Francisco, *O Populismo na Política Brasileira*. Rio de Janeiro: Paz e Terra, 1980.

Weinstein, Barbara, *For Social Peace: Industrialists and the Remaking of the Working Class in São Paulo, 1920–1964*. Chapel Hill: University of North Carolina Press, 1996.

——— 'Racializing Regional Difference: São Paulo versus Brazil, 1932', in Anne S. Macpherson, Nancy P. Applebaum, and Karin Alejandra Rosemblatt (eds), *Race and Nation in modern Latin America*. Chapel Hill: University of North Carolina Press, 2003.

Willis, Paul, 'L'école des ouvriers', *Actes de la Recherche en Sciences Sociales*, 24 (1978), pp. 50–61.Witter, José Sebastião, 'Futebol: várzea e cidade de São Paulo', in *Estudo de Tombamento do Parque do Povo*. São Paulo, Condephaat, 1994.

Wisnik, J.M., *Veneno remédio: o futebol e o Brasil*. São Paulo: Companhia das Letras, 2008.

Yallop, David A., *Como Eles Roubaram O Jogo: segredos dos subterrâneos da FIFA*. Rio de Janeiro: Record, 1998.

BIBLIOGRAPHY

Documents

Employee records of Companhia Riograndense de Mineração (CRM), Arquivos CRM, Minas do Leão, Rio Grande do Sul, Brasil.

Minutes of Atlético Mineiro Football Clube, Anos 1950 a 1970, Arquivos da CRM, Minas do Leão, Rio Grande do Sul, Brasil.

INDEX

257

INDEX

INDEX

INDEX

INDEX

INDEX

INDEX

INDEX

INDEX

INDEX

INDEX